An Annotated Bibliography
of
French Language and Literature

Garland Reference Library of the Humanities (Vol. 26)

An Annotated Bibliography
of
French Language and Literature

Fernande Bassan   **Paul F. Breed**
Donald C. Spinelli

Wayne State University

Garland Publishing, Inc., New York & London

1977

Library of Congress Cataloging in Publication Data

Bassan, Fernande.
  An annotated bibliography of French language and literature.

  (Garland reference library of the humanities ; v. 26)
  Includes index.
  1. French philology--Bibliography. I. Breed, Paul
Francis, 1916-   joint author. II. Spinelli,
Donald C., joint author. III. Title.
Z2175.A2B38 [PC2071] 016.44   75-24079
ISBN 0-8240-9986-9

Printed in the United States of America

PREFACE

This annotated bibliography of French language and literature is conceived as a guide to the student, scholar, and librarian interested in these fields. The book can be used as a textbook for the student of French bibliography; in addition, it will update the knowledge of library resources for scholars and librarians.

Putting together an annotated bibliography is not an easy endeavor. The various reputable national, retrospective, and current bibliographies do not always provide the same information, and their inconsistencies necessitate time-consuming verifications. The selection of materials from an abundance of documentation is a difficult task; to keep within the limits of about three hundred pages, we have had to exclude many books in spite of their excellence, and to eliminate articles except in rare cases.

Many books have been here annotated for the first time. In almost all instances our annotations are original; we have aimed at keeping them as informative and concise as possible while taking into account the complex variations of some series. Considering that the titles are rarely indicative of the content of the books, these comments should prove useful.

As we address ourselves mostly to English-speaking readers with some knowledge of French, we have primarily selected books written in those two languages; we have tried to list the most recent and complete ones.

Our book is divided into three parts devoted to (1) bibliographical tools concerning the field, (2) the French language, and (3) French literature. The ten chapters of our first part, which contain basic research tools, have been annotated with precision and detail. We have kept the annotations to a minimum in the two other parts. The second part lists various aspects of the study of French language. Part three deals with French literature; we limit ourselves to general works and indicate where to find editions of the writers and literary criticism on them. The general works include studies on literature as well as selective studies on history, civilization, philosophy, and religion. However, because of lack of space, we generally omitted books on other subjects. Our last chapter concerns the literature of French expression in countries other than France.

The alphabetical author-title index which concludes the work will help the reader to easily find his way in the book.

i

We would like to express our gratitude to René Rancoeur, *conservateur en chef* at the Bibliothèque Nationale in Paris, for his invaluable advice, and to Wayne State University for providing us with typing funds.

Fernande Bassan   Paul F. Breed   Donald C. Spinell
Prof. of French   Librarian and Bibliographer   Asst. Prof. of Fr

February 1st, 1976

Beginning with this printing, we have made some changes and updating; they are incorporated in the text or indicated at the end of the book in an "Addenda and Errata" list.

F. B.

P. F. B.

D. C. S.

February 1st, 1977

TABLE OF CONTENTS

	Numbers	Pages

vii

ABBREVIATIONS AND ACRONYMS

Am.	America, American
assn.	association
Aufl.	*Auflage* (G. for edition)
augm.	*augmenté(e)* (Fr. for enlarged)
AUPELF	Association des Universités Partiellement ou Entièrement de Langue Française
av.-pr.	*avant-propos* (Fr. for foreword)
Bd.(e).	*Band(e)* (G. for volume(s))
BELC	Bureau pour l'Enseignement de la Langue et de la Civilisation Françaises à l'Etranger
B.N.	Bibliothèque Nationale
CARDAN	Centre d'Analyse et de Recherche Documentaires pour l'Afrique Noire
CDU	Centre de Documentation Universitaire
ch.(s).	chapter(s); Fr.: *chapitre(s)*
CLE	Centre de Littérature Evangélique
CNRS	Centre National de la Recherche Scientifique
coll.	collection
collab.	collaboration
compl.	completed; Fr.: *complété(e)*
comp.(s).	compiler(s), compiled; Fr.: *compilateur(s), compilé*
corr.	corrected; Fr.: *corrigé(e)*
dept./dépt.	department; Fr.: *département*
dir.	directed, director; Fr.: *dirigé, direction*; G.: *Direktor*
diss.	dissertation(s)
ed.(s).	edited, edition(s), editor(s)
éd.(s).	*édité, édition(s), éditeur(s)* (Fr. for edited, edition(s), editor(s)
enl.	enlarged
ent.	*entièrement* (Fr. for entirely)
Fr./fr.	French; Fr.: *français*
Frankfurt a/M.	Frankfurt am Main
G.	German
gén.	*général* (Fr. for general)
gen. ed.	general editor
GmbH	*Gesellschaft mit beschränkter Haftung* (G. for limited liability company)
gov.	government
imp.	*imprimerie* (Fr. for printing)
intr.	introduction
ISBN	International Standard Book Number
L.C.	Library of Congress
lib.	library
litt.	*littéraire* (Fr. for literary)
M.I.T.	Massachusetts Institute of Technology
MLA	Modern Language Association of America
MS(S)	manuscript(s); Fr.: *manuscrit(s)*
nat.	national
no.	number
nouv.	*nouveau, nouvelle* (Fr. for new)
NUC	National Union Catalog
nuova ed.	*nuova edizione* (Italian for new edition)
P.	Paris
p./pp.	page(s)
P.M.L.	Pierpont Morgan Library
Pr.	Press

pref./préf.	preface/*préface* (Fr.)
pub.	published, publishing, publisher
pt(s).	part(s)
PUF	Presses Universitaires de France
renouv.	*renouvelé(e)* (Fr. for renewed)
rev.	revised; Fr.: *revu(e)*
RHLF	*Revue d'Histoire Littéraire de la France*
rpt(s).	reprint(s)
s.d.	*sans date* (Fr. for no date)
SEDE	Société d'Edition de Dictionnaires et d'Encyclopédies
SEDES	Société d'Edition d'Enseignement Supérieur
ser./sér.	series/*série* (Fr.)
SEVPEN	Société d'Editions et de Vente des Publications de l'Education Nationale
soc.	society; Fr.: *société*
SUNY	State U. of N.Y.
sup.	*supérieur* (Fr.)
supp(s).	supplement(s); Fr.: *supplément(s)*
tr.	translator, translated; Fr.: *traduit, traducteur*
U.	University; Fr.: *Université*
univ.	*universitaire(s)*
UCLA	University of California at Los Angeles
U.D.C.	Universal Decimal Classification
Unesco	United Nations Educational, Scientific and Cultural Organization
vol(s).	volume(s)

PART I

GENERAL BIBLIOGRAPHIES AND REFERENCE WORKS

CHAPTER 1

BIBLIOGRAPHIES OF BIBLIOGRAPHIES

1 (International Federation for Documentation.) *Abstracting
        Services*. 2nd ed. 2 vols. The Hague: International
        Federation for Documentation, 1969.
        I: *Science, Technology, Medicine, Agriculture*.
        II: *Social Sciences and Humanities*.

> Lists and briefly describes ca. 1,500 abstracting
services—journals or card services—current in 1969.
They are listed alphabetically by title, then by subject in
English, French, Russian and Spanish and finally by title
under name of country (twenty-seven countries).
> Vol. 2 lists about 200 items in the social sciences
and humanities. Of interest to students in literature are
several abstracts of a general nature, and others in linguistics and literature.

2 Besterman, Theodore. *A World Bibliography of Biblio-
        graphies and of Bibliographical Catalogues,
        Calendars, Abstracts, Digests, Indexes and
        the Like*. 1939-40. 4th ed. rev. and greatly
        enl. throughout. 5 vols. Lausanne: Societas
        Bibliographica, 1965-66.

> Mainly separately published bibliographies—
books, pamphlets, special library catalogs, etc.—
but includes many bibliographical periodicals and
series.
> Valuable for its coverage of subjects (ca.
16,000), retrospective record (the beginning through
1963), major and obscure bibliographies, but it
tends to be incomprehensive in many individual subjects.
Size of bibliographies (no. of titles cited) is indicated
in brackets. Alphabetical subject sequence with full
index of authors, corporate entries and titles.
> Listed for French language are sixteen general and
twenty-two special dialect bibliographies; for French lit.
about twenty pages, classed in eight parts including manuscripts, general, specific periods, translations and
writings on French lit. There also are entries for individual authors and for the French lit. of other nations (Belgian,
Canadian, Swiss, etc.).

3 *Bibliographical Services Throughout the World; Annual Report*.
        1950-. P.: Unesco, 1951-. Annual.
        Cumulations: *1950-1959*, by Robert Lewis Collison,
        1961; by Paul Avicenne: *1960-1964*, 1969; *1965-1969*,
        1972.

The reports and the cumulations are pub. also in French under the title *Les Services bibliographiques dans le monde*.

Provides information on bibliographical publishing (or lack of it), including the following: national bibliographies (current and retrospective), lists, union lists, and indexes of periodicals, theses and dissertations, government documents, and bibliographies of special subjects. Arranged alphabetically by country with a convenient synoptic table. A very useful source for quickly finding a country's national bibliography, etc. The earlier annual reports and cumulations must sometimes be used for complete information and special subject bibliographies.

4 *Bibliographic Index: A cumulative Bibliography of Bibliographies*. N.Y.: H. W. Wilson, 1938-.

Semiannual with annual and multi-year cumulations (i.e., 1937-42).

An alphabetical subject index (no author or title index) to the following forms of bibliography: separately published books and pamphlets, serial bibliographies (annuals, etc.), topical lists appearing regularly in certain journals, and those included in books and articles. Annotated bibliographies are noted and size (no. of pages) is indicated. Over 1,700 journals are regularly searched with international coverage of all types of publication (mostly European and American).

History and criticism of French literature is included (general and by period) with additional entries for French drama, fiction, language, poetry, French literature in other countries, individual authors and aspects of comparative literature.

A first-rate source for many current bibliographies but far from exhaustive.

5 (France. Direction des bibliothèques de France.) *Bibliographies internationales spécialisées courantes françaises ou à participation française (Les)*. P: B.N., 1958. (Texte préparé par Andrée Lhéritier.)

A useful inventory of continuing bibliographies appearing as separates (annuals, irregular serials, etc.), bibliographical journals and bibliographies published regularly in journals. Among many other subjects, "Bibliologie, Linguistique, Littérature," are covered. A detailed description is provided of the starting date, periodicity, purpose, subjects, countries and languages surveyed, number of journals scanned and other types of publications examined.

6 Collison, Robert Lewis. *Bibliographies, Subject and National. A Guide to Their Contents, Arrangement and Use.*

1st ed. 1951; 2nd ed. 1962; 3rd ed. rev. and
enl. London: Crosby Lockwood, 1968.

Avoids all reference works of the dictionary
type, concentrates on a selection of bibliographies,
mostly British. Twenty-four pages of general bibliographies. The 3rd ed., like the 2nd, is updated rather
than radically revised.

7 Gray, Richard A. *Serial Bibliographies in the Humanities
       and Social Sciences.* Ann Arbor, Mich.: Pierian
       Pr., 1969.

Included are separately published serial bibliographies (annuals, yearbooks, handbooks, abstracts,
periodical indexes) and those appearing regularly in
journals on certain subjects. The author makes a special effort to reveal "concealed" bibliographies which
otherwise would be difficult to find. He includes de-
funct as well as current publications. International
in scope (Western European languages only).
       Arranged by Dewey classes 100-900 with useful
indexes to titles, authors, publishers, sponsors, and
subject key-words.
       Except for defunct pubs. it repeats much infor-
mation found in the *Bibliographic Index*, but it is occasionally useful for retrospective searching and elusive
bibliography in French language and literature, Canadian
literature, etc.

8 Malclès, Louise-Noëlle. *Les Sources du travail biblio-
       graphique.* 3 tomes en 4 vols. Genève: Droz,
       1950-58; rpt. 1965-66.

This work is a must for librarians and researchers; it is informative and clear. It lists and annotates
all the source books and bibliographic tools up to 1950.
After reviewing   bibliographies of bibliographies,
international and national bibliographies, and catalogs
of books and periodicals, it concentrates on various subjects.
       Tome I is devoted to general bibliographies;
Tome II, parts 1 and 2: to specialized bibliographies
in the humanities; Tome III: to specialized bibliographies
in the sciences including medicine and pharmacy.
       There are author, subject, and title indexes at
the end of each of the three tomes.

9 _____. *Manuel de bibliographie.* 2e éd. entièrement
       refondue et mise à jour. P.: PUF, 1969. (1st ed.
       1963.)

Essential book. Consult Chs. i-x, xviii and xix.
This work contains in an abbreviated form some of the
bibliographies and reference materials given in *Les
Sources*, and adds many recent publications. It is espe-

4

cially useful to the lay person, for much of the detailed historical matter has been deleted. As in the larger work, emphasis is on French and European materials, but works from other countries are included. There is an index of authors, anonymous titles and subjects.

3rd ed. considerably revised, completed and updated by Andrée Lhéritier, January 1977.

10 Taylor, Archer. *A History of Bibliographies of Bibliographies*. New Brunswick, N.J.: Scarecrow Pr., 1955.

Concerned only with universal bibliography of bibliography, not subject or national bibliography, this history begins with the earliest times, but covers mainly from the 17th century to the mid 20th century. The work of the major bibliographers is discussed in detail; among others, Peignot, Petzholdt, Sabin, Vallée, Stein and Besterman. Some of the cooperative serial bibliographies of recent times are also surveyed. A bibliography and index concludes the book.

CHAPTER 2

INTERNATIONAL GENERAL BIBLIOGRAPHIES

See Ch. 1: Besterman (no. 2), and Malclès (no. 8).

A. CUMULATIVE AND CURRENT BIBLIOGRAPHIES

11 Bouvier, Emile, et Jourda, Pierre. *Guide de l'étudiant en littérature française.* 6e éd. P.: PUF, 1968.

Reading lists, research methods and advice.

12 *Bulletin Signalétique 523: Histoire et Science de la Littérature.* P.: CNRS, 1940-. Quarterly. General title in 1940-56 was: *Bulletin Analytique du CNRS.*

This is one of the many bulletins published by the CNRS on various disciplines. Titles and contents vary.
Each issue has a list of international periodicals abstracted, index of concepts, index of authors, classification table and abstracts section. Annual cumulated author and concept indexes. The *Table annuelle* (in the last issue of the year) for 1974 lists about 600 periodicals selectively abstracted. In addition it covers dissertations, reports, congress and colloquium publications, and *volumes de mélanges*. Abstracts are brief and descriptive.
French literature is covered chronologically from the Middle Ages through the twentieth century. Each chronological period is further subdivided to treat generalities, genres, authors, etc. The concept subject index is very useful for locating material on individual authors, bibliography, comparative literature, and the literatures of Switzerland, Belgium, Canada, etc.
In the *Table annuelle*, one finds *Théâtre* in the Subject Index. It is classified first by countries, then by period or century, then by playwright, A-Z. There is a section for Belgium, Canada, France, *Noire, littérature*, Switzerland, etc. Then there is a section on different types of theatre, including: committed, poetical, political, popular, and religious, and one on the theory of the theatre.

13 Cabeen, David Clark, gen. ed. *A Critical Bibliography of French Literature.* Syracuse: Syracuse U. Pr., 1947-

    I. *The Medieval Period*, ed. by Urban Tignor Holmes, 1947, rev. 1952.
    II. *The Sixteenth Century*, ed. by Alexander H. Schutz, 1956.

III. Cabeen, David Clark, and Brody, Jules, gen. eds.
The Seventeenth Century, ed. by Nathan Edelman,
1961.
IV. *The Eighteenth Century*, ed. by George R. Havens
and Donald F. Bond, 1951.
IV. *Supplement*, ed. by Richard A. Brooks, 1968 (no
gen. ed.)

The entries are selected and annotated by
specialists. Intended for scholars and advanced students,
this excellent work provides critical opinion on the
most significant writings of European and American
scholars. Books and articles are included, about 3,000
items in each volume. Index of authors, titles and subjects
in each volume. Further volumes are planned for the nineteenth century and for the twentieth century to 1945.

14 Cioranescu, Alexandre. *Bibliographie de la littérature fran-
çaise du XVIe siècle*. Collab. et préf. de V.-L.
Saulnier. P.: Klincksieck, 1959; rpt., Genève:
Slatkine, 1975. (No reference after 1950.)

_____. *Bibliographie de la littérature française du
XVIIe siècle*. 3 vols. P.: CNRS, 1965-67. (For
this book and the next, no reference after 1960.)

_____. *Bibliographie de la littérature française du
XVIIIe siècle*. 3 vols. P.: CNRS, 1969-70.

This is the pattern followed: a general section of
historical character (surroundings, institutions, society,
intellectual life, themes, sources of inspiration, traditions, etc.); a section by authors: editions of their
works, critical and biographical studies. More than twenty
thousand references in each volume. The idea of "literature"
changes as it is applied to periods after the sixteenth century. Scientific, juridical and medical works, admitted in
the first volume, are excluded in the following ones.

15 Cordié, Carlo. *Avviamento allo studio della lingua e della
letteratura francese*. Milano: Marzorati, 1955.

An annotated selective bibliography of French
language and literature, from the Middle Ages to 1955,
arranged by periods. Attempts to stress the most valuable
and recent material. Index of writers, characters, subjects,
themes, critics, etc.

16 Kirsop, Wallace. "The Bibliography of French Literary History, Progress, Problems, Projects." *Australian Journal
of French Studies*, 1, No. 3 (Sept.-Dec. 1964), 325-64.

A survey of special bibliographies in French literature, noting gaps in coverage and pointing out shortcomings
of existing bibliographies covering 1501-1800.

17 Klapp, Otto. *Bibliographie der französischen Literatur-*
    wissenschaft/Bibliographie d'histoire littéraire
    française. Frankfurt a/M.: Klostermann, vol.· I-:
    1956-1958-, 1960-. Biennial: 1961-69. *Supplément*
    aux tomes I-VI, Index rerum, 1970. Annual since
    vol. VII: *1969*, 1970.

        Registers editions and criticism of French liter-
    ature, from the Middle Ages to now. Index of authors, index
    of subjects. Vol. XIII: *1975*, came out in 1976.

18 Langlois, Pierre, et Mareuil, André. *Guide bibliographique*
        des études littéraires. 5e éd. P.: Hachette, 1968.

        A didactic presentation of useful editions and
    works of criticism. It recommends studies written in French
    but in the appendix it lists some contributions in foreign
    languages. Index of authors. 1st ed. 1958, 3rd ed. 1965.

19 Lanson, Gustave. *Manuel bibliographique de la littérature*
        française moderne. XVIe, XVIIe, XVIIIe et XIXe
        siècles. Nouv. éd. avec Supp. et Index général.
        P.: Hachette, 1921; nouv. éd. rev. et corr., 1931.

        Classified by centuries, then by literary genres
    or periods, and by writers. For each century there is a
    general section containing bibliography, language, social
    environment, academies, education, influences, etc. For
    each author there are editions of texts and critical works.
    1st ed. 1913. Continued by:

20 Giraud, Jeanne. *Manuel de bibliographie littéraire pour*
        les XVIe, XVIIe et XVIIIe siècles français (1921-
        1935). P.: Vrin, 1939; 2e éd., 1958.

        Vol. II: for the works of *1936-1945*. P.: Nizet,
    1956. Vol. III: *1946-1955*. P.: Nizet, 1970.

21 Lecoy, F.; Lebègue, Raymond; et Van Tieghem, Philippe. "Les
        Etudes sur la langue et la littérature française de
        1940 à 1945." *Modern Language Review*, 41, No. 3
        (1946), 269-297 (in French, with an English title:
        "Reports Concerning French Literary and Linguistic
        Studies in the Period 1940-1945".) Reproduced in
        Bulletin de l'Association G. Budé, 1947, pp. 82-129.

        In three parts: I: Middle Ages, II: Renaissance and
    Seventeenth Century, III: Eighteenth Century and after. Surve
    of important books, articles, bibliographies and notable
    editions published during the period 1940-45, i.e. the war
    years--material difficult to find elsewhere.
        Each major historical period covered by an expert,
    i.e., Middle Ages by F. Lecoy, Renaissance and Seventeenth Ce

tury by R. Lebègue, Eighteenth Century and after by Ph. Van Tieghem.

22 Modern Language Association of America. Its bibliographies varied through the years in title and content.

"American Bibliography for 1921" (through 1955). Published annually in the periodical *PMLA (Publications of the Modern Language Association of America)*, from 1922 through 1956. Reprinted with title: *MLA American Bibliography of Books and Articles on the Modern Languages and Literatures, 1921-1955*. N.Y.: Kraus, 1964.

Limited to the works of American scholars on language and literature of various countries, mainly of the U.S., England, France, Germany, Italy, Spain, and Portugal. Continued as:

"Annual Bibliography," *PMLA*, 1956-62. Reprinted as *MLA International Bibliography. . . 1956-1962*. N.Y.: Kraus, 1964. Continued as:

MLA International Bibliography of Books and Articles on the Modern Languages and Literatures, 1963-. Published as part of *PMLA* until 1968; separately since 1969 in 3 vols.; French literature is in vol. II; vol. III is devoted to linguistics. Last one pub. to date: *1974 MLA International Bibliography*, 1976.

Coverage has increased through the years. Currently about 2,800 periodicals (a list is provided) are indexed, plus books, dissertations, *Festschriften*, etc. It is the most important literary bibliography in America. The arrangement is by language, subdivided chronologically by century, with individual authors in alphabetical order. An index of authors (authors of articles, books, etc.) has been added since 1964.

23 Modern Language Association of America. *French III. Bibliography of French Seventeenth Century Studies*. No. 1-. 1952/53-. (Publisher varies. No. 22, 1974, pub. by Colorado St. U. for French III Group.)

International coverage of books and articles with emphasis on scholarly writing. Considerable expansion in indexing of journals since the beginning; e.g., No. 1 indexed fifty-two titles; No. 21, 123 titles. In five parts: (1) Bibliography and Linguistics, (2) Political and Social Background, (3) Philosophy, Science and Religion, (4) Literary History and Criticism, (5) Authors and Personages (alphabetically arr.). A bibliography with brief annotations giving a short summary of contents, often with an evaluation of the contribution to scholarship. Citations to book reviews are also given.

24 (MLA) *French VI Bibliography: Critical and Biographical
        References for the Study of Nineteenth-Century French
        Literature. 1954/55-1966/67.* N.Y.: French Institute
        1965-69. Biennial. Ceased publication. (Issued by
        the French Institute and the Bibliography Committee
        of the French VI Section of the MLA of Am.)

            Modelled after *French VII* (now called *French XX) B
        liography*, and similar to that publication in indexing polic
        and arrangement. Late 19th century authors, e.g. Rimbaud, a
        placed in *French VII (French XX) Bibliography*.

25 (MLA) *Bibliography of Critical and Biographical References
        for the Study of Contemporary French Literature.
        Books and Articles Published from 1940 to 1948.* Ed.
        by Douglas W. Alden; G. R. Jasper; and R. P. Waterman
        N.Y.: Stechert-Hafner, 1949 (MLA, French VII, Pub. 1)
        Suppléments 1949-1952, N.Y.: Stechert-Hafner, 1950-53
        (MLA, French VII, Pub. 2-5); Pt. 1: General Subjects
        Pt. 2: Authors. (A total of 8,654 references.) (Vol
        Continued by:

    (MLA) *French VII Bibliography: Critical and Biographical
        References for the Study of Contemporary French Liter
        ture (1953-1967).* Ed. by Douglas W. Alden, et al. V
        nos. 1-5, N.Y.: Stechert-Hafner, 1954-58. Vol. III,
        no. 1-vol. IV, no. 5, N.Y.: French Institute, 1959-68
        French VII, Pub. 6-20). Author indexes for vols. I-I
        III-IV. Continued by:

    (MLA) *French XX Bibliography: Critical and Biographical
        References for the Study of French Literature since
        1885.* Ed. by Douglas W. Alden, et al. Annual. *1968*
        vol. V, no. 1-, N.Y.: French Institute, 1970- (MLA,
        French VII, Pub. 21-). Index to vol. V (Pub. 21-25),
        1968-1972, issued in 1974.

            As of vol. VI, issue no. 26, 1974, *French XX* has
        become a joint publication of The French Institute, Alliance
        Française de New York, and The Camargo Foundation, Cassis,
        France, under the direction of Ruth Elaine Tussing; the
        numbering starts at A1-.
            This bibliography, and the two above, were com-
        piled by the Bibliography Committee for French VII of the
        MLA. There is considerable duplication of material with the
        MLA Bibliography, but it was thought that a separate bib-
        liography was justified because of the more complete coverag
        of books, the attention paid to essays within collections of
        essays and *Festschriften*, and the efforts to include materia
        not in the *MLA Bibliography*. Over the years coverage has
        expanded, especially for European publications, and in
        recent years there has been considerable retrospective in-
        dexing to pick up references omitted in earlier volumes.

Indexes an international range of books, chapters
in books, annuals, series, articles, and newspapers (selectively). Arranged in three sections. Pt. 1 covers general
aspects, bibliography, literary genres, æsthetics, themes,
literary history, philosophy, religion, surrealism, symbolism
and theatre; pt. 2 treats authors and is arranged alphabetically by name, citing critical editions of works and criticism; pt. 3 deals with cinema, including directors, actors
and authors.
  Reviews of books, plays and films are indicated,
and a careful internal cross reference system refers one
from authors' names to additional material about them in
the subject sections. There are no annotations.

26 Rancoeur, René. *Bibliographie de la littérature française
      du Moyen Age à nos jours*. P.: A. Colin.

      This is the present title; here are the former ones:

_____. *Bibliographie littéraire*. *1953-1961*. P.: A.
Colin, 1953-62; rpt., N.Y.: Johnson, 1966.

      Annual reprint of the bibliography as it appeared
quarterly in the *Revue d'Histoire Littéraire de la France*.
Index 1953-1955, in 1955; *1956-1958*, in 1958; *1959-1961*, in
1961. (Earlier R. Rancoeur's bibliographies were published
only in the periodical, 1949-52.) (In 1949-62, it excluded
Medieval literature and living authors.)

_____. *Bibliographie de la littérature française moderne
(XVIe-XXe siècles)*. *1962-1965*. 4 vols. P.: A. Colin,
1963-66. (Living authors are included as of the production of 1962.)

_____. *Bibliographie de la littérature française du Moyen
Age à nos jours*. *1966-*. P.: 1967-. (Medieval literature is included as title shows.)

      Content: after bibliographies and generalities,
classification is done by period or century. For each
period, first it lists group studies and themes, then the
writers (editions of texts, biographical and critical works).
Studies on literary genres and comparative literature are
retained only if they treat writers of French expression.
      Since 1964 (for 1963), the annual *Bibliographie* is
not a duplication of the *RHLF*, but provides important complementary information. The *1974* volume contains 6,680
items, followed by addresses of periodicals and an index.
      The scope of the work, its exhaustive aspect in
terms of studies of interest to researchers and critics,
and its accuracy are admirable. This reference work by R.
Rancoeur, impatiently awaited every year, is indispensable
for all libraries and research centers, professors, students,
and critics.

27 *Romanische Bibliographie/Bibliographie Romane/Romance Bibli-*
       ography, 1961/62-. Tübingen: Niemeyer, 1965-.
       Biennial. Continuation of the bibliographical sup-
       plement of:

    Zeitschrift für Romanische Philologie. Supplementheft:
       Bibliographie 1875/76-. Halle, subsequently
       Tübingen: Niemeyer, 1877-1964.

            This supplement was an extensive, international bib-
    liography of books, articles, theses, etc. on Romance lan-
    guages, culture and literatures. Three general sections
    covered (1) philology and history of culture, (2) Middle Ages
    and Modern Times, and (3) Romance philology followed by sepa-
    rate sections for Italian, French, Catalan, Spanish and Por-
    tuguese language and literature. There was an alphabetical
    index of names (authors written about, writers of books and
    articles), and anonymous titles.
            In general the arrangement and coverage of *R. B.*
    are similar to the above, but with some changes and additions.
    Last volume published: *1967-68*, 3 vols., 1975. Vol. 1 con-
    tains a systematic table, or classification, of the bibliog-
    raphy, a list of the 740 periodicals indexed, lists of
    society and congress publications, *Festschriften*, etc., and
    indexes of writers, literary authors and subjects. Vol. 2
    is devoted to the several Romance languages, and vol. 3 to
    Romance literatures. With regard to French literature, like
    other literatures, there is a general section for bibliog-
    raphy, literary history, poetry, drama, themes, comparative
    literature, etc., followed by a chronological treatment by
    centuries and individual authors alphabetically within each
    century (biographical and critical works). Included also in
    the bibliography are works about French literature in Canada,
    Louisiana, Martinique, the Near East, Africa, and East Asia.

28 Ronge, Peter. *Studienbibliographie Französisch*. 2 vols.
       Frankfurt a/M.: Athenäum Verlag GmbH, 1971.

            A good selective bibliography on French studies,
    with brief annotations.

29 Spaziani, Marcello. *Introduzione bibliografica alla lingua*
       e alla letteratura francese. Palermo: Manfredi
       editore, 1969.

            A good bibliographical introduction to French lan-
    guage and literature studies.

30 Talvart, Hector, et Place, Joseph. *Bibliographie des auteurs*
       de langue française. (1801-1927-). (Continued as of
       vol. XV by Georges Place.) P.: Chronique des lettres
       françaises, 1928-.

            A very good selective bibliography. Writers are
    given a long biographical notice, then comes an enumeration

and description of their works in chronological order. Current editions, original editions, deluxe editions are given. Also prefaces, introductions and collaborations of the author on journals are all mentioned. Finally, works and articles to consult. Up to 1976, the following volumes have appeared:
I-XV: up to Mirbeau, 1928-63.
XVI and XVII: Index of titles of works, of names and pseudonyms of the authors and collaborators of vols. I-XV.
XVIII-XXII: from Mirecourt to Claude Morgan.
Each volume treats the literature up to the date it goes to the printer, e.g.: 1927 for vol. I, 1962 for vol. XV, 1967 for vol. XVIII, 1974 for vol. XXI (pub. in 1975), 1976 for vol. XXII (pub. in 1976).

31 Thieme, Hugo Paul. *Bibliographie de la littérature française de 1800 à 1930.* 3 vols. P.: Droz, 1933; rpt., 2 vols. Genève: Slatkine, 1971.

A revision of the author's *Guide bibliographique de la littérature française de 1800 à 1906.* P.: H. Welter, 1907.
Vols. I and II are an alphabetical list of authors who have written after 1800 (ca. 2,000). Editions of their texts and works devoted to them are listed chronologically. Useful: only completed cumulative bibliography of 19th century French literature. Some errors. Vol. III, *La Civilisation*, is a classified list of books and articles on literature, language and general culture. Continued by the two following bibliographies:

32 Dreher, Silpelitt, et Rolli, Madeleine. *Bibliographie de la littérature française. (1930-1939). Complément à la Bibliographie de H. P. Thieme.* Genève: Droz, 1948.

Same format as the preceding entry, plus list of pseudonyms. Continued by:

33 Drevet, Marguerite L. *Bibliographie de la littérature française (1940-1949). Complément à la Bibliographie de H. P. Thieme.* Genève: Droz, 1954.

Same format, adds many clandestine publications and a number of foreign periodicals, indexes vols. of *Mélanges* and general works. Also adds lists of patronyms, pseudonyms, etc.

34 *Year's Work in Modern Language Studies (The).* Cambridge: Cambridge U. Pr. Vol. 1-: 1931 (for 1929-). Published by the Humanities Research Association.

Analyses of works relative to languages and literatures including Medieval Latin, Romance Languages, Germanic Languages (excluding English which has its own separate bibliography), and Slavic Languages.

B. BIBLIOGRAPHY OF SPECIAL INTERESTS

35 Brunet, Jacques-Ch. *Manuel du libraire et de l'amateur
    de livres.* 5e éd. refondue et augm. 6 vols. P.:
    Firmin-Didot, 1860-65.

    Supplément par Pierre Deschamps et P.-Gustave Brunet.
    2 vols. 1878-80. Rpt. with the *Manuel*, 8 vols.
    P.: Maisonneuve et Larose, 1965-66.

    Vols. 1-5 list the authors and anonymous titles,
in alphabetical order, of about 7,500 noteworthy books
published since the beginning of printing, in a variety of
languages (the French titles are the majority), list their
various editions, forgeries, sale prices reached in France
and England over a century. Vol. 6 classifies those books
into: Theology, Jurisprudence, Sciences and Arts, Literature, History. The *Supplément* adds about 12,500 titles.

C. COMPARATIVE LITERATURE

36 Baldensperger, Fernand, and Friederich, Werner Paul. *Bib-
    liography of Comparative Literature.* Chapel Hill:
    U. of North Carolina Pr., 1950.

    The standard bibliography and still the most ex-
tensive work in the field with about 33,000 entries. There
is no index, but a very detailed table of contents serves
fairly well. It includes universal literary themes, genres,
motifs and international literary influences, national literatures by country and individual authors. The scheme
throughout is to list material according to the author,
country, etc., exerting influence. Continued by the *Yearbook*, see below.

37 Betz, Louis-Paul. *La Littérature comparée. Essai biblio-
    graphique.* Intro. par Joseph Texte. 2e éd. augm.,
    pub. avec un index méthodique, par Fernand Balden-
    sperger. Strasbourg: Trübner, 1904.

    Bibliography of books and periodicals, articles
on comparative literature from the Middle Ages through the
nineteenth century. Completes Baldensperger's *Bibliography*
for the nineteenth century.

38 *Yearbook of Comparative and General Literature.* Annual. 1-
    9, Chapel Hill: U. of North Carolina Pr., 1952-60; 10-
    Bloomington: Indiana U. Pr., 1961-; rpt., vols. 1-11,
    N.Y.: Russell and Russell, 1975.

    Contains: "Reviews of Professional Works," and a

"List of Translations" into English from various foreign languages (since 1961). The editors decided to substitute reviews in essay form for the bibliography, as of the 1970 issue (covering 1969).

39   *Bibliographie générale de littérature comparée, 1949/50-1957/58.* P.: Boivin, then Didier. Biennial. Reprint of the bibliography published in the *Revue de Littérature Comparée.* This journal contained a bibliography from 1921 to 1960.

D. TRANSLATIONS

40   *Chartotheca Translationum Alphabetica/Internationale Bibliographie der Übersetzungen auf Karteikarten/ International Bibliography of Translations.* Vol. 1-. Frankfurt a/M.: Bentz, 1961-. Annual.

Arranged alphabetically by names of authors, anonymous titles, corporate names, etc., giving original language, title, nationality of the author, imprint and price; then translator, title, imprint and price for translations. Coverage is much less intensive than the *Index Translationum.* Reported translations vary greatly according to language. It contains translations of German, British, and American authors into many languages, and also translations of French authors into German.

41   Fromm, Hans. *Bibliographie deutscher Übersetzungen aus dem Französischen, 1700-1948/Bibliography of German Translations from the French, 1700-1948/Bibliographie des traductions allemandes d'imprimés français, 1700-1948.* 6 Bde. Baden-Baden: Verlag für Kunst und Wissenschaft, 1950-53.

Three lists. A: Alphabetical list of French authors, titles, German translators, titles and imprints. B: Alphabetical list of German authors, translated titles and French authors. C: Alphabetical list of German collections, series, miscellaneous anthologies, etc., containing translations from the French.
There is an index of German titles which appear in list A. Includes a total of 28,740 citations in the main list (A). Besides the information on translations this serves as an extensive bibliography of French drama for the period.

42   Horn-Monval, Madeleine. *Répertoire bibliographique des traductions et adaptations françaises du théâtre étranger du XVe siècle à nos jours conservées dans les bibliothèques et archives de Paris.* 9 vols. P.: CNRS, 1958-67.

Each volume covers the theatres of one or more countries or languages. Vol. 1: in ancient Greek; vol. 2:

15

Latin (all periods); vol. 3: Italian; vol. 4: Spanish, Portuguese, Latin American; vol. 5: English and American; vol. 6: German, Austrian, and Swiss; vol. 7: Scandinavian, Flemish, Dutch, Northern countries; vol. 8: Slavic countries and other European countries, Asia and Africa, addenda to the American theatre; vol. 9 is a general index of authors in the first eight volumes.

43 *Index Translationum/Répertoire international des traductions International Bibliography of Translations.* P.: Pr. l'Unesco, 1949-. Annual. Vol. 26 (for 1973), pub. 197

   Called New Series in continuation of *Bibliographie internationale des traductions,* covering 1932-40, by the International Institute of Intellectual Cooperation, So- ciété des Nations, etc.
   This index has increased its coverage of transla- tions over the years. Besides Europe and the Americas, it includes Oriental, Near Eastern and African countries. Ar- ranged alphabetically by country, subdivided by ten major subject areas according to the U.D.C. method. Full bibliographic data is given, including the original and translated title, translator and price. There is an alpha- betical author index.

44 Parks, George B. *The Literatures of the World in English Translation. A Bibliography. Vol. III: The Romance Literatures.* 1 vol. in 2. N.Y.: Ungar, 1970.

   Pt. I: Catalan, Italian, Portuguese and Brazilian, Provençal, Rumanian, Spanish and Spanish-American Literatures; Pt. 2: French Literature.

   The volume for French literature covers French literature in general, Medieval literature, and a separate section for each century from the sixteenth through the twentieth. Another part covers French literature in Belgium Switzerland, Canada, Louisiana, West Indies, and Africa. Each section is edited by a specialist and each is preceded by reading lists of background material, a bibliography of the period and pertinent literary studies in French and English.
   The bibliography of translations first lists col- lections of poetry, romances, plays, stories, then works of individual authors. The attempt has been to be as complete as possible for all English translations, except for those in periodicals and collections, through 1968.
   Each volume has an index of translated authors and anonymous works.

CHAPTER 3

NATIONAL AND TRADE BIBLIOGRAPHIES

A. BIBLIOGRAPHY OF NATIONAL BIBLIOGRAPHIES

See Ch. 1: Besterman (no. 2), and Malclès (no. 8).

45 Conover, Helen F. *Current National Bibliographies.*
Washington, D.C.: Gov. Printing Office, 1955; rpt., 1968.

      Compiled by H. F. Conover on the basis of publi-
cations received at the Library of Congress as of 1954. An
annotated bibliography of national and trade bibliographies
issued in sixty-seven countries. It also includes periodical
indexes, published lists of newspapers and periodicals,
and lists of government publications.

B. RETROSPECTIVE BIBLIOGRAPHIES

FRENCH ANTILLES AND GUIANA, HAITI, FRENCH-SPEAKING AFRICA
See Ch. 20: nos. 1486 to 1488.

46 Arnaud, Jacqueline et al. *Bibliographie de la littérature
nord-africaine d'expression française. 1945-1962.*
Pub. sous la dir. de Albert Memmi. P.-La Haye:
Mouton, 1965.

47 Baratte, Thérèse, et Beningo, Eno. *Bibliographie. Auteurs
africains et malgaches de langue française.* 3e éd.
revue et mise à jour avec la collaboration du Service
"Etudes et Documentation," ORTF/DAEC. P.: Office de
Radiodiffusion Télévision Française, 1972.

      List of works by country, and bibliography of
anthologies and criticism of African and Madagascan writers
of French expression.

BELGIUM

48 *Bibliographie Nationale. Dictionnaire des écrivains belges
et catalogue de leurs publications, 1830-1880.*
4 vols. Bruxelles: Weissenbruch, 1886-1910.

      Alphabetical classification by authors and anony-
mous titles of works published in Belgium, of works by
Belgian authors published abroad, of foreign works pertaining
to Belgium. Approximately 65,000 citations for books,
pamphlets, theses, music, etc. Brief biographical information on authors included.

17

49 *Bibliographie des écrivains français de Belgique, 1881-1950.*
Bruxelles: Palais des Académies, 1958-. Vol. 1-.

Vols. 2-4 have title: *Bibliographie . . . 1881-
1960,* 1966-72.

50 *Bibliotheca belgica. Bibliographie générale des Pays-Bas,*
fondée par Ferdinand van der Haeghen. Ré-éditée sous
la direction de Marie-Thérèse Lenger. 6 vols.
Bruxelles: Culture et Civilisation, 1964-1970.

Originally published in irregular order, 1880-
1964. Reassembled in alphabetical order in this edition.
Mostly fifteenth and sixteenth century works, but includes
some later works. Covers Belgian and Dutch authors published in Belgium, Holland, and abroad. Frequent bibliographical or historical notes are added, as well as
biographical information on authors.

CANADA

51 Lochhead, Douglas. *Bibliography of Canadian Bibliogra-
phies/ Bibliographie des bibliographies canadiennes.*
2nd ed. rev. and enl. Comp. by Douglas Lochhead.
Index comp. by Peter E. Greig. Toronto: Pub. in
association with the Bibliographical Soc. of Canada
by U. of Toronto Pr., 1972.

The material in the first ed., compiled by
Raymond Tanghe, 1960, and three supplements to the first
ed. issued by the Society, covering the years 1961-65, have
been incorporated into this edition with additional new
material.
Includes bibliographies appearing as books, pamphlets, government publications, theses, library catalogs,
series, periodical articles, etc. However, bibliographies
included in, or appended to, books, articles, theses, etc.
are excluded. A broad range of subjects is covered in the
humanities, social sciences and the sciences. French
language, literature, poetry and individual authors are
represented. The arrangement is alphabetical by author or
anonymous title, with a fine bilingual index of authors,
titles and subjects. There are 2,325 bibliographies listed
No annotations.

52 Dionne, Narcisse Eutrope. *Québec et la Nouvelle France.
Bibliographie.* 4 vols. Québec: Soc. Royale du
Canada, 1905-12. *Premier Supplément, 1905-12.* Québec
Soc. Royale du Canada, 1912; rpt., 5 vols. in 2, N.Y.
Burt Franklin, 1969.

Vol. 1: Books, pamphlets, newspapers, periodicals published in French in Quebec, 1764-1905. Vol. 2:
Books, etc. published in foreign countries about New France

and Quebec, 1534-1906. Vol. 3: Books, etc. published in
English in Quebec, 1764-1906. Vol. 4: Maps, charts, plans,
and atlases of New France and Quebec, 1508-1908, published
in Canada or elsewhere. Supplement: Books, etc. published
1904-11, in French, English, etc. in Quebec or outside
Quebec.

  A total of about 8,745 titles recorded: no annotations. Each volume has an index; vols. 1-3 have an author-
title-subject index; vol. 4 has an index of places, and a
bibliography of 102 items. Preface to vol. 1 has a summary
of the highlights of publishing, noteworthy literary
authors, etc. in various periods.

53 Tremaine, Marie. *A Bibliography of Canadian Imprints,*
   1751-1800. Toronto: U. of Toronto Pr., 1952.

  A chronological record of 1,204 publications with
a detailed author-title-subject index. Includes all types
(books, pamphlets, leaflets, broadsides, newspapers, periodicals, etc.), with full descriptions and notes. Newspapers have a separate section and they are given detailed
histories and extensive commentary. Appendices include
printing offices, printers (with biographical notes), a
list of public archives with their manuscript holdings, and
a bibliography of published sources.

54 Haight, Willet Ricketson. *Canadian Catalogue of Books,*
   1791-1897. 3 vols. Toronto: Haight, 1896-1904;
   rpt., Vancouver: Devlin; London: Pordes, 1958.

  Only pt. 1 of a projected record for 1791-1895
was published, listing 1,006 titles published from 1791
through 1895. Arrangement is alphabetical by author, with
title and chronological indexes. Books, etc. of a wide
variety are listed, including literature, poetry, essays
and novels. The first and second supplements cover 1896
and 1897; they are entitled: *The Annual Canadian Catalogue
of Books* and together add about 900 titles.

55 Hare, John Ellis, et Wallot, Jean-Pierre. *Les Imprimés dans
   le Bas-Canada, 1801-1810: bibliographie analytique.*
   Montréal: Pr. de l'U. de Montréal, 1967.

  A chronological bibliography of books, pamphlets,
government documents, newspapers and periodicals with annotations and locations of copies.

56 Martin, Gérard. *Bibliographie sommaire du Canada français,
   1854-1954.* Québec: Secrétariat de la province de
   Québec, 1954.

  A classified bibliography of 900 titles covering
History, Economics, Education, French Canadians, Fine arts,
and Literature. There are 368 items on literature which is

subdivided into poetry, theatre, novels, history and criticism and bibliography. No annotations.

57 Tod, Dorothea, and Cordingley, Audrey. *A Check List of
    Canadian Imprints, 1900-1925/ Catalogue d'ouvrages
    imprimés au Canada.* Preliminary checking ed.
    Ottawa: Canadian Bibliographical Centre, 1950.

    An alphabetical list by authors' names. Excludes
pamphlets of less than fifty pages, gov. publications, and
serials. No index.

FRANCE

58 Quérard, Joseph-Marie. *La France littéraire ou Dictionnaire
    bibliographique des savants, historiens et gens de
    lettres de la France ainsi que des littérateurs
    étrangers qui ont écrit en français plus parti-
    culièrement pendant les XVIIIe et XIXe siècles.*
    12 vols. P.: Firmin-Didot, 1827-1864; rpt. 12
    vols. P.: Maisonneuve et Larose, 1964.

    Vols. I to X, for A-Z. Vols. XI and XII (pub. in
1854-1864) form a supplement from A up to "Rog." Contains
also writers who published anonymously or under a pen-name.
This work concerns mostly the writers of the eighteenth
century. Continued by:

59 Quérard, Joseph-Marie; Louandre, Charles; Bourquelot,
    Félix; et Maury, Alfred. *La Littérature française
    contemporaine.* 6 vols. P.: Daguin, 1840-1857; rpt.
    P.: Maisonneuve et Larose, 1965.

    Vol. I and II up to page 282 are by Quérard. They
go up to 1840. The following volumes go up to 1842 for the
letters B through F, and up to 1849 for the letters G to Z.
    This work has the same format as *La France litté-
raire,* but with more succinct annotations. It contains only
works signed, no anonymous works.
    Quérard, having been rejected by his publisher,
published in revenge: *Omissions et bévues au livre intitulé
"La Littérature française contemporaine."* P.: Quérard, 1848.

60 Quérard, Joseph-Marie. *Les Supercheries littéraires dé-
    voilées. Galerie des écrivains français de toute
    l'Europe qui se sont déguisés sous des anagrammes,
    des astéronymes, des cryptonymes, des initialismes,
    des noms littéraires, des pseudonymes facétieux ou
    bizarres.* 1e éd. 5 vols. P.: l'éditeur, 1847-53;
    rpt., 3 vols. P.: Maisonneuve et Larose, 1964.

61 Barbier, Antoine-Alexandre. *Dictionnaire des ouvrages
    anonymes.* 3e éd. rev. et augm. par Olivier Barbier,
    René et Paul Billard. 4 vols. P.: Daffis, 1877-1879.

rpt., 4 vols. Maisonneuve et Larose, 1964.

These two books are supplemented by Gustave
Brunet's *Dictionnaire des ouvrages anonymes. . . Supplément
à la dernière édition de ces deux ouvrages*. (P.: Fechoz,
1889), and by an article of Henry Celani in *Revue des
Bibliothèques*, 11 (1901), 333-361: "Additions et corrections
au Dictionnaire des anonymes de Barbier."

62 *Catalogue général de la librairie française*, par Otto Lorenz.
Continué par Daniel Jordell, puis Henri Stein et Edouard
Champion, puis le Service bibliographique Hachette.
34 vols. P., 1867-1945. I-XI, *1840-1885*, Lorenz,
1867-85; XII-XVIII, *1886-1905*, Nilsson, 1892-1908; XIX,
1900-1905, Jordell et Nilsson, 1909; XX-XXVII, *1909-
1915*, Jordell, 1910-20; XXVIII-XXXII, *1916-1925*,
Champion, 1924-34; XXXIII-XXXIV, *1916-1925*, Hachette,
1945. Rpt., 34 tomes en 35 vols., Nendeln, Liechtenstein: Kraus, 1966; P.: Cercle de la Librairie, 1975.

SWITZERLAND

63 Société des Libraires et Editeurs de la Suisse Romande.
Genève: *Catalogue des éditions de la Suisse Romande*,
rédigé par Alexandre Jullien. 2 vols. Genève:
Jullien, 1902-12. Continued by:

_____. *Catalogue des ouvrages de langue française publiés
en Suisse, 1910-1945*, rédigé par Alexandre Jullien.
2 vols. Genève: Jullien, 1929-48.

64 Bern. Schweizerische Landesbibliothek. Bibliothèque
Nationale. *Katalog. . .Systematisches Verzeichnis
der schweizerischen oder die Schweiz betreffenden
Veröffenlichungen/Catalogue de la Bibliothèque
Nationale Suisse. Répertoire méthodique des publications suisses ou relatives à la Suisse, 1901-20,
1921-30, 1931-40, 1941-47*. Bern: Huber, 1922-54.

65 *Schweizer Bücherverzeichnis/Répertoire du livre suisse/
Repertorio del libro svizzero. 1948/50-*. Zürich:
Schweizerischer Büchhandler und Verlegerverein,
1951-. (Called Pt. 1 of the Switzerland Nat. Bibliography from 1951.)

First vol. covers 1948-50, published every five
years since 1951, continues the *Katalog* (see above). Cumu-
lates the entries in *Das Schweizer Buch*, except for periodicals which are published separately in the *Schweizer Zeit-
schriftenverzeichnis* (see Ch. 6, no. 172).

C. BOOKS IN PRINT

CANADA

66 *Catalogue de l'édition au Canada français, 1965-*. Montréal:
    Le Conseil supérieur du livre, avec le concours du
    Ministère des Affaires culturelles du Québec, 1965-.

          French Canadian books in print arranged in Dewey
    Classification order with author and title indexes and a
    list of publishers. Separate list for textbooks.

67 *Canadian Books in Print/Catalogue des Livres Canadiens en
          Librairie, 1967-*. Toronto: Canadian Books in Print
          Committee, 1968-. Annual.

          From 1967 through 1972 this source lists English
    and French books in print; in the 1967 ed. ca. 11,300
    English and ca. 5,400 French titles in print. Beginning
    with the 1973 ed. mostly English works are listed (some
    French titles are included if published by predominantly
    English language publishers). French titles were dropped
    because of the appearance of the *Répertoire de l'édition au
    Québec*. Excluded by policy from all volumes are maps, sheet
    music, newpapers, periodicals, catalogs, annuals (not of
    general interest), and most government publications (some
    of general interest are included). Pamphlets of less than
    fifty pages are excluded, but poetry and children's books
    are included.
          Separate author, title and publisher indexes. The
    1973 edition contains 14,295 entries including 1,890 titles
    published in 1973. The cut-off date was August 31, 1973.

68 *Répertoire de l'édition au Québec, 1972-*. Montréal: Assn.
          des éditeurs canadiens, Soc. des éditeurs de manuels
          scolaires du Québec, 1972- (*1974* ed. Québec: Edi-
          Québec). Annual.

          The *1974* edition lists ca. 13,000 books in print
    published in Quebec as of June 30, 1974. It has author and
    title indexes, a subject guide, list of publishers, list of
    publishers' series, lists of Quebec French literary periodica
    French-Canadian, French, Swiss and Belgian criticism, as well
    as book-trade publications in French. Kept up to date by
    the *Bibliographie du Québec*, and *Vient de paraître: Bulletin
    du Livre au Canada Français* (quarterly), Montréal: Le Conseil
    supérieur du livre.

69 *La Librairie française. Catalogue général des ouvrages en
    vente au 1er janvier 1930.* 3 vols. P.: Cercle de
    la Librairie, 1931-32. I-II: *Répertoire par noms
    d'auteurs*, 1931. III: *Répertoire par titres d'ouvrages
    (anonymes ou non anonymes)*, 1932.

    _____. *Supplément au 1er janvier 1933. Répertoire par
    auteurs et répertoire par titres.* P.: Cercle de la
    Librairie, 1933. 2 parties en 1 vol.

    _____. *Catalogue général des ouvrages parus du 1er
    janvier 1933 au 1er janvier 1946.* 3 vols. P.:
    Cercle de la Librairie, 1947-49. I-II: *Répertoire
    par auteurs*, 1947-48. III: *Répertoire par titres*,
    1949.

    _____. *Catalogue général des ouvrages parus du 1er
    janvier 1946 au 1er janvier 1956. Tables décennales.*
    3 vols. P.: Cercle de la Librairie, 1957-(58). I-
    II: *Auteurs et anonymes*, 1957. III: *Titres*, s.d.

    _____. *Tables décennales. Catalogue général des ouvrages
    parus en langue française entre le 1er janvier 1956
    et le 1er janvier 1966.* 4 vols. P.: Cercle de la
    Librairie, 1968. I-II: *Auteurs*. III-IV: *Titres*.

         All reprinted in P.: Cercle de la Librairie; vols.
    concerning years 1929-45 reprinted in Nendeln, Liechtenstein:
    Kraus.

         Report books in print, 1930-66, of French,
    Belgian, Swiss, and Canadian publishers.
         Fullest information including pagination, price,
    series and publisher is under the author entry.
         These repertories are based on *Les Livres de
    l'Année.*

70 *Catalogue des livres disponibles. Littérature et sciences
    humaines.* P.: Cercle de la Librairie, 1969.

         The publisher, in an *avertissement*, cautions that
    this edition is not complete, or free from errors, they will
    be corrected in a second edition.
         Pt. 1 is a *table méthodique* in literature and
    humanities. For literature there are twelve sections; each
    one is arranged alphabetically by author's name. Pt. 2 is
    an alphabetical list of titles. Pt. 3 is an index of
    authors, publishers and distributors.

71 *Catalogue de l'édition française. Une liste exhaustive des
    ouvrages disponibles publiés en français, de par le
    monde. 1970.* 4 vols. P.: VPC Livres, 1971 (1st
    ed.). (Published simultaneously in France, the U.S.A.
    and Canada.) 3e éd. 6 vols., 1974 (authors, titles,
    and subjects); 4e éd., 1975, 4 vols. (authors and
    titles); 5e éd. Cercle de la Librairie, 1976 (4 vols.
    authors and titles; 2 vols. subjects to be published
    in Jan. 1977).

         In early Nov. 1976, *Catalogue de l'édition fran-
    çaise,* the Cercle de la Librairie and France Expansion decide
    to pool their resources in order to form only one bank of
    bibliographic data. They will issue a *Répertoire des livres
    disponibles* on paper and on microfiche which will replace
    Catalogue de l'édition française and *Répertoire des livres de
    langue française disponibles.* The Cercle de la Librairie wil
    publish and distribute it for the association. The first
    repertory will be issued by the end of 1977. Apart from this
    common publication, the Cercle de la Librairie and France
    Expansion will pursue their own activities (information
    printed in *Bulletin du livre,* Nov. 15, 1976).
         The 5th ed. contains 209,000 titles of books in
    print in French, concerning 4,527 publishers and distributors
    and 5,800 collections.

72 *Répertoire des livres de langue française disponibles.* 2 vol
    P.: France Expansion, 1972 (1st ed.). 2e éd. 6 vols.,
    1975-76 (authors, titles, and subjects).

         Lists books pub. in French around the world.
    Repertory established by computer in cooperation with
    numerous national libraries. Second ed. gives separate lists
    of series and publishers. See no. 71 above.

D. CURRENT BIBLIOGRAPHIES

BELGIUM

73 *Bibliographie de Belgique. Liste Mensuelle des Publications
    Belges ou Relatives à la Belgique Acquises par la
    Bibliothèque Royale.* Bruxelles: Bibliothèque Royale,
    1875-.

         The plan, scope, contents, title, and arrangement
    have varied over the years. For some of these see Fernand
    Remy, *Bibliographie de Belgique,* vol. 57 (1931), 356-98.
         The official national bibliography for Belgium
    Currently reports publications of many kinds: books, brochure
    of five pages or more, new periodicals, photographs, govern-
    ment publications, geographic maps accompanied by commentary,
    etc. Published monthly with a special yearly issue for
    Belgicana, or foreign works about Belgium and works by
    Belgian authors published abroad.

There is also an annual cumulated index plus an additional alphabetical subject index (French and Flemish). Some years have an alphabetical title list of literary works.

CANADA

74 *Canadian Catalogue of Books Published in Canada, about Canada, as Well as Those Written by Canadians.* 28 nos. Toronto: Toronto Public Lib., 1923-50. Annual.

Covers books, pamphlets, and government publications (selectively) in French and English published in 1921-49. A cumulated edition of the English titles was published in 1967 (same title). Continued by *Canadiana*.

75 *Canadiana. Publications of Canadian Interest Received by the National Library/Publications se rapportant au Canada reçues par la Bibliothèque nationale, 1950-.* Ottawa: Nat. Lib., 1950-.

Monthly with annual cumulations. Indexes are monthly, with monthly, quarterly, semi-annual and annual cumulations.

This national bibliography of Canada ·includes material deposited in the National Library by law, plus other titles acquired by purchase or gift, i.e. books of Canadian interest published abroad and material by Canadians also published abroad. The types of material presently included are books, pamphlets, music scores, new periodicals and newspapers, films, microforms, recordings, theses, and government publications (federal and provincial). However, some of these types have been added after *Canadiana* began publication. For a detailed account see Ryder, Dorothy E. *Canadian Reference Sources: a Selective Guide.* Ottawa: Canadian Lib. Assn., 1973. Appendix A.

Canadiana is issued in a classified arrangement (Dewey Decimal Classification) and both the classified part and the indexes are bilingual. The cumulations of the indexes are excellent, listing authors, titles, subjects and key words of titles in alphabetical order; theses on microfilm (an extensive coverage) are listed alphabetically by author; there are two separate indexes of subjects keyed to the classification scheme, in English and French. A cumulated index for the years 1950-62 was published in 1965.

76 *Bibliographie du Québec. Liste trimestrielle des publications québécoises ou relatives au Québec, établie par la Bibliothèque nationale du Québec, 1968-.* Québec: Ministère des Affaires culturelles, 1968-.

One volume covering 1968 was published; in 1969 it became a quarterly with a cumulated annual index (authors,

titles and subjects in one alphabet). Monthly issues list
books, pamphlets and new serials deposited in the library,
and works published outside Quebec about the province, in
classified order according to the Library of Congress scheme.
A separate section lists publications of the Government of
Quebec. Works on French Canadian language and literature
can be found via the classified sections or through the
annual index.

FRANCE

77 *Annales typographiques ou Notice des progrès des connoissance
      humaines. . . .* P., 1759-63. Continued by:

78 *Catalogue hebdomadaire ou liste des livres qui sont mis en
      vente chaque semaine tant en France qu'en pays
      étrangers.* 27 vols. P., 1763-89. Takes the title
      of *Journal de la librairie ou Catalogue hebdomadaire*
      in 1782-89. In it, national books are separated
      from foreign books.

79 *Journal de Paris* (daily paper founded in 1777, P.) publishes
      from 1 July 1785 till 13 January 1786 a "Supplément":
      "Etat des livres, estampes. . . dont les exemplaires
      ont été fournis en vertu de l'arrêt du Conseil du
      roi." (Books, etchings. . . copies of which have
      been deposited according to the decree of the King's
      Council.)

80 *Journal général de la littérature de France ou Répertoire
      méthodique des livres nouveaux, cartes géographiques,
      estampes et oeuvres de musique qui paraissent en
      France.* 44 vols. P., 1798-1841.

            Parallels the *Journal typographique* and its
      sequels. (See below.)

81 *Journal typographique et bibliographique.* Founded in 1797,
      P. Becomes:

82 *Journal général de l'imprimerie et de la librairie* in 1810.
      P. Becomes:

83 *Bibliographie de l'Empire français* on 14 October 1811. P.
      Becomes:

84 *Bibliographie de la France ou Journal général de l'im-
      primerie et de la librairie.* P.: Cercle de la
      Librairie, 1814-; rpt. of years 1810-56, Nendeln,
      Liechtenstein: Kraus.

            A detailed description of this very important
      bibliography, and an account of the modifications occurring,
      is to be found in Malclès, *Manuel de bibliographie* (no. 9).

In Jan. 1972, the *Bibliographie de la France* absorbed *Biblio* (no. 86), formerly published by Hachette, and the title became *Bibliographie de la France-Biblio*. Here is its presentation in 1976:

It is a weekly review (48 fascicules in a year) of the book trade. Each week, its *Chronique* section (more than 2,000 pages over the year) contains: news of the publishing trade, new series, new books, etc. Each week also, the "Notices" (*Annonces*) section (preceded by a subject table entitled "Books of the Week," *Les Livres de la Semaine*) contains publishers' own announcements of their new books (over 12,000 titles a year, practically all the new publications), U.D.C. classification.

In addition, there is an "Official Bibliography" (*Bibliographie Officielle*) compiled by the Bibliothèque Nationale (entries concerning publications deposited at the B.N. in compliance to the law). It contains:

    a. "New Books" (*Livres*) (weekly)
    b. "Supplements" (*Suppléments*):
        1. "Serials" (*Publications en série*) (monthly)
        2. "Official Publications" (*Publications officielles*) (bi-monthly)
        3. "Music" (*Musique*)
        4. "Maps and Plans" (*Cartes et plans*) (2 issues per year)

The weekly *Bibliographie de la France* is supplemented mainly by:

Les Livres du Mois ("Books of the Month"): list by subjects, with an index of authors and titles. U.D.C. classification.

Les Tables Trimestrielles des Nouveautés ("Quarterly Lists of New Publications"): recapitulation of the production of the last three months.

Les Livres de l'Année-Biblio (see no. 85).

Since January 1975, the *Bibliographie Officielle* is automated. The computer provides expeditiously: registration of new titles, production of indexes, cumulative lists, and the texts of the *Livres*.

The *Bibliographie Officielle* is placed on tape and sent to other national bibliographical centers, which send their own in return.

The supplements will be automated in the near future. Already supplement 1, *Publications en Série*, follows the international norm of cataloging ISBD(S), International Standard Book Description (Serials), and gives moreover the ISSN, International Standard Serial Number, of all the new French serials.

85 *Les Livres de l'Année, 1922-1970.* P.: Cercle de la Librairie 1923-71. Annual. *1922-1933*, rpt., Nendeln, Liechtenstein: Kraus. (*1934-*, available at P.: Cercle de la Librairie.)

Cumulated from the *Annonces* of the *Bibliographie de la France*, with in addition unannounced books published in French in France and abroad.
Classified list (U.D.C.), followed by separate title and author indexes which refer to page number in the classified part for the most complete entry. The classified part is preceded by an "Index de mots usuels et des mots vedettes" (with page references), to help find books in the classification by more specific subjects. Continued by:

Les Livres de l'Année-Biblio, 1971-. P.: Cercle de la Librairie, 1972-. Annual.

Formed by the merger of *Les Livres de l'Année* and *Biblio*, this is the only French *catalôgue-dictionnaire*; it has become the most comprehensive and convenient annual source for finding all publications in French throughout the world. It is all the more important since the *Bibliographie de la France* also merged with *Biblio* in 1972, thus combining into one bibliographical system: the commercial or trade bibliography with the French national bibliography of France; they add information drawn from foreign bibliographies. The titles published (25,000 in *1975*) are entered by names of authors and translators; by general titles and vol. title; by editors, prefacers, illustrators; and by subjects and keywords, in one alphabetical sequence.

86 *Biblio. Catalogue des ouvrages parus en langue française dans le monde entier. 1934-1970.* Tomes 1-37. P.: Hachette, 1935-71; rpt., t. 1-36, Nendeln, Liechtenstein: Kraus, 1935-70. (All available at P.: Cercle de la Librairie.)

An annual *catalogue-dictionnaire* of the bibliographical section of the monthly periodical *Biblio*. It is based on the *Bibliographie de la France*, but is expanded greatly to encompass French publications from all parts of the world (Canada, Switzerland, Belgium, Algeria, etc.). For the period covered, it is the most comprehensive and convenient source for searching French publications in general.

In 1971, *Biblio* merged with *Les Livres de l'Année* (see no. 85), in 1972 it was absorbed by the *Bibliographie de la France* (see no. 84).

87 *Francophonie-Edition*. P.: France Expansion, nov. 1972-. Three issues in May, July, and October.

An annual repertory of ca. 700 pp., pub. in March, under a different title. Last vol. pub.: *Douze Mois d'édition francophone 1975*, 1976.

This repertory gives a complete bibliographical documentation on the new books, journals, audio-visual materials, microfiches, and literary records, published in French all over the world in the preceding year. Every item is classified under authors, titles, and subjects.

The content of this publication is entered simultaneously in specialized repertories undertaken also by France Expansion: *Répertoire des livres de langue française disponibles, Répertoire de l'édition au Québec, Répertoire des matériels audiovisuels, Répertoire de la micro-édition*, etc.

88 *L'Année francophone 1974*. P.: CEF, 1975.

In 648 pages, it records 29,609 books, classified by authors and by titles, with their prices on Jan. 1, 1975. This work contains also a list of 3,941 publishers recorded in forty-three countries, and of 5,715 collections.

Selective Bibliographies

89 *Bulletin Critique du Livre Français*. P.: Assn. pour la diffusion de la pensée française, 1945-. Reprinted.

Monthly bibliographical journal. Drawn up by a committee composed of professors and librarians who retain only those publications of real interest. More than 200 analyses per issue; mentions of bibliographies, encyclopedias, literature, sciences, humanities, followed by a summary of main French journals. Monthly and annual indexes. Since Jan. 1971, the *Bulletin Critique* publishes quarterly reviews in English (*New French Books*) and Spanish (*Nuevos libros franceses*); they will be discontinued in 1977.

Since 1974, it mentions for each book its ISBN number.

90 *Les Livres. Bulletin Bibliographique mensuel*. P.: Institut Pédagogique Nat., SEVPEN, 1951-.

The works, selected by the "Commission des livres" of the "Institut pédagogique national," are presented briefly with publisher and price, under a systematic classification. For each title, notices are followed by a critical analysis; the category of readers to which the books might be best suited is indicated. The analyses are signed.

SWITZERLAND

91 *Bibliographie und literarische Chronik der Schweiz/ Bibliographie et chronique littéraire de la Suisse.* 31 vols. Zürich: Schweiz antiquariat, 1871-77; Basel: George, 1878-1901. (Title 1871-77: *Bibliographie der Schweiz/Bibliographie de la Suisse.)*

Monthly, with annual author index.
Content: books, maps, atlases, music, new periodicals, theses, official publications, *Helvetica.* Continued by:

92 *Bibliographisches Bulletin der Schweiz/Bulletin Bibliographique de la Bibliothèque Nationale Suisse.* Berne, 1901-42.

Monthly, with annual index of authors up to 1916, then of subjects only; since 1938: author and subject index. Cumulated in a *Katalog.* . . (no. 64). Continued by:

93 *Das Schweizer Buch/Le Livre suisse/Il libro svizzero. Bibliographisches Bulletin der Schweizerischen Landesbibliothek/Bulletin Bibliographique de la Bibliothèque Nationale Suisse.* Zürich, 1943-.

In two series. Series A (semi-monthly) lists book trade titles, including works about Switzerland published abroad; Series B (every two months) lists non-book trade items such as theses, society and institutional publications. Non-book types such as maps, phonodiscs and new periodical titles are included in Series A. Arranged in a classified order with the indexes for both Series A and B cumulating together semi-annually and annually. (Alphabetical author-title index.)
Since January 1976, Series A and B are published together semi-monthly.

The content of the two series forms, since 1948, the official retrospective bibliography of Switzerland: *Schweizer Bücherverzeichnis* (no. 65).

The *Schweizer Buch* is complemented by: *Der schweizer Buchhandel/La Librairie suisse/La libreria svizzera.* Jan. 1943-.

Semi-monthly publication of the Swiss associations of publishers and book-dealers. In two parts: *"Chronique"* (on the book-trade), and *"Annonces."*

CHAPTER 4

REFERENCE WORKS

See Ch. 1: Malclès (no. 8)

A. MAIN REFERENCE WORKS

94 Beaudiquez, Marcelle, et Zundel-Benkhémis, Anne. *Ouvrages
    de référence pour les bibliothèques publiques. Réper-
    toire bibliographique.* P.: Cercle de la Librairie, 197█

        Contains the following parts (all items except
    Ch. 10 concern France mainly): Generalities (Encyclopedias
    and Dictionaries, biographies, yearly publications, bib-
    liographies, periodicals, French administration and everyday
    life); 1. Philosophy and psychology; 2. Religion; 3. Social
    Sciences; 4. Linguistics; 5. and 6. Pure and Applied Sci-
    ences; 7. Fine Arts; 8. Literature; 9. Geography and History;
    10. Countries other than France; Index.

95 Calot, Frantz, et Thomas, Georges. *Guide Pratique de bi-
    bliographie.* 2e éd. refondue avec le concours de
    Clément Duval. P.: Delagrave, 1950.

        Lists, describes, and analyzes: encyclopedias,
    biographies, specialized repertories, and general bibliog-
    raphies. 1,361 items with annotations. Index of authors
    and subjects.

96 Walford, Albert John. *Guide to Reference Material.* 2nd ed.
    3 vols. London: Library Assn., 1966-1970.
    I. Science and Technology, 1966.
    II. Philosophy and Psychology, Religion, Social
    Sciences, Geography, Biography and History, 1968.
    III. Generalities, Languages, The Arts and Lit-
    erature, 1970.

        Much enlarged from the first ed. (1959) and its
    suppl. (1963), this edition approximates, or exceeds slightly
    the number of sources cited by Winchell (8th ed. plus three
    supps.). Walford has about 10,000 principal entries plus
    about 3,500 additional titles in the annotations, while
    Winchell has ca. 11,000 citations plus an uncounted number
    of additional references.
        While duplication is considerable between the two
    works, they complement one another, and are both very useful.
    Walford stresses recency of publication, is strong in British
    reference sources and has given greater emphasis in this
    edition to foreign language sources, Africa, author bib-
    liographies, linguistics, manuscript collections, etc.

For the subjects covered in vol. 3, this edition
has about 3,700 items plus ca. 1,000 more in notes. The
annotations are brief, descriptive and occasionally evalu-
ative. Frequently one finds annotations for works not in
Winchell, or more informative annotations. Walford often
cites a critical review, or other source of criticism, about
the reference works listed. Includes publications with imprints up to March, 1970. Authors, titles and subjects index.
       Third edition in progress, vols. I and II
pub. in 1975.

97 Winchell, Constance Mabel. *Guide to Reference Books.* 8th
            ed. Chicago: Am. Lib. Assn., 1967. *First Supplement,*
            1965-1966, 1968. *Second Supplement, 1967-1968,* 1970.
            Third Supplement, 1969-1970, 1972. 9th ed., 1976.

       The standard, most widely used, American guide
covering general reference works, the humanities, social
sciences, history and area studies, and the pure and applied
sciences. The 8th ed. has ca. 7,500 titles plus those noted
in annotations. The three supplements add ca. 3,500 titles.
It is updated regularly in the Jan. and July issues of *College*
and Research Libraries, a feature edited by Eugene P. Sheehy.
The updating is very useful, for there is about a two year
lag from coverage date to publication date.
       There is a natural emphasis on American reference
works; but foreign works are well represented with particularly strong coverage of national and subject bibliography,
academic rather than popular subjects, and retrospective
reference sources. It is reputed to be especially valuable
in the humanities and social sciences. It is also notable
for its accuracy and completeness in regard to bibliographic
data and description.
       Winchell has provided useful introductory remarks
for most sections discussing the nature of reference work,
the kinds of information frequently wanted, and the more
important basic reference sources involved.
       Annotations vary greatly in length, from a column
or more to a brief descriptive sentence. However, most of
the major works are annotated, some in great detail. Eval-
uative or comparative judgements are rare. Critical reviews
are cited only in the supplements.
       The alphabetical index lists authors, main entries,
subjects and some titles.

98 Wynar, Bohdan S. *Introduction to Bibliography and Reference*
            Work; A Guide to Materials and Sources. 4th ed. rev.
            Rochester, N.Y.: Libraries Unlimited, 1967.

       A guide for library science students in bibliog-
raphy and general reference work which discusses the historical development and current aspects of bibliography of
bibliography, several national and trade bibliographies, library catalogs (U.S., British and French), and with separate

chapters for indexes and other types of reference books. It provides the student a good initiation to the areas covered, about 270 first-rate annotations of specific works, book review citations and reading lists.

B.   ON SCHOLARLY PUBLICATION

I.   SCHOLARLY ADVICE

99   Cargill, Oscar; Charvat, William; and Walsh, Donald D. *The Publication of Academic Writing.* N.Y.: MLA, 1966.

100   Chicago. University Press. *A Manual of Style for Authors, Editors, and Copywriters.* 12th ed. rev. Chicago: U. of Chicago Pr., 1967.

> A detailed manual on preparation of manuscripts, books and articles, written by editors of one of the principal university presses.

101   Pell, William. "Facts of Scholarly Publishing." *PMLA,* 88 (Sept. 1973), 639-670.

> An important article on the various journals and university presses in the U.S. which accept work in the fields of the languages.
> Each journal and press is listed with a brief summary of the kind of material accepted for publication.
> A table at the end lists journals, their circulation, and statistics. It indicates how many manuscripts have been accepted and refused, the time involved from acceptance to publication, whether reviews are accepted, etc.

102   Thorpe, James. *The Use of Manuscripts in Literary Research; Problems of Access and Literary Property Rights.* N.Y.: MLA, 1974.

> "Guides the researcher in the use of manuscripts held by libraries and private collectors. Valuable for the inexperienced scholar and a handy reference for the seasoned one."

II.   STYLE MANUALS

103   Dufour, M.-L. *Le Tapuscrit. Recommandations pour la présentation et la dactylographie des travaux scientifiques (Sciences Humaines)* réunies par M.-L. Dufour. P.: Ecole Pratique des Hautes Etudes. VIe section. Service des Publications, 1971.

> How to document, organize, and present a typescript.

04 Gouriou, C. *Mémento typographique*. P.: Hachette, 1961.

            A very detailed style sheet for publications in
France.

05 *MLA Style Sheet*. 2nd ed. rev. N.Y.: MLA, 1970.

            "The indispensable reference on the preparation
of material for publication. Special attention is given to
the preparation of theses and term papers." Official style
sheet of most publishers.

06 Turabian, Kate L. *A Manual for Writers of Term Papers,
        Theses, and Dissertations*. 4th ed. Chicago: U. of
        Chicago Pr., 1973.

            "Designed as a guide to suitable style in the
typewritten presentation of formal papers in both scientific
and non-scientific fields." It provides many precious details and examples; but the user should be aware that it
differs sometimes from the rules of the *MLA Style Sheet*.

CHAPTER 5

CATALOGS OF BOOKS AND MANUSCRIPTS OF MAIN LIBRARIES

See Ch. 1: Malclès (no. 8), and Ch. 4: Walford (no. 96), and Winchell (no. 97).

A. MAIN RESEARCH LIBRARIES AND DOCUMENTATION CENTERS

107 *International Library Directory. A World Directory of Libraries*. 3rd ed. London: A. P. Wales, 1968.

Covers 150 countries. Primary arrangement is by name of country, then by provinces, states (if any), and names of cities. Indicates address, librarian, type of library, main subjects, languages, and number of volumes in collection. Lack of an index reduces its effectiveness.

108 Paris. Bibliothèque Nationale. *Répertoire des Bibliothè-ques et organismes de documentation 1971*, par Mireill Olivier, avec la collab. de Marie-Bernadette Jullien et Jacqueline Mallet. P.: B.N., 1971.

Supersedes three earlier repertories pub. by the B.N., i.e., *Guide pratique des bibliothèques de Paris*, by Emile Leroy, 1937; *Répertoire des bibliothèques de France*, 1950-51; and *Répertoire des bibliothèques d'étude et orga-nismes de documentation*, 1963.
Contents: *Région parisienne* et *Départements*. Ind
A directory and survey of 3,210 libraries and doc-umentary centers of France. Gives names, addresses, per-sonnel, regulations, catalogs, resources, history, publi-cations, etc. Special collections on French language and literature and individual French authors are noted, as well as collections of documents and MSS. Index includes *départ ments*, names of libraries, subjects, etc.

_____. *Supplément 1973*, par M. Olivier avec la collab. de M.-B. Jullien. P.: B.N., 1973.

The announcement for this supp. reads as follows:
"In this supplement 957 institutions are added to the 3,210 which were listed in the 1971 edition: 30% of th have opened since 1968. In the descriptions one can find: practical information such as addresses, telephone numbers, hours, conditions of entrance, lending and research; main aspects of the holdings, their nature, importance and his-tory, the catalogs available, etc. The dictionary index (3,696 entries on all subjects) is a useful complement to this repertory.
A twenty-four page leaflet gives updated (to Oct. 1973) information on university and interuniversity li-

braries and adds some complementary data to the descriptions included in the 1971 *Répertoire*."

B. CATALOGS OF BOOKS

FRANCE

109 Paris. Bibliothèque Nationale. *Catalogue général des livres imprimés de la Bibliothèque Nationale. Auteurs.* P.: Imprimerie Nationale, 1897-(in progress).

In 1974, vol. CCXXI reached word "Wetzstein."

A catalog of inestimable importance of one of the world's greatest libraries. The last volumes cover works published through 31 December 1959. Supplements are issued to continue the catalog of books in latin alphabet, a five year cumulation: *Catalogue général des livres imprimés: auteurs, collectivités-auteurs, anonymes, ouvrages parus de 1960 à 1964.* 12 vols. Paris: B.N., 1965-1967; and a ten year cumulation: *1960-69*, 1972- (12 vols. pub. by 1975, out of the twenty-four announced).

It is important to remember that the basic catalog does not include collective authors (government agencies, societies, etc.), anonymous works, titles for collections of documents, etc. Moreover, it has bypassed many twentieth century authors over the years because of its A-Z alphabetical author entries and the slow publishing schedule.

However, for authors included, the catalog is done with great care and accuracy. The titles within an author's collected works are listed volume by volume; voluminous author's works are systematically classified; reprints, extracts of periodical articles, etc. are cited, if separately published.

For many famous authors, the library has issued about sixty-six off-print catalogs; some of these catalogs include books in other P. libraries. Many other catalogs have been pub. for periodicals, documents, manuscripts, exhibitions, and several subject or classified catalogs in history, of great bibliographical importance; e.g., *Catalogue de l'histoire de France* (18 vols., 1855-1895, rpt. in 16 vols. in 1968); *Catalogue de l'histoire de la Révolution Française* par A. Martin et G. Walter (6 vols., 1936-1955), and *Répertoire de l'histoire de la Révolution Française. Travaux publiés de 1800 à 1940* (2 vols., 1941-1951).

GERMANY

110 *Deutscher Gesamtkatalog. Hrsg. von der Preussischen Staatsbibliothek. . . .*Vols. 1-14. Berlin: Preussische Druckerei-und-Verlags Aktiengessellschaft, 1931-1939.

Vols. 1-14: A-Beethordnung. No more published.
Vols. 1-8: A (1931-1935), as *Gesamtkatalog der*

Preussischen Staatsbibliotheken, lists the holdings of
eleven large Prussian libraries as well as those of the
Bavarian State Library and the Austrian National Library,
Vienna. Includes about 2,500,000 items ranged over the
whole alphabet. Includes books published up to 1930, excluding Orientalia, maps, music and dissertations. With
vol. 9 and the letter "B," scope was extended to cover 110
German and Austrian libraries. An author, anonymous-title
catalog. This catalog is incomplete.
     Supplemented by: *Deutsche Gesamtkatalog. Neue
Titel* (1892-1944), the annual cumulations of which are
partly cumulated in *Berliner Titeldrucke: Fünfjahrs-
Katalog,* 1930/34-1935/39 (1935-1940), two sequences each
in eight vols.
     The title *Berliner Titeldrucke* is now used for the
present Deutsche Staatsbibliothek's *Jahreskatalog* (e.g.,
Berliner Titeldrucke. Jahreskatalog 1964). 2 vols.
Berlin, 1966.

GREAT BRITAIN

111 British Museum. Dept. of Printed Books. *General Catalogue
      of Printed Books. Photolithographed Edition to 1955.*
      263 vols. London: Trustees of the British Museum,
      1965-66.

     For the history and evolution of this edition see
Ch. 4: Winchell (no. 97), AA67.

          . *Ten-year Supplement, 1956-65.* 50 vols. London,
1968. (Further 10-year supplements are planned.)

          . *Five-year Supplement, 1966-70.* 26 vols. Lon-
don, 1971-72.

     The printed catalog of a massive, general collec-
tion from the beginning of printing to the present; the
principal source for British publications before 1950, when
the *British National Bibliography* began. All languages
(except Oriental) are cataloged, primarily by names of
authors in alphabetical order. Initials, pseudonyms, etc.
are included; anonymous works and collections of documents,
etc. are interfiled by title. Publications of academies,
societies, institutions, and governments are found under
place-names. Large collections such as England, France,
U.S.A., Bible, Liturgies, have special indexes. Voluminous
authors' works are **systematically** classified, usually with
an index of titles.
     In a limited way the catalog serves as a subject
catalog for books about persons, places. Certain topics are
added to such entries via addenda, see-references, etc.
Many catchword subjects (i.e., Europe, French Literature,
French Poets) are used by selecting key words from titles,
but the number of books found through such subjects is too

small for effective bibliographical searching. For literary scholars, perhaps the most valuable aspect of the subject approach is that biographical and critical works about authors may be found under names of authors.

_____. *Subject Index of the Modern Works Added to the Library of the British Museum, 1881-1900.* 3 vols. London: British Museum, 1902-03. Continued by:

_____. *Subject Index of the Modern Works Added to the British Museum Library.* Vol. 1-: *1901/05-* (quinquennial). Number of vols. in quinquennial eds. vary; 11 vols. in 21 through 1965.

112 Peddie, Robert Alexander. *Subject Index of Books Published up to and Including 1880.* 4 vols. London: Grafton, 1933-48. (Vol. 1 has title: *Subject Index of Books Published Before 1880.*) Rpt., London: Pordes, 1962.

Mainly, but not exclusively, books in the British Museum Library.
The three above subject indexes are arranged alphabetically by subject, A-Z. Several limitations to their usefulness are apparent: they represent a small selection from the library's large collection, works of pure literature are excluded, and they are difficult to use due to the lack of a systematic, logical order of entries under the subjects consulted.

113 Adams, Herbert Mayow. *Catalogue of Books Printed on the Continent of Europe, 1501-1600, in Cambridge Libraries.* Comp. by H. M. Adams. 2 vols. Cambridge: U. Pr., 1967.

Vol. 1: A-M; Vol. 2: N-Z.
Contains an author list of about 30,000 items numbered under each letter of the alphabet, abridged titles, full imprints, signature collations. Locations in thirty-five libraries (British Museum, Cambridge U. Lib., Fitzwilliam Museum, Whipple Museum, plus college and departmental libraries). Vol. 2 includes index of printers (name, date, works printed) and index of places, with names of printers.

114 London Library. *Catalogue of the London Library.* New ed. 2 vols. London: London Lib., 1913-14. Supps.: *1913-20* (1920), *1920-28* (1929), *1928-50* (1953).

First published in 1847.
Entries give author, title (sometimes abbreviated) and date, and note inclusion of bibliographies. Uses cataloging rules akin to those of the British Museum. Well over 500,000 entries; the third supp. alone lists

about 150,000 vols. Particularly rich in such subjects as history, philosophy and literature. Frénch authors are wel represented. Biographical and critical works about them follow a listing of their works, editions, etc.

_____. *Subject Index of the London Library, St. James's Square, London,* by C. T. Hagberg Wright, Secretary and Librarian. London: London Lib., 1909-55.
   Vol. 2: *Additions, 1909-22.* Vol. 3: *Additions, 1923-38.* Vol. 4: *Additions, 1938-53.*

Alphabetical subject arrangement, A-Z. Entries are found under countries, literary genres, places, etc. In French studies, entries beginning with French (Drama, Language, Fiction, Poetry, etc.) are useful. There are also headings for Belgian, Canadian, and Swiss literatures.

ITALY

115 Roma (City). Centro Nazionale per il catalogo unico delle biblioteche italiane e per le informazioni bibliografiche. *Primo catalogo collettivo delle biblioteche italiane.* Roma: Centro Nazionale per il Catalogo Unico delle Biblioteche Italiane, 1962-. Vol. 1

A union catalog of the holdings of books printed between 1500 and 1957 in the national libraries of Rome, Florence, Naples and Milan, and in seven other state libraries in Rome.

UNITED STATES

116 California University. Library (Los Angeles). *Dictionary Catalog.* 129 vols. Boston, Mass.: G. K. Hall, 1963.

2,703,000 photolithographed card entries. The UCLA Library has collections of materials on Near Eastern Studies, Folklore, African Studies, Latin American Studies International Relations. Also maintained are holdings in the history of science, Medieval and Renaissance Studies, etc.

117 U.S. Library of Congress. *A Catalog of Books Represented by Library of Congress Printed Cards Issued to July 31, 1942.* 167 vols. Ann Arbor, Mich.: Edwards, 1942-46. *Supplement:* cards issued August 1, 1942-December 31, 1947. 42 vols. 1948.
   Continued by:

_____. *Library of Congress Author Catalog: A Cumulativ List of Works Represented by Library of Congress Printed Cards, 1948-1952.* 24 vols. Ann Arbor, Mich Edwards, 1953.
   Vols. 1-23, Authors. Vol. 24, Films.

Continued by:

118 *National Union Catalog: A Cumulative Author List Representing Library of Congress Printed Cards and Titles
Reported by Other American Libraries, 1953-1957.* 28
vols. Ann Arbor, Mich.: Edwards, 1958.
    Vols. 1-26, Authors. Vol. 27, Music and Phono-
records.
    Vol. 28, Motion Pictures and Filmstrips.

_____. *Pre-1956 Imprints.* *A Cumulative Author List
Representing Library of Congress Printed Cards and
Titles Reported by Other American Libraries.* Comp.
and ed. with the cooperation of the L.C. and
the *NUC* Sub-Committee of the Resources and Technical
Services Division, Am. Lib. Assn. London: Mansell,
1968-.

    In progress. To be completed in ten years in about
610 vols. Together with the 1958-1962 cumulation listed
below, this catalog supersedes (when completed) the three
catalogs above through 1957, except for music and phonorecords, motion pictures and filmstrips.

_____. *A Cumulative Author List . . . 1958-1962.*
54 vols. N.Y.: Rowman and Littlefield, 1963.
    Vols. 1-50, Authors. Vols. 51-52, Music and
Phonorecords.
    Vols. 53-54, Motion Pictures and Filmstrips.
    Includes all 1956-57 imprints in the 1953-57
cumulation above.

_____. *1963-1967.* 67 vols. Ann Arbor, Mich.: Edwards,
1969.
    Vols. 1-59, Authors. Vols. 60-67, Register of
Additional Locations. Music and Phonorecords, 3
vols. Motion Pictures and Filmstrips, 2 vols.

_____. *1968-1972.* 119 vols. Ann Arbor, Mich.: Edwards,
1973.
    Vols. 1-104, Authors. Vols. 105-119, Register of
Additional Locations. Music and Phonorecords, 5
vols. (Motion Pictures and Filmstrips issued separately).

_____. *1973-.* Washington, D.C.: L.C., 1974-.
    Monthly, with quarterly, annual and quinquennial
cumulations.

    The current continuation of the cumulations above.

Listed above, from the basic L.C. catalog to date, are the catalogs necessary for a thorough search. For a more complete record and detailed description see Ch. 4: Winchell (no. 97) and supps.

There are two cumulations issued by commercial publishers used by many libraries, i.e., *Library of Congress and National Union Catalog Author Lists, 1942-1962: A Master Cumulation*. 152 vols. Detroit: Gale Research, 1969. And *The National Union Catalog 1956 through 1967. A Cumulative Author List Representing Library of Congress Printed Cards and Titles Reported by Other American Libraries*. 125 vols. Totawa, N.J.: Rowman and Littlefield, 1970-72.

The L.C. *Catalog* . . . through 1952 includes most copyrighted books and other material having printed cards. It includes some material in certain governmental libraries and in a small number of university and research libraries who participated in a limited cooperative cataloging program. Generally the catalog reflects a very strong collection of American imprints, important holdings for Great Britain, Germany and France, but less important for other countries. Beginning in 1953, the *National Union Catalog* added material from about 500 American and Canadian libraries (increased to 750 in 1958-62, and to ca. 1,100 later), resulting in a dramatic expansion of material included, particularly in foreign languages. During this period also, the L.C. itself greatly expanded its own aquisitions program for foreign material, especially in Europe (West and East), Israel, Egypt, India, Pakistan, etc. Mainly books are involved, but the catalog also has entries for pamphlets, maps, atlases, periodicals, serials, and government documents with separate catalogs for music, recordings and films. Consequently the NUC has become an extremely important current international bibliographic source.

As noted above, the *National Union Catalog. Pre-1956 Imprints* is to supersede the *Library of Congress Catalog* . . . . This project is based on a Union Catalog card file at the L.C.; the printed catalog, when complete, will represent the holdings of about 700 American and Canadian libraries, plus L.C., together about ten million entries. The catalog has a great many helpful *see* and *see also* references, many serials and some manuscripts. Materials in non-Latin alphabets are limited to those with L.C. printed cards. Its great strong point is its very extensive coverage of monographs in many languages, from the beginning of printing,   through 1955.

119   U.S.   Library of Congress. *The Library of Congress Catalog. Books: Subjects*. Washington, D.C.: L.C., 1950-. Quarterly (with annual and five year cumulations). Publisher for cumulations varies, i.e *1950-54* (20 vols.), Ann Arbor, Mich.: Edwards, 1955. *1955-59* (22 vols.), Paterson, N.J.: Pageant Books, 1960. *1960-64* (25 vols.), Edwards, 1965. *1965-69*

(42 vols.), Edwards, 1970.

A-Z subject arrangement: the quarterly parts list recent publications, but cumulations include publications from 1945. Omits the notes and tracings given in the author catalog.

For modern books this is the fullest and most up to date subject catalog, giving many more specific entries than the British Museum's *Subject Index*. It is extremely useful for critical material on French authors, literary genres, history, bibliography and similar materials on French literature in Belgium, Canada, etc.

120 New York (City). Public Library. Research Libraries. *Dictionary Catalog of the Research Libraries: A Cumulative List of Authors, Titles, and Subjects Representing Books and Book-Like Materials Added to the Collections since January 1, 1971.* N.Y.: N.Y. Pub. Lib., 1972-. (Issued as basic volumes with monthly cumulative supps.; the basic vols., cumulating all previous volumes and supps., are reissued from time to time.)

The printed catalog of one of the major research libraries in the U.S. It represents from 65,000 to 75,000 titles added per year and includes books, microfilms and music scores. Beginning Jan. 1974, non-book materials such as maps, phonorecords and motion pictures were added. Entries in the catalog are alphabetical by author (including corporate bodies such as societies, government agencies, names of conferences or symposia, co-authors, editors, compilers, etc.), by title, by subject, and by series title. Critical material about authors may be found under their names and there are subject headings (with subdivisions) for French Drama, French Language, French Poetry, French Literature, etc. Works on Belgian, Canadian, Swiss literature, etc. may also be found under subject entries.

C. CATALOGS OF MANUSCRIPTS

121 Richardson, Ernest Cushing. *A List of Printed Catalogs of Manuscript Books.* N.Y.: Burt Franklin, 1972. (Rpt. of vol. 3 of *A Union World Catalog of Manuscript Books: Preliminary Studies in Method.* N.Y.: Wilson, 1935.)

An extensive bibliography of lists of manuscripts published in various ways--books, library catalogs, archives, periodical articles, learned society publications, etc. It is arranged first by city or place, then alphabetically by author, title, library, etc., under the place.

The author used a bibliography on cards at the L.C. as a basis for this list and there are a great many abbreviations and incomplete references, making it a difficult tool to use. While locations for many of the lists in American libraries are indicated, a great many would have to be searched in the *National Union Catalog* or other sources.

There are no indexes of writers, or subjects, or other approach to the nature of the manuscript collections listed.

FRANCE

122 Bibliothèque littéraire Jacques Doucet. *Catalogue de manuscrits de la bibliothèque littéraire Jacques Doucet.* Boston: G. K. Hall, 1972.

A catalog of an important collection of literary manuscripts and correspondence of numerous French literary figures.

123 France. Ministère de l'Instruction Publique. *Catalogue général des manuscrits des bibliothèques publiques des départements.* 7 vols. P.: Imprimerie Impériale, 1849-85. (Rpt., Farnborough: Gregg, 1969). Continued by:

France. Ministère de l'Education Nationale. *Catalogue général des manuscrits des bibliothèques publiques de France. Départements.* . . . P.: Plon et B.N., 1885-. (58 vols. up to 1974.)

Each vol. is devoted to a *département,* or group of them, and presents a detailed catalog of the manuscripts in each library, archive, or museum. Each has a forward touching on the history, and the most important types of manuscripts collected. The items in the main part of each catalog are numbered in sequence and described. There follows an index of place names, subjects and personal names.

The wealth of research material in history, biography, religion, science, literature, etc. which can be recovered through these catalogs is almost beyond estimate. In literature, for example, using the indexes under names of authors one finds photographs, journals, correspondence, separate letters, bibliographies, literary works in manuscript, fragments of incomplete works, critical and biographical works, copies, facsimiles, published editions, proof copies, etc.

124 Gallet-Guerne, Danielle. *Les Sources de l'histoire littéraire aux Archives Nationales.* Préf. d'André Chamson. P.: Imprimerie Nationale, 1961.

A survey and description of the collections, or series, in the Archives Nationales, with particular attention to material of value in literary research on French literary history, drama and specific French authors. The

analysis of the archives points out documents, correspondence, records, personal papers, literary manuscripts,
etc., having biographical, historical and critical importance. There are many footnote references to inventories
of the archives, and to published articles, books, bibliographies and theses. An index of authors helps one to
quickly find sources scattered throughout the archives.

125 Paris. Bibliothèque Nationale. *Les Catalogues imprimés
de la Bibliothèque Nationale. Liste établie en 1943,
suivie d'un supplément. 1944-1952. 1. Manuscrits.*
P.: B.N., 1953.

     Manuscript lists are grouped as follows: "Géné-
ralités, Fonds orientaux, Fonds grec, Fonds latin et français, Fonds français, Anciens fonds spéciaux, Histoire des
provinces. . . Bibliographie."

126 Paris. Bibliothèque Nationale. Département des Manuscrits. *Les Catalogues du Département des manuscrits
occidentaux* par Lydia Mérigot et Pierre Gasnault.
P.: B.N., 1974.

     _____. *Nouvelles Acquisitions du département des manu-
scrits pendant les années 1891-1910. Répertoire alphabétique des manuscrits latins et français,* par Henri
Omont, Paris: B.N., 1912.

     _____. *Catalogue général des manuscrits français. Table
générale alphabétique des anciens et nouveaux fonds
(nos. 1-33,264) et des nouvelles acquisitions (nos.
1-10,000).* Comps. A. Vidier et P. Perrier. 6 vols.
P.: B.N., 1931-48.

     _____. *Nouvelles Acquisitions françaises 1946-1957
(nos. 13,005-14,061 et 24,219-25,100).* P.: B.N., 1967.

     _____. *Nouvelles Acquisitions latines et françaises
du département des manuscrits pendant les années
1958-1964, 1965-1968, 1969-1971.* P.: B.N., 1966-1973.

GREAT BRITAIN

127 British Museum. Department of Manuscripts. *Catalogue of
Romances in the Department of Manuscripts in the
British Museum.* 3 vols. London: British Museum,
1883-1910. (Rpt. 1962.)

     Selected from the various manuscript collections
in the British Museum and providing historical background
information and bibliographical details. Vol. 1 covers
Classical romances, British and English traditions, French
traditions (Cycle of Charlemagne, etc.), miscellaneous
romances, allegorical and didactic romances. Vol. 2 in-

cludes Northern legends and tales, Aesopic fables, Reynard the Fox. Vol. 3: Exempla and moralized tales in prose and verse.

In regard to French MSS, frequent references of a comparative nature are made to other MSS in the B.N. and other French MS collections.

SWITZERLAND

128 Bibliotheca Bodmeriana. *Manuscrits et autographes fran-çais.* Catalogue établi par Bernard Gagnebin. Cologny-Genève: Fondation Martin Bodmer, 1973.

This catalogue lists all the MSS and autographs written in French, as of the sixteenth century, owned in this private and precious collection.

129 _____. *Manuscrits français du Moyen Age.* Catalogue établi par Françoise Vielliard. Cologny-Genève: Fondation Martin Bodmer, 1974.

This catalogue lists twenty-eight medieval MSS of importance in literature and art with detailed descriptions, excerpts, and a record of owners. A selective bibliography and index is included.

UNITED STATES

130 Hamer, Philip M. *A Guide to Archives and Manuscripts in the United States.* Comp. for the National Historical Publications Commission. New Haven: Yale U. Pr., 1961.

A list of archival and MS repositories arranged alphabetically by state and city. It includes historical societies, public, academic, corporate, and other types of libraries and archives. Collections are described generally as to subject, number and type of archives or MSS. In the case of large collections descriptions are extensive. There is an alphabetical index of names and subjects. While the materi is mostly concerned with U.S. historical subjects, it is frequently possible to find documents and MSS in other areas, including literature which are omitted from th *National Union Catalog of Manuscript Collections.*

131 *National Union Catalog of Manuscript Collections.* *1959/ 61-.* Imprint varies: *1959-61,* Ann Arbor, Mich.: Edwards; *1962,* Hamden, Conn.: Shoe String Press; *1963-,*Washington, D.C.: L.C. Frequency: *1959/61,* 1962; *1963/64-,*annual, 1965-.

Each vol. has index, with cumulated indexes every two to four years, e.g., 1959-62, 1963-66, 1967-69, 1970-72.

Through 1972 the catalog reports on 31,256 collections in 883 repositories, with a total of nearly 202,300 citations. Manuscripts include diaries, account books, maps, photocopies, literary MSS or typescripts, records, documents, correspondence, journals, etc. Large groups only are reported, i.e., those formed around an individual, family, corporation or theme. Regrettably, small groups of a few pieces, or single MSS are usually omitted, but they are sometimes reported in connection with larger collections.

The basic arrangement is by L.C. card number in numerical sequence, with access via the general index which is alphabetical and lists subjects, places, personal names, corporate bodies, historical events, etc. There are entries under France, French Language and Literature and authors' names.

132   New York   Public Library. *Dictionary Catalog of the Manuscript Division.* 2 vols. N.Y.: N.Y. Pub. Lib., 1967.

25,000 entries including names, subjects, geographical areas and types of manuscripts (e.g., account-books, diaries, log-books, maps, literary typescripts). Not a strong collection in French MSS but includes some modern French authors. Subjects include Drama, French; Literature, French; Poetry, French.

133   New York   Public Library. Research Libraries. *Catalog of the Theatre and Drama Collections.* 21 vols. Boston: G. K. Hall, 1967.

Contents: Pt. 1 (Section 1), Drama Collection: Author Listing, 6 vols. Pt. 1 (Section 2), Drama Collection: Listing by Cultural Origin, 6 vols. Pt. 2, Theatre Collection: Books on the Theatre, 9 vols.

The alphabetical author part (Section 1) includes more than 120,000 plays in major and minor languages (excluding Cyrillic, Hebrew and Oriental languages), published in anthologies, periodicals, collected works, or appearing as separate editions, or recordings. Anonymous titles are interfiled with names of authors. The listing by cultural origin rearranges the same play by country, i.e., Drama: Belgian (French), Canadian (French), French, Swiss (French), etc., and adds translations into other languages.

Pt. 2 has 121,000 entries representing 23,500 vols. on the theatre (which includes radio, TV, cinema, circus, vaudeville, etc.), arranged alphabetically under subject headings. Periodical articles are indexed selectively. This part includes bibliographies, biographies, criticism, history, etc., and under authors a large number of plays in the form of typescripts, prompt books and radio and television production scripts.

134   Pierpont Morgan Library, New York. *Books and Manuscripts
        from the Heineman Collection.* N.Y.: Pierpont Morgan
        Library, 1963.

            Catalog of the exhibition of items from this col-
        lection. Especially strong in French and German literature
        of the eighteenth and nineteenth centuries.

            _____. *Major Acquisitions of the Pierpont Morgan Library
        1924-1974.* 4 vols. N.Y.: Pierpont Morgan Library,
        1974.
        (I):   Autograph Letters and Manuscripts
        (II): Drawings
        (III): Early Printed Books
        (IV): Mediaeval and Renaissance Manuscripts

135   Ricci, Seymour de, and Wilson, W. J. *Census of Medieval and
        Renaissance Manuscripts in the United States and
        Canada.* 3 vols. N.Y.: Wilson, 1935-1940; rpt.,
        N.Y.: Kraus, 1961.

            Covers from the beginning to 1600 and lists about
        10,000 MSS, giving probable date and place, material
        written upon, size, no. of leaves, binding, former owners,
        and bibliographical references to printed material.
            Arranged by states, cities and libraries, including
        private collections. Vol. 3 is an index of authors, names
        of persons, titles and subjects (for anonymous works only).
        A limited number of subjects such as "Chansons françaises,"
        "Poems," "France," "Paris" are directly useful in French
        studies. The index also has separate parts for scribes,
        illuminators and cartographers, incipits, and present and
        previous owners.

            _____. *Supplement to the Census.* . . . Originated by
        C. U. Faye; continued and edited by W. H. Bond.
        N.Y.: Bibliographical Soc. of Am., 1962.

            Similar in pattern, with corrections, additions
        and with cross references to the main work.

CHAPTER 6

PERIODICALS

A. BIBLIOGRAPHIES AND CATALOGS

I. BIBLIOGRAPHIES OF PERIODICALS

36 "Births, Deaths and Magazine Notes: A Record of New Titles,
Changed Titles, and Deaths in the Periodical World."
Bulletin of Bibliography (Boston: Faxon), April 1900-.

A regular feature published in most issues of the
journal. Gives address, size, date of founding, and price.

a. REPERTORIES BY NATIONS

37 Duprat, Gabrielle; Lutova, Ksenia; et Bossuat, Marie-Louise.
*Bibliographie des répertoires nationaux de pério-
diques en cours.* P.: Unesco; London: IFLA, 1969.

Lists national directories of current newspapers
and periodicals published in 183 countries or territories.
Arranged under countries A-Z. Data on each directory include scope, number of periodicals listed, and a typical
example of an entry. To be updated.

BELGIUM

38 *Annuaire officiel de la presse belge/Officieel jaarbook
van de Belgische pers.* Assn. Générale de la Presse
Belge, 1921-. (Irregular)

A list of newspapers by place of publication, and
information on press associations and journalism in Belgium.

39 Archives de la Ville de Bruxelles. *Catalogue des journaux
et périodiques conservés aux Archives de la Ville de
Bruxelles/Catalogus van de dagbladen en Tijdschriften
bewaard op het Stadsarchief van Brussel.* 3 vols.
Bruxelles: Ville de Bruxelles, 1965.

An alphabetical title list of the newspaper and
periodical collection in the Archives. Included are Flemish,
Belgian French titles, and some foreign publications, but
most are of Belgian origin. About 3,000 titles.

_____. *Catalogue des journaux et périodiques conservés
aux Archives de la Ville de Bruxelles.* Index fait par
Guy Michaux. (Classement systématique du Catalogue
des journaux et périodiques conservés aux Archives de

la Ville de Bruxelles, catalogués par Van Impe.)/
*Catalogus van de dagbladen en tijdschriften bewaard
op het stadsarchief van Brussel.* Index opgesteld
door Guy Michaux. (Systematische classificatie van
de Catalogus van de dagbladen en tijdschriften bewaar
op het stadsarchief van Brussel, gecatalogiseard door
Van Impe). Bruxelles: Ville de Bruxelles, 1971.

A classified arrangement of the alphabetical
catalog above.

140   Hove, Julien van. *Répertoire des périodiques paraissant
en Belgique/Repertorium van de in België verschij-
nende tijdschriften.* Bruxelles: Librairie Encyclopédique, 1951. *Suppléments* 1-4, 1955-72.

Three supplements in 1955, 1960 and 1964.
The basic repertory consists of 2,387 periodicals
in circulation in 1950. Alphabetical classification. In
the supplements are found new titles, modifications made
to the titles used as the basis, and titles of periodicals
that have disappeared. Three indexes for each volume:
subjects, publishers, and places.

141   Maréchal, Yvon. *Répertoire pratique des périodiques belges
édités en langue française.* Louvain: Vander, 1970.

Provides a list of national daily newspapers
(twenty-eight titles), followed by a classified section of
periodicals arranged alphabetically by subject (i.e.,
Bibliographie, Histoire, Langue, Littérature) or type
(i.e., *Magazines de la Femme*). There is an alphabetical
title index of about 1,100 titles. Excludes publications
of only local or regional interest. Updated ed. 1974.

142   Vandenberghe-Robert, Christiane. *Répertoire des périodiques littéraires français de Belgique   (Bibliothèque
royale de Belgique) 1830-1880.* Mémoire présenté à
l'Ecole provinciale de Bibliothécaires du Brabant,
Session 1961. Bruxelles: Commission belge de bibliographie, 1964.

143   Vermeersch, Arthur J. *Répertoire de la presse bruxelloise/
Repertorium van de Brusselse pers, 1789-1914.* 2 vols
Louvain: Nauwelaerts, 1965-68.

A list of 2,615 newspapers and periodicals, arranged alphabetically by title, which were published in
Brussels from 1789 through 1914. Information includes
title, subtitle, periodicity, publisher, dates, purpose,
political bias, content, etc., and the files found in the
Archives de la Ville de Bruxelles, the Bibliothèque Royale
de Belgique, the Fonds Mertens and the Musée International
de la Presse.

144   Beaulieu, André, et Hamelin, Jean. *La Presse québécoise
      des origines à nos jours.* Nouv. éd. rev. et augm.
      Québec: Pr. de l'U. Laval, 1973-. Tome 1: *1764-1859.*

          First edition entitled: *Les Journaux du Québec de
      1764 à 1964,* pub. 1965, has a twelve page bibliography on
      the history of the Canadian press (including periodicals),
      a list of newspapers arranged by city, a chronological
      index 1764-1964, and an alphabetical index of titles.
          The main list has 2,293 titles, giving beginning
      date, frequency, political affiliation, publisher, circu-
      lation, final date if any, and libraries having the title.
      Notes are added for many titles providing further details
      of publishing history, changes in title, characteristics,
      sponsors, etc. Many have literary interests and many are
      bilingual.

145   Bibliothèque Nationale du Québec. *Répertoire des pério-
      diques québécois.* Ie partie par Ginette Henry.
      Montréal: Ministère des Affaires Culturelles, B.N. du
      Québec, 1974-.

          An inventory of the newspapers and periodicals
      received by the library in original print or microform.
          There are 1,221 French and English (mostly French)
      titles classified by subject with an alphabetical index of
      titles, key words, societies, institutions, places, etc.,
      with many see-references. A broad range of subjects is
      represented, including generalities, history, art, language,
      and literature.

146   *Canadian Serials Directory/Répertoire des Publications
      Sériées Canadiennes.* Toronto: U. of Toronto Pr.,
      1972-. (Annual.)

          Periodicals and series published in Canada.
      Series include annotated reports, yearbooks, memoirs, pro-
      ceedings, transactions, numbered monographs, serially pub-
      lished reports and documents compiled by the U. of British
      Columbia, National Lib. of Canada, and B.N. du Québec.
          About 8,000 titles. Alphabetical title list,
      subject index (i.e., linguistics, literature, bibliography,
      French-Canadian culture), publishers index, list of indexing
      and abstract services.

FRANCE

History of the French press from its origins to the present.

147   Hatin, Eugène. *Bibliographie historique et critique de la
      presse périodique française ou Catalogue systématique
      et raisonné de tous les écrits périodiques. . . depuis
      l'origine du journal jusqu'à nos jours, avec ex-
      traits, notes historiques, critiques et morales. . .*

*Précédé d'un Essai historique et statistique sur la
naissance et les progrès de la presse périodique dans
les deux mondes.* P.: Firmin-Didot, 1866; rpt., P.:
Ed. Anthropos, 1965.

The periodicals of the old period, 1631-1789, are
classified systematically by genres. Those of the modern
period, 1789-1865, are classified year by year and alphabetically. Detailed descriptions, and abundant historical
notes are included. At the end there is a table of the
Parisian press in 1865. Alphabetical index of titles.

148 Livois, René de. *Histoire de la presse française.* 2 vols.
Lausanne: Editions Spes, 1965.

Vol. 1: *Des origines à 1881.* Vol. 2: *De 1881 à
nos jours.*

149 *Histoire générale de la presse française,* pub. sous la dir.
de Claude Bellanger, Jacques Godechot, Pierre Guiral
et Fernand Terrou. Préf. de P. Renouvin. 5 vols.
P.: PUF, 1969-1976. Ills.

1: *Des origines à 1814.* 1969.
2: *De 1815 à 1871.* 1969.
3: *De 1871 à 1940.* 1972.
4: *De 1940 à 1958.* 1975.
5: *De 1958 à nos jours.* 1976.

Each volume contains twenty-four plates, numerous
ills. and indexes. This *Histoire,* following the sequence of
events, presents a general history of the French
press and stresses its evolution.

150 Paris. Bibliothèque Nationale. Département des Périodiques. *Bibliographie de la presse française
politique et d'information générale, 1865-1944.*
P.: B.N., 1964-. (27 fascicules pub. by 1975.)

Established with the collab. of librarians and
archivists of each *département.* One section per *département.* Lists not only the titles of journals conserved in
libraries, but also those which have disappeared (the
documents which mention them are indicated). Gives titles,
subtitles, periodicity, places of issuance, format, places
of storage with state of the collection. B.N. call numbers. Chronological tables are given with the year of
founding and of ending of each periodical.

151 *Annuaire de la presse et de la publicité,* sous la dir. de
Raymond Mery. 87e éd. P.: Soc. d'éd. de l'Annuaire
de la presse, 1973. 1e éd. 1880.

Publisher varies.
Volumes for 1906, 1940-41, 1945 not pub. Super-

sedes E. Mermet's *La Publicité en France,* 1878-80.
Title varies. *1880-91: Annuaire de la presse française; 1892-1905: Annuaire de la presse française et du monde politique; 1907-64: Annuaire de la presse française et étrangère et du monde politique; 1965 : Annuaire de la presse française et étrangère.*

A directory of organizations, professional associations, suppliers, public relations agencies, administrative offices, etc., connected to the French press. Includes French newspapers and periodicals classified by subject and a short list of current foreign newspapers by country. Includes several indexes for the various sections and an alphabetical index of newspapers and periodicals.

152 *Annuaire des journaux, revues et publications périodiques publiés à Paris.* 43 vols. P.: H. Le Soudier, 1881-1914; 1922-30.

Provides an alphabetical title list and a separate list arranged by subjects.

153 Place, Jean-Michel, et Vasseur, André. *Bibliographie des revues et journaux littéraires des XIXe et XXe siècles.* P.: Chronique des Lettres Françaises, 1973-. Tome 1, 1973; tome 2, 1975; tome 3, 1977.

The authors seek to enhance the understanding of French literature through an in depth analysis of certain literary periodicals, particularly *"les petites revues."* Tome 1 makes an analysis of fourteen titles of the nineteenth century including: *La Variété* (1840), *Le Réveil* (1858-59), *La Renaissance* (1872-74), *Le Jeune France* (1878-88), *Les Grimaces* (1883-84), *La Syrinx* (1892-94), and *La Coupe* (1895-98). For each of the fourteen titles there is: an essay discussing its origin, purpose, editors, contributors, significance, etc.; a detailed description of publication; an author-title summary of the tables of contents number by number. There are also many extracts of letters, parts of articles, etc., written by French authors, and which are of interest to literary historians.

154 Caron, Pierre, et Jaryc, Marc. *Répertoire des périodiques de langue française, philosophiques, historiques, philologiques et juridiques.* P.: Maison du Livre Français, 1935.

_____. *Premier Supplément.* 1937.

_____. *Deuxième Supplément.* 1939.

While this is not primarily a list of literary periodicals, it is important for its inclusion of many

general, cultural, historical and learned society journals
useful in literary research; also includes several Belgian,
Canadian and Swiss periodicals. Altogether there are 1,900
titles, listed alphabetically and indicating those in the
B.N., and the Sorbonne. Index of subjects, places, persons, societies, etc.

155 Paris. Bibliothèque Nationale. Département des Pério-
      diques. *Répertoire de la presse et des publications
      périodiques françaises.* 5e éd. *1965-71.* 2 vols.
      P.: B.N., 1973.

          This was first published by H.-F. Raux,
P.: La Documentation française. The first four eds. are
out of print: 1958, 1961, 1964, 1968. It is now compiled
under the direction of Monique Lambert.
          The descriptions are systematically divided in
sixteen divisions, and 143 subdivisions. A general alphabetical index completes each volume.
          The last edition contains all the serial publi-
cations received, through the Legal Deposit, at the Department of Periodicals of the B.N. from Oct. 1965 to
Dec. 31, 1971.

SWITZERLAND

156 Blaser, Fritz. *Bibliographie der schweizer Presse mit
      Einschluss des Fürstentums Liechtenstein/Bibliographie
      de la presse suisse/Bibliografia della stampa svizzera*
      2 vols. Basel: Birkhaüser Verlag, 1956-1958.

          Lists all the journals and periodicals of Switz-
erland and Liechtenstein until 1803. After this date only
the political journals are listed. Classified by titles.
Historical and bibliographical notes, locations in Swiss
libraries. Numerous indexes.

b. INTERNATIONAL GENERAL REPERTORIES

157 *Irregular Serials and Annuals: An International Directory.
      A Classified Guide to Current Foreign and Domestic
      Serials, Excepting Periodicals Issued More Frequently
      than Once a Year.* Ed. by E. Koltay. N.Y.: Bowker,
      1961; 2nd ed. 1972; *Fourth Edition, 1976-1977,* 1976.

          4th ed. covers about 30,000 U.S. and foreign irregu-
serials which include proceedings, transactions, advances,
yearbooks, annual reviews, periodical supplements, etc.,
published from 1963 on.
          The arrangement and information provided is closely
similar to *Ulrich's International Periodicals Directory*
(no. 159).
          Index to titles and subjects.

158   *Ulrich's International Periodicals Directory: A Classified*
      Guide to a Selected List of Current Periodicals, For-
      eign and Domestic. N.Y.: Bowker, 1932-. New eds.
      pub. biennially; supps. in alternate years. 16th ed.
      pub. 1975-76.

      55,000 selected titles, classified under 450
headings of subjects. Index of titles and year of founding,
circulation, periodicity, price and indexes or abstracts
in which periodical is listed. Index to new periodicals,
list of periodicals which have gone out of print since last
edition. Four supps. issued from 1966 to 1970.

159   *Bowker Serials Bibliography Supplement, 1972-.* N.Y. and
      London: Bowker, 1972-.

      Issued intermittently as a supplement to *Ulrich's*
International Periodicals Directory and *Irregular Serials
and Annuals, 1972* and *1974* issued to date.
      Supersedes *Supplement* to *Ulrich's.* . . .

160   *Willing's European Press Guide 1965-.* London:
      Hutchinson-Willing, 1966/67-. Irregular. 2nd ed.
      1968. Supplements 1968-69.

      Lists 50,000 newspapers, magazines, periodicals,
annual bulletins of western Europe, except for Finland,
Spain, and the United Kingdom. Titles listed under subject
headings A-Z. Headings in four languages: English, German, French, and Italian. Alphabetical index, by countries
A-Z, subdivided by titles A-Z. Subject index in four
languages.

                  c.   JOURNALS IN THE HUMANITIES

      See Ch. 2: *MLA Bibliography* (no. 22), Rancoeur (no. 26),
and Ronge, II, 343-54 (no. 21); Ch. 4: Walford (no. 96),
Winchell (no. 97), Pell (no. 101).

161   *Directory of Journals and Series in the Humanities. A Data
      List of the Periodical Sources on the Master List of
      the MLA International Bibliography.* Comp. by Har-
      rison T. Meserole and Carolyn James Bishop. N.Y.:
      MLA, 1970.

      Gives bibliographical and subscription data for
1,524 of the journals and series central to the field of
modern languages and literatures.

                  II.   CATALOGS OF PERIODICALS

                        CANADA

      See also *Union List of Serials in Libraries of the United
States and Canada* (under United States, below).

162   Goggio, Emilio; Corrigan, Beatrice; and Parker, Jack H.
      *A Bibliography of Canadian Cultural Periodicals
      (English and French from Colonial times to 1950) in
      Canadian Libraries.* Toronto: U. of Toronto, Dept.
      of Italian, Spanish and Portuguese, 1955.

        A union list of Canadian periodicals in literature
      and history, listing the location of the most complete
      files found. Updates and expands: Tod, Dorothea, "A Biblio
      graphy of Canadian Literary Periodicals, 1789-1900."
      Royal Soc. of Canada, *Proceedings and Transactions,* vol.
      26, 1932.

FRANCE

163   Paris. Bibliothèque Nationale. Département des Pério-
      diques. *Catalogue collectif des périodiques con-
      servés dans les bibliothèques de Paris et dans les
      bibliothèques universitaires des départements.* P.:
      B.N., 1967-.

          I : A-B, to appear in 1978.
         II : C-I, 1973.
        III : J-Q, 1969.
         IV : R-Z, 1967.

        Union list of 75,000 French and non-French peri-
      odicals, published between 1631 and 1939. Union catalog of
      about seventy-five French libraries. This work gives for
      each title the holdings in each library. Overall entries
      give information on the history of each periodical, with
      mergers, splits, etc. Alphabetical order of titles.
        This catalog does not list official publications,
      calendars, clergy news bulletins, newspapers after 1849;
      Slavic periodicals in Cyrillic are cataloged   separately.
        This catalog is the result of a collective work
      started in 1936 at the Bibliothèque de la Sorbonne and at
      the B.N., where it has continued since 1939. This work has
      been prepared with the help of all the libraries listed,
      under the direction of Mlle. Fanny Petitbon, then of Mlle.
      France Pascal, librarians at the B.N.
        A supplement listing of the periodicals of 1940-
      1959, plus additional entries and indexes, is in prepara-
      tion, and will bring the total number of periodicals to
      about 100,000.

164   Paris. Bibliothèque Nationale. Département des Pério-
      diques. *Répertoire collectif des quotidiens et
      hebdomadaires publiés dans les départements de la
      France métropolitaine de 1944 à 1956 et conservés
      dans les archives et bibliothèques de France.*
      P.: B.N., 1958.
      Followed by:

_____. *Catalogue collectif des journaux quotidiens d'information générale publiés en France métropolitaine de 1957 à 1961.* P.: B.N., 1962.

This catalog records all the editions of daily newspapers (and those published two or more days per week), and provides information on where to find them in the B.N., or in a number of municipal and university libraries or archives. Usually the B.N. keeps one edition, but it is occasionally useful to know how to locate others due to varying contents of the several editions. This catalog includes weeklies because they are kept (originals or microfilms) in the B.N.

165   _____. *Catalogue des périodiques clandestins diffusés en France de 1939 à 1945, suivi d'un catalogue des périodiques clandestins diffusés à l'étranger.* Comps. R. et P. Roux-Fouillet. P.: B.N., 1954.

1,106 numbered entries. Index.

166   _____. *Inventaire des périodiques étrangers reçus en France par les bibliothèques et les organismes de documentation.* 1e éd. P.: B.N., 1956; 3e éd. 1962.

_____. *Inventaire des périodiques étrangers et des publications en série étrangères (IPPEC) reçus en France par les bibliothèques et les organismes de documentation en 1965.* 4e éd. P.: B.N., 1969. Mise à jour *1965-70*, 1973.

Union list of foreign periodicals, received by 2,000 libraries and documentation centers in France.

_____. *Catalogue des périodiques étrangers reçus par la Bibliothèque Nationale de 1960 à 1963.* P.: B.N., 1964. *Supp. jan. 1964-juin 1965*, 1966. *Supp. juil. 1965-déc. 1968*, 1970.

GREAT BRITAIN

167   *British Union Catalogue of Periodicals: A Record of the Periodicals of the World, from the Seventeenth Century to the Present Day, in British Libraries.* Ed. by J. D. Stewart, with M. E. Hammond and E. Saenger. 4 vols. London: Butterworths, 1955-1958.

Lists more than 140,000 titles filed in about 440 libraries of Great Britain. Excludes newspapers after 1799. Covers completely many general libraries and incompletely others. Periodicals are arranged by their earliest names, with references to these from later titles, and providing changes of titles, vol. numbering, dates, and cumulated indexes.

_____. *Supplement to 1960.* London: Butterworths, 1962.

Includes entries for new periodicals appearing since publication of the main vols., some amended entries and some entries for earlier periodicals not previously reported.
Further supplemented by:

168 *British Union Catalogue of Periodicals, Incorporating the "World List of Scientific Periodicals": New Periodical Titles.* Ed. for the National Central Library by K. I. Porter. London: Butterworths, 1964-. Cumulation *1960-1968* pub. in 1970.

Appears quarterly with an annual cumulation which takes two forms: one lists all the new periodicals from the quarterly lists; and the second lists periodicals of science and technology.

SWITZERLAND

169 Bern. Schweizerische Landesbibliothek. *Verzeichnis der laufenden schweizerischen Zeitschriften/Catalogue des périodiques suisses, revues, journaux, annuaires, almanachs, collections, etc., reçus par la Bibliothèque Nationale à Berne.* (2nd ed.) Bern-Bümpliz: Benteli, 1925.

_____. *Nachtrag/Supplément, 1926-30.* 5 vols. Bern-Bümpliz: Benteli, 1926-31.

Classified list with a title index.

170 *Schweizerischer Zeitschriften-und Zeitungskatalog/ Catalogue des revues et journaux suisses.* Olten: Schweizerisches Vereinssortiment, 1945.

Classified list with title index of newspapers and periodicals currently published at the time of publication.

171 *Zeitungskatalog der Schweiz/Catalogue des journaux suisses.* Zurich: Verband Schweizerischer Annoncen Expeditionem, 1950-. (Irregular, mostly annual.)

List of current Swiss newspapers and periodicals. In German and French.

172 *Schweizer Zeitschriftenverzeichnis/Répertoire des périodiques suisses/Repertorio dei periodici svizzeri,* 1951/55-. Zurich: Verlag des Schweizerischen Buchhändlerund Verlagvereins, 1956-. Quinquennial: *1956-60,* 1961; *1961-65,* 1966, etc.

Forms part of the Swiss national bibliography.
Lists all periodicals (but not newspapers) published during
the five-year period; includes official and local government
periodicals, and directories and annuals. Classified sequence, with index of titles and key words. States title,
publisher, address, date of foundation, date of last issue
received, frequency and price.

UNITED STATES

173 *Union List of Serials in Libraries of the United States and
       Canada*. 3rd ed. by Edna Brown Titus. 5 vols. N.Y.:
       Wilson, 1965.

    1st ed. 1927; 2nd ed. 1943. *Supplements, 1941-
1949*, 2 vols., 1945-1953.
    3rd ed.: 156,449 serials in 956 libraries; covers
periodicals published through 1949 only.

    International in scope, including many annuals,
irregular serials, but excluding: foreign newspapers after
1820, American newspapers, most governmental serials and
conference proceedings. For a more complete list of ex-
clusions, see Ch. 4: Winchell (no. 97).
    There is a very useful "Place Index to French
Societies" preceding entries beginning *"Société. . . ."*
This index is arranged alphabetically by name of French
city, or place, listing the full name of each society located there. Serials can then be found under the name of
the society.
    Continued by:

174 *New Serial Titles, 1950-1970; A Union List of Serials
       Commencing Publication after December 31, 1949.
       1950-1970 Cumulative*. 4 vols. Washington, D.C.:
       L.C., 1973. *1971-1974 Cumulation*, 2 vols., 1975.

    New Serial Titles is published in eight monthly
issues, four quarterly issues, in annual and multi-
year cumulations.

    The 1950-1970 cumulation lists 220,000 titles in
U.S. and Canadian libraries (about 7,800 titles from
France). An excellent tool for searching serials under
various titles or issuing bodies. All issues and cumulations have a separate section listing changes in serials
which includes title changes, cessations, changes in name
of corporate authors, resumptions and suspensions. These
changes are for all serials regardless of beginning date.

175 U.S. Library of Congress. General Reference and Bib-
       liography Division. *Union List of Serials: A
       Bibliography*. Comp. by Ruth S. Freitag. Washington,
       D.C.: U.S. Govt. Printing Office, 1964.

Lists 1,218 union lists--books, articles, parts of books, etc., published from 1859 to 1964. Covers fifty-six countries or geographical areas. For France, 116 catalogs are mentioned. Index of names, of subjects, and places.

176 Wall, C. Edward. *Periodical Title Abbreviations*. Detroit: Gale Research Co., 1969.

Over 8,800 abbreviations of titles as used in many indexes, bibliographies, abstracts and journals, including such major works as *PMLA*, *Studies in Philology*, and *Year's Work in Modern Language Studies*.
Arranged alphabetically by abbreviations giving equivalent titles. A very useful list for verifying or identifying serial titles which are frequently incomplete in bibliographical citations.

B. BIBLIOGRAPHIES OF ARTICLES, INDEXES TO PERIODICALS, TABLES TO INDIVIDUAL JOURNALS

I. BIBLIOGRAPHIES OF ARTICLES

177 Golden, Herbert Hershel, and Simches, Seymour O. *Modern French Literature and Language: A Bibliography of Homage Studies*. Cambridge, Mass.: Harvard U. Pr., 1953.

An index of articles in 309 homage and *Fest-schriften* vols. on French language and literature from 1500 to the present.

178 Jaffe, Adrian H. *Bibliography of French Literature in American Magazines in the 18th Century*. East Lansing: Michigan State College Pr., 1951.

A specialized bibliography intended mainly to re-flect general popular American intellectual interests in French literature.
Lists 189 references from ninety-one periodicals published in the U.S. from 1741 to 1799, mostly general circulation magazines. Citations are restricted to French literature, articles on French authors, translated works, French history, culture and contemporary affairs.

179 Modern Language Association of America. *MLA Abstracts of Articles in Scholarly Journals, 1970-*. N.Y.: MLA of Am., 1972-. Annual.

In three vols., available separately or bound in one vol. Vol. 1 includes sections on General, English, American, Medieval and Neo-Latin, Celtic literatures and folklore. Vol. 2 covers European, Asian, African and Latin-American literature. Vol. 3 concentrates on various aspects of linguistics.

The arrangement follows that of the *MLA International Bibliography*, and the intent is to provide abstracts of citations which have appeared in the bibliography. (An asterisk preceding the item number in the bibliography indicates an abstract in *MLA Abstracts*. . . .) The abstracts are about 150 words long, written by the authors of the articles. In addition, abstracts from *LLBA (Language and Language Behavior Abstracts)* are included in this publication through an exchange arrangement. Such abstracts end with the initials *LLBA*. Beginning in 1972, a subject index was added to provide an approach by themes, genres, styles, structures, techniques and many other subjects.

The *1970 MLA Abstracts* contained 1,744 abstracts and some increase is apparent in subsequent vols.

II. INDEXES TO PERIODICALS

CANADA

180 *Canadian Periodical Index,* 1928-1947.

Publisher varies. Pub. first by Windsor Pub. Lib. (for the years 1928-1932), later in Toronto by the Pub. Libs. Branch, Ontario, Dept. of Education.

Published 1928-30, quarterly; 1931, annual; 1932, quarterly; 1933-37, not published; 1938-47, annual (cumulations of quarterly indexes published in the *Ontario Library Review*).

An author-subject index to thirty to forty Canadian periodicals.

Continued by:

181 *Canadian Periodical Index/Index de périodiques canadiens.*
Vol. 1-. 1948-. Ottawa: Canadian Lib. Assn. and Nat. Lib. of Canada, 1948-.

Title varies: 1948-50, *Canadian Index; A Guide to Canadian Periodicals and Films;* 1952-63, *Canadian Index to Periodicals and Documentary Films.* There is also a one vol. cumulation entitled: *Canadian Index to Periodicals and Documentary Films; An Author and Subject Index, Jan. 1948-Dec. 1959.* Ed. by Margaret E. Wodehouse. Ottawa: Canadian Lib. Assn., 1962.

Monthly subject index with annual and quinquennial cumulations which include author indexes.

A bilingual index to about ninety Canadian periodicals (ca. sixty English, ca. fourteen French, ca. ten bilingual). There is a separate section for book reviews.

Films were dropped from the index in 1964; they are covered in *Canadiana.*

182 *Index Analytique*, vols. 1-6. Feb. 1966-1972. Québec:
        Centre de documentation, Bibliothèque de l'U. Laval,
        1966-1972.

        Monthly, with annual cumulations.
        Computer produced. Indexes about 120 French lan-
    guage periodicals (about 25 Canadian).
        List of periodicals by title, then by subject
    (no addresses given), followed by 6 sections: *Index alpha-
    bétique, Index méthodique, Index méthodique des ouvrages
    recensés, Auteurs des articles et des comptes rendus,
    Références bibliographiques.*
        Continued by:

183 *Periodex; index analytique de périodiques de langue
        française.* Vol. 1-. Sept. 1972-. Montréal:
        La Centrale des bibliothèques, 1972-.
                                                                •
        Monthly (except July and Aug.) with annual cumu-
    lations.
        Indexes about 160 periodicals in French; wide sub-
    ject coverage, including general (thirty titles), arts
    (nine), cinema (five), education (eleven), history (twelve)
    linguistics (two), and literature (ten).
        Three sections: A, an alphabetical subject list
    using key words in titles; B, a classified subject list
    grouped by broad disciplines; C, an alphabetical author of
    articles list.

                                FRANCE

        See *Bulletin*(s) *Signalétique*(s) *523* and *524* (nos. 12
    and 370).

                               GERMANY

184 *Internationale Bibliographie der Zeitschriftenliteratur
        aus allen Gebieten der Forschung.* Leipzig/(später)
        Osnabrück, Dietrich, 1897-.

        Title in English and French: *International Bib-
    liography of Periodical Literature Covering All Fields of
    Knowledge/Bibliographie internationale de la littérature
    périodique dans tous les domaines de la connaissance.*

        Founded in 1896. Interrupted at various times.
    Still referred to by the name of the founder "Dietrich."
    Originally composed in three pts.: A. *Bibliographie der
    deutschen Zeitschriftenliteratur. 1896-1964.*
    B. *Bibliographie der fremdsprachigen Zeitschriften-
    literatur/Répertoire bibliographique international des
    revues/International Index to Periodicals. 1911-64.*

C. *Bibliographie der Rezensionen und Referate.* *1900-43.*

In 1965 (for the periodicals of 1963-64), parts
A and B have merged into one: *Internationale Bibliographie.*
Alphabetical order of subjects using German terms. About
8,000 periodicals are searched, 600 of which are French.
About 1,250,000 articles. Index of authors produced semi-
annually. Covers all fields of research. The most extensive of periodical indexes.

UNITED STATES

185 Kujoth, Jean Spealman. *Subject Guide to Periodical Indexes
and Review Indexes.* Metuchen, N.J.: Scarecrow Pr.,
1969.

A guide to periodical indexes, abstracts and book
review indexes. The first part is an alphabetical list of
academic subjects listing under each subject the pertinent
indexes. The second part is an alphabetical title list of
the indexes indicating form, periodicity, content (number
of periodicals, or kinds of publications covered and special
kinds of indexing or abstracting), and subjects included.
For both parts a code is used to indicate further details
such as indexing of various types of reviews (plays, films,
music, phonorecords, criticism, etc.).

III.   INDEXES TO INDIVIDUAL JOURNALS

Apart from yearly indexes, certain journals publish from time to time indexes of past issues.

UNITED STATES

186 New York Public Library. *A Check List of Cumulative Indexes
to Individual Periodicals in the New York Public Library.* Compiled by Daniel C. Haskell. N.Y.: N.Y.
Pub. Lib., 1942; rpt., Detroit: Gale Research Co.,
1969.

An alphabetical list of thousands of entries arranged by titles of periodicals in various languages,
mainly of the nineteenth and twentieth centuries, which are
available in the N.Y. Public Lib., with the addition of a
few not available in the library.
"A cumulative index is to be understood as one
which indexes at least three volumes of a file and makes
at least a slight attempt at the classification of the
periodicals' contents, either an arrangement by authors or
by subjects." (Preface)
Lists ca. 2,000 periodical indexes under subjects
A-Z: code letters indicate type of material indexed. Appended is a descriptive list of the indexes, A-Z by title.

C. MAIN PERIODICALS ON FRENCH STUDIES

See Ch. 2: R. Rancoeur's *Bibliographie littéraire* (no. 26). At the end of each annual volume, since 1962, he gives a complete list, including addresses of periodicals used in that specific volume under the title: "Adresses des périodiques français et étrangers."

See also, in Chs. 2 and 3: *Bibliographie de la France* (no. 84), *MLA Bibliography* (no. 22) ("Master List," pub. since 1960), and Langlois and Mareuil's *Guide bibliographique des études littéraire* (no. 20), pp. 262-64.

Journals devoted to one particular period or author will be listed under the proper period. Bibliographical journals are mentioned in Chs. 2 and 3. We indicate here only some of the most important journals in print, which publish on French language and/or literature in general, and comparative literature.

AUSTRALIA AND NEW ZEALAND

AUMLA, Journal of the Australasian Universities Language and Literature Association. Christchurch, New Zealand; Townsville, Queensland, Australia.
Australian Journal of French Studies. Clayton, Victoria, Australia.
Essays in French Literature. Nedlands, Western Australia.

BELGIUM

Bulletin de l'Académie Royale de Langue et de Littérature Françaises. Bruxelles.
Lettres Romanes (Les). U. Catholique de Louvain.
Revue Belge de Philologie et d'Histoire. Bruxelles.
Revue de l'Université de Bruxelles. Bruxelles.
Revue des Langues Vivantes. Bruxelles.

CANADA

See also U.S.

Canadian Literature/Littérature Canadienne. Vancouver, British Columbia.
Canadian Review of Comparative Literature/Revue Canadienne de Littérature Comparée. Edmonton, Alberta.

Etudes françaises. Montréal, Province de Québec.
Etudes littéraires. Québec, Province de Québec.
Revue de l'Université d'Ottawa. Ottawa, Ontario.

DENMARK

Revue Romane. Copenhague.

FINLAND

*Neuphilologische Mitteilungen. Bulletin of the Modern
Language Society of Helsinki.* Helsinki.

FRANCE

Banque des Mots (La). P.
Bulletin analytique de linguistique française. Nancy.
Bulletin des Bibliothèques de France. P.
*Cahiers de l'Association Internationale des Etudes
Françaises.* P.
Europe. P.
Français dans le Monde (Le). P.
Français Moderne (Le). Revue de linguistique française. P.
Information Littéraire (L'). P.
Jeune Afrique. P.
Langue Française. P.
Lettres Nouvelles (Les). P.
Littérature. P.
Monde des livres (Le). P.
Nouvelle NRF. P.
Nouvelles Littéraires (Les). P.
Poétique. Revue de théorie et d'analyse littéraire. P.
Présence Africaine. P.
Revue de Linguistique Romane. Strasbourg.
Revue de Littérature Comparée. P.
Revue des Deux Mondes. P.
Revue des Langues Romanes. Montpellier.
Revue des Lettres Modernes (La). P.
Revue des Sciences Humaines. Lille.
Revue d'Histoire du Théâtre. P.
Revue d'Histoire Littéraire de la France. P.
Travaux de Linguistique et de Littérature, publiés par le
Centre de philologie et de littérature romanes de
l'Université de Strasbourg.
*Unesco. Bibliography, Documentation, Terminology/Bibliographie,
Documentation, Terminologie.* P.
*Unesco. Bulletin for Libraries/Bulletin de l'Unesco à l'in-
tention des bibliothèques.* P.

GERMANY

Zeitschrift für Französische Sprache und Literatur. Wiesbaden.

GREAT BRITAIN

Forum for Modern Language Studies. The U. of St. Andrews, St. Andrews.
French Studies. Oxford.
Modern Language Review. Edinburgh.
Nottingham French Studies. Nottingham.

ITALY

Giornale Italiano di Filologia. Napoli.
Rivista di Letterature Moderne e Comparate. Firenze.
Saggi e Ricerche di Letteratura Francese. Roma.
Studi Francesi. Torino.

NETHERLANDS

Neophilologus. Groningen.
Rapports-het Franse Boek. Amstelven.

SWEDEN

Studia Neophilologica. A Journal of Germanic and Romance Philology. Uppsala.

SWITZERLAND

Journal de Genève (Samedi littéraire). Genève.

UNITED STATES

Fiber, Louise A. "A Selected Guide to Journals in the Field of French Language and Literature." *French Review*, 47 (May 1974), 1128-1141.

Limited to the major journals of the U.S. and Canada. Excludes bulletins of various state level Departments of Education, and news letters or publications of regional and local modern language teachers' associations, as well as graduate student reviews.
Gives conditions and requirements, if any, for publishing in the ninety-one journals mentioned. Other essential information on these journals is also listed.

Comparative Literature. Eugene, Oregon.
Comparative Literature Studies. Champaign, Illinois.
Esprit Créateur (L'). Lawrence, Kansas.
French Review (The). Chapel Hill, North Carolina.
Kentucky Romance Quarterly. Lexington, Kentucky.
Modern Language Journal (The). Boulder, Colorado.
Modern Language Notes. Baltimore, Maryland.
Modern Language Quarterly. Seattle, Washington.
Modern Philology. Chicago, Illinois.

66

ublications of the Modern Language Association, PMLA.
      New York, N.Y.
omance Notes. Chapel Hill, North Carolina.
omance Philology. Berkeley, California.
omanic Review (The). New York, N.Y.
tudies in Philology. Chapel Hill, North Carolina.
ymposium. A Quarterly Journal in Modern Foreign Litera-
      tures. Syracuse, N.Y.
ale French Studies. New Haven, Connecticut.

CHAPTER 7

PH.D. DISSERTATIONS AND THESES

See in Ch. 1: Besterman (no. 2); in Ch. 2: *MLA Bibliog-phy* (no. 22), Rancoeur (no. 26); in Ch. 3: *Bibliographie de la France* (no. 84); in Ch. 4: Winchell (no. 97).

A. BIBLIOGRAPHIES OF DISSERTATIONS AND THESES

188 Paris. Bibliothèque Nationale. Département des Impri-més. *Catalogue des dissertations et écrits acadé-miques provenant des échanges avec les universités étrangères et reçus par la Bibliothèque Nationale, 1882-1924.* 43 vols. P.: Klincksieck, 1884-1925.

Diss. received by the B.N. from European univer-sities, arranged by universities.

189 (AUPELF) *Répertoire des thèses de doctorat soutenues devan-universités de langue française.* Québec: Université Laval, Centre de Documentation nationale, 1970-74. Semi-annual. (Ceased publication.)

Prepared for the "Association des Universités Partiellement ou Entièrement de Langue Française" (AUPELF). No. 1 lists about 2,400 doctoral theses, mostly of 1969 and 1970, granted by sixty-nine universities in Africa, Belgium, Canada, France, Switzerland, South Viet-nam, etc. Produced by computer, provides a subject approach by geographic area or by academic discipline, and an alpha-betical list by author. There is also a list of directors of theses. Rather difficult to use for French literature since subjects are not divided by period or main authors.

B. NATIONAL GENERAL LISTS OF PH.D. DISSERTATIONS

AUSTRALIA

190 *Union List of Higher Degree Theses in Australian University Libraries. Cumulative Edition to 1965.* Edited by Enid Wylie. Hobart: U. of Tasmania Lib., 1967.

Union list of master's and doctor's theses in nine university libraries through 1965. Includes information on availability of theses through loan or photocopy. A classified subject arrangement with an alphabetical index of subject headings and an author index.

191 Wien Universität. Philosophische Fakultät. *Verzeichnis über die seit dem Jahre 1872 an der Philosophischen Fakultät der Universität in Wien, eingereichten und approbierten Dissertationen.* 3 vols. Wien, 1935.

  Index of submitted and approved dissertations since 1872 in the College of Philosophy at the University of Vienna up to 1933.

  Arranged by broad subjects, with a catchword subject index at end of each group and an author index for each vol.

  _____. Bd. 4, *Nachtrag: Verzeichnis der 1934 bis 1937 an der Philosophischen Fakultät der Universität in Wien u. der 1872 bis 1937 an der Philosophischen Fakultät der Universität in Innsbruck eingereichten und approbierten Dissertationen.* Wien.

  This vol. 4 is a Supplement containing the Index of submitted and approved dissertations in the College of Philosophy at the University of Vienna in 1934-37, and at the College of Philosophy at the University of Innsbruck in 1872 to 1937.
  Continued by:

192 Alker, Lisl. *Verzeichnis der an der Universität Wien approbierten Dissertationen, 1937/1944-.* Wien: Kerry, 1950-.

  An Index of approved dissertations at the University of Vienna 1937/1944-. Classified, with combined author and subject index.
  Note: Since 1949, Austrian diss. have been listed in *Osterreichische Bibliographie.*

193 *Gesamtverzeichnis Osterreichischer Dissertationen.* Vol. 1-. 1966-. Wien: Notring der Wissenschaftlichen Verbände Osterreichs, 1967-. Annual.

  General Index of Austrian doctoral diss., listed by university, with author and subject indexes.

194 Liège. Université de. Bibliothèque. *Répertoire des thèses de doctorat européennes, année 1969-1970-.* Liège: Bibliothèque de l'U. de Liège, 1970-.

  A list of theses received in the library of Liège U. Classified in five broad subject areas including *Philosophie et Lettres,* and sublisted by name of university

in random order as theses are received. Following each
classification is an index by languages of key words in
titles. The 1969-70 vol. covers 10,673 theses from universities in Germany, France, Scandinavia, etc.

195 Louvain. Université Catholique. *Bibliographie académique.*
Louvain: Bibl. de l'U., 1880-1937.

196 _____. *Résumé des dissertations présentées pour
l'obtention du grade de docteur en philosophie et
lettres.* Louvain: Bibliothèque de l'U., 1933-.

CANADA

The main Canadian Universities publish lists of their
doctoral theses. Canadian theses are also listed in
Canadiana (Ch. 3, no. 74), and in *Doctoral Dissertations
Accepted by American Universities,* etc. (below, nos.
237-40).

197 Ottawa. Canadian Bibliographic Centre. *Canadian Graduate
Theses in the Humanities and Social Sciences, 1921-
1946/Thèses des gradués canadiens dans les humanités
et les sciences sociales, 1921-1946.* Ottawa: E.
Cloutier, 1951.

A briefly annotated list of 3,043 theses arranged
by college or university under broad subjects. There is
an author index, English and French subject indexes.

198 Ottawa. National Library. *Canadian Theses/Thèses canadiennes. 1960/61-.* Ottawa: Queen's Printer, 1962-.
Annual.

Arrangement is by broad subject classification,
then by university or college, with an author index.
Theses listed in this series are not necessarily
included in *Canadian Theses on Microfilm.*

199 _____. *Canadian Theses on Microfilm; Catalogue, Price
List/Thèses canadiennes sur microfilm; catalogue,
prix.* Ottawa: National Lib., 1969.

Supps. Nos. 1-6 issued through 1971.
Theses are listed according to accession number
from 1965 (but some theses prior to 1965 are included).
Some 7,450 titles from eighteen cooperating universities
are listed. This list also included in *Canadiana,* Pt. 3,
since 1967.

200 Naaman, Antoine Youssef. *Guide bibliographique des thèses
littéraires canadiennes de 1921 à 1969.* Montréal:
Eds. Cosmos, 1970.

Includes theses in English and French on Canadian, French and other literatures. Author index and keyword subject index including names of authors written about. The introduction contains a list of French language periodicals and reference works for French literary studies. Supplemented by:

01 Brodeur, Léo A. *Répertoire des thèses littéraires canadiennes (janvier 1969-septembre 1971): 1786 sujets/ Index of Canadian Literary Theses (January 1969-September 1971): 1786 Subjects.* Sherbrooke: U. de Sherbrooke, Centre d'étude des littératures d'expression française, 1972.

DENMARK

Theses of Denmark are also listed in the national bibliography: *Dansk Bogfortegnelse, 1851-.* Købnhavn: Gads, 1851-. Annual.

02 Copenhagen. Universitet Bibliotek. *Danish Theses for the Doctorate and Commemorative Publications of the University of Copenhagen, 1836-1926. A Bio-bibliography.* Copenhagen: Munksgaard, 1929.

In two pts.: (1) class list, arranged by main classes of the U.D.C.; (2) alphabetical author list with references to fuller biographies elsewhere, and also serves as an author index to the class list. Bibliographical detail given for each thesis includes: author's name, title, English translation of a Danish title sometimes with a brief abstract in English, date, paging, ills., date of oral defense. Subject index.
Continued by:

_____. *Danish Theses for the Doctorate, 1927-1958. A Bibliography.* Copenhagen: U. Lib., 1962.

Alphabetically listed by author with subject index.

FINLAND

See also Sweden.

03 Hjelt, Otto Edvard August. *Det Finska universitets disputations-och program-litteratur under aren 1828-1908 systematiskt ordnad/Dissertationes academicae et programmata Universitatis litterarum Fennorum Helsingforsiae annis 1828-1908 edita.* Helsingfors: Helsingfors Centraltryckeri, 1909.

Finnish theses in literature, 1828-1908. Systematically classified.

204 Kärmeniemi, Kaija. *Opinnäytteiden bibliografia: luettelo Helsingin yliopistossa, Turun yliopistossa ja Yhteiskunnallisessa Korkeakoulussa vuoteen 1956 mennessä humanististen tietei den aloilta laadituist tutkielmista.* Helsinki: Suomalaisen Kirjallisuuden Seura, 1959.

Bibliography of unpublished essays and theses, and of printed Ph.D. diss. written up to 1956, in the Humanities and Social Sciences at the Universities of Helsinki and Turku. Pub. by the Finnish Literary Soc.

205 Sajavaara, Karl. "Finnish Theses and Dissertations in Modern Languages and Literatures. Work in Progress. *Neuphilologische Mitteilungen*, 1964-.

A continuing feature appearing usually once each year since 1964. Arranged by language (English, French, German, etc.); giving author, title, university, and indicating theses that have been published.

FRANCE

(Atelier de Reproduction des Thèses Françaises (Lille) publishes P

206 Mourier, Louis-Athénaïs, et Deltour, Félix. *Notice sur le doctorat ès lettres, suivie du Catalogue et de l'analyse des thèses françaises et latines admises par les Facultés des lettres depuis 1810.* 4e éd. rev. et considérablement augm. P.: Delalain, 1880. Annual supps. 21 vols., 1880/81-1901/02.

The U. of Paris is at the beginning and the other universities follow alphabetically. Chronological order of *Doctorats d'Etat* in the Arts for each university. Summary of theses and biographical information on doctors. Table of subjects and of doctors.

207 Maire, Albert. *Répertoire alphabétique des thèses de doctorat ès lettres des universités françaises (1810-1900), avec table chronologique par université et table détaillée des matières.* P.: Picard, 1903.

2,182 theses in alphabetical order by author indicating form of publication. Subject index.

208 France. Ministère de l'Education Nationale. *Catalogue des thèses de doctorat soutenues devant les universités françaises. 1884/1885-1971.* 75 vols. P.: Cercle de la Librairie, 1885-1973.

Prepared from 1884 to 1925 by the Ministère de l'Instruction Publique; 1926 to 1929 by the Bibliothèque de la Sorbonne; then, by the university libraries and the B.N., with the help of the "Service des échanges universitaires."

72

From 1884 to 1913, classification is by university and then by *Faculté* (College). From 1914 on, the classification is by *Faculté*. Subject and author indexes up to and including 1928. No index from 1929 to 1956. Author index taken up again from 1958 (for 1957) on. From 1947 to 1972, the *Catalogue* forms the *Supplément D* of the *Bibliographie Officielle* of the *Bibliographie de la France*. New series since 1960: *Catalogue des thèses et écrits académiques*. Some changes in the presentation in 1970-71. Continued by:

Secrétariat d'Etat aux Universités. Direction des bibliothèques et de la lecture publique. *Catalogue des thèses de doctorat soutenues devant les Universités françaises en 1972-*. Nouv. série. P.: Cercle de la Librairie, 1974-.

Uses a developed U.D.C. system, with authors index. Indicates the institutions which provide a copy of the dissertations. Dissertations list is classified by subjects, disciplines and universities.

)9 Association Internationale des Docteurs (Lettres) de l'Université de Paris. *Annuaire des docteurs (lettres) de l'Université de Paris et des autres universités françaises. Bibliographie analytique des thèses (1899-1965)*. P.: L'Association, Nizet diffuseur, 1969.

.0 Paris. Université. Faculté des Lettres et Sciences Humaines. *Positions des thèses de troisième cycle, soutenues devant la Faculté, 1960/61-1970*. 10 vols. P.: PUF, 1962-72. (No more published.)

Excellent summaries or abstracts of theses, with an alphabetical index of authors and a subject index.

.1 Quémada, Bernard. "Bibliographie des thèses littéraires d'intérêt lexicologique (1940-1960). 1e série." *Cahiers de Lexicologie* 2, 1960, pp. 152-174.

GERMANY

2 Mundt, Hermann. *Bio-bibliographisches Verzeichnis von Universitäts und Hochschuldrucken (Dissertationen) vom Ausgang des 16. bis Ende des 19. Jahrhunderts*. 2 vols. Leipzig: Carlsohn, 1936-42; rpt., N.Y.: Johnson, 1966.

Bio-bibliographical Index of university dissertations (and publications) from the end of the Sixteenth Century to the end of the Nineteenth Century. Interrupted at the name "Ritter." The library of the U. of Leipzig intends to finish it. Chiefly German diss., with some Dutch and Scandinavian diss.

213 *Jahresverzeichnis der deutschen Hochschulschriften*, Berlin
       1887-1936; Leipzig: VEB Verlag für Buchund Biblio-
       thekswesen, 1937-.

       Annual Index of German university publications. Clas-
    sified by universities, then by authors, with an annual
    table of authors and subjects.
       Includes theses from all German universities, *Technisch*
    Hochschulen, etc. Provides citations for theses published
    as books, articles, etc.

GREAT BRITAIN AND IRELAND

214 Taylor, Alan Carey. *Bibliography of Unpublished Theses on*
       French Subjects Deposited in University Libraries of
       the United Kingdom (1905-1950). Oxford: Blackwell,
       1964.

          Sections on linguistics, stylistics, literature,
    studies of French authors, anonymous works.

215 Green, F. C. "Thèses inédites de littérature, histoire,
       philosophie et art français soutenus devant les
       universités de Grande-Bretagne de 1939 à 1949."
       Cahiers de l'Association Internationale des Etudes
       Françaises, No. 2 (mai 1952), 112-121.

216 *Index to Theses Accepted for Higher Degrees in the Univer-*
       sities of Great Britain and Ireland. Vol. 1,
       1950/51-. London: Aslib, 1953-. Annual.

          Classified systematically as well as by univer-
    sities. Author and subject indexes.

217 Cambridge University. *Abstracts of Dissertations Approved*
       for the Ph.D., M.Sc., and M.Litt. Degrees in the
       University of Cambridge, 1925-1957. Cambridge:
       U. Pr., 1927-1959.

          Arranged by Faculties and departments, then by
    type of degree. Index of authors.
          Continued by:

    _____. *Titles of Dissertations Approved for the Ph.D.,*
       M.Sc., and M.Litt. Degrees in the University of
       Cambridge, 1957/58-. Cambridge: U. Pr., 1958-.
       Annual.

          Arranged like the above, but gives titles only.

218 Oxford University. Committee for Advanced Studies. *Ab-*
       stracts of Dissertations for the Degree of Doctor of
       Philosophy. 13 vols. Vols. 1-13: *1925/28-1940.*
       Oxford: U. Pr., 1928-1947.

_____. *Successful Candidates for the Degree of D.Phil.,
B.Litt., and B.Sc., with Titles of Their Theses.*
Vol. 1-: *1940/49-*. Oxford: U. Pr., 1950-. Annual.

NETHERLANDS

19 *Catalogus van academische geschriften in Nederland
verschenen, 1924-*. Utrecht, 1925-.

Annual with cumulations for *1941-45*, 1949; and
1946-49, 1952.

Catalog of university publications of the Netherlands as of 1924. Arranged by name of university. Author
index. Title varies, includes the Netherlands Indies up
to 1945. Prepared since 1952 by the Utrecht U. Lib.

NEW ZEALAND

20 *Union List of Theses of the Universities of New Zealand,
1910-1954*. Ed. D. L. Jenkins. Wellington: New
Zealand Lib. Assn., 1956.

Doctoral theses arranged chronologically, Master's theses in alphabetical subject order. Includes
foreign theses, about New Zealand, and theses presented by
New Zealand students while overseas. Index of authors.
Supplemented by:

_____. *Supplement 1955-1962, with some additions and
corrections to the 1910-1954 list.* Comp. by D. G.
Jamieson. Wellington: New Zealand Lib. Assn., 1963.

Continued by:

*Union List of Higher Degree Theses of the Universities of
New Zealand. Supplement 1963-1967*. Comp. by
Catherine G. Swift. Wellington: New Zealand Lib.
Assn., 1969.

In the 1963-67 supplement, the arrangement within
subjects is alphabetical by author rather than chronological.

NORWAY

21 Andressen, Gunnar W. *Doctors kreert ved Universitet i
Oslo, 1817-1961; en bibliografi. . .med en historisk
innledning; om doktorgraden ved vart universitet* av
Leiv Amundsen. Oslo: Universetets Forlaget, 1962.

Index of doctoral dissertations at the University of
Oslo 1817-1961. A bibliography with a historical introduction about the doctorate at this university by Leiv A-
mundsen.

SOUTH AFRICA

222 Robinson, Anthony Meredith Lewin. *Catalogue of Theses and Dissertations Accepted for Degrees by the South Afri Universities/Katalogus van proefskrifte en verhandelinge vir grade deur die Suid-Afrikaanse universiteite goedgekeur, 1918-1941.* . . . Capetown: pub. by the author at the South African Public Lib., 1943.

       1,757 theses classified, with subject and author indexes.
Continued by:

223 Malan, Stephanus I. *Gesamentlike katalogus van proefskrifte en verhandelinge van die Suid-Afrikaanse universiteite/Union Catalogue of Theses and Dissertations of the South African Universities, 1942-1958.* Potchefstroom: U. for Christian Higher Education, 1959. Annual supplement, *1959-*.

       A classified list with author index.

SPAIN

224 Madrid Universidad. *Catalogo de las tesis doctorales manuscritas existentes en la Universidad de Madrid.* Madrid: Gonzalez, 1952.

       Catalog of unpublished doctoral dissertations at the U. of Madrid. Arranged alphabetically under broad subjects. No author or subject index.

SWEDEN

225 Marklin, Gabriel. *Catalogus disputationum in academiis Scandinaviae et Finlandiae Lidenianus continuatus a Gabr. Marklin.* Upsaliae: Reg. Academiae Typ., 1820.

       Lidenian Index of diss. in universities of Scand navia and Finland, continued by Marklin. Covers 1778-181 Contents: 1) Uppsala diss.; 2) Lund diss., Oslo diss.; 3) Åbo diss.

       _____. *Ad Catalogum disputationum in academiis et gymnasiis Sveciae Lidenianum supplementa addidit Gabr. Marklin.* Upsaliae: Reg. Academiae Typ., 1820.

       Supp. to the Lidenian Index of diss. in universi ties and institutions of higher learning in Sweden, by Marklin.

       _____. *Catalogus disputationum in academiis Sveciae et Fenniae habitarum Lidenianus iterum continuatus a Gabr. Marklin.* Upsaliae, 1856.

Index of diss. in universities continued by Gabr.
Marklin. Covers 1820-55. Contents: 1) Uppsala diss.;
2) Lund diss.; 3) Finland diss.

26 Josephson, Aksel Gustav Salomon. *Avhandlingar ock program
uitg. svenska ock finska akademier ock skolor, 1855-
1890.* 2 vols. Uppsala, 1891-97.

Author list with classified index of both Swedish
and Finnish theses. It should be noted that many Scandinavian theses on French language and literature are written
in French, and have a reputation for a high quality of
scholarship.
Continued by:

27 Nelson, Axel Herman. *Akademiska afhandlingar vid Sveriges
Universitet och Högskolor läsären 1890/91-1909/10,
jämte förteckning öfver svenskars akademiska
afhandlingar vid utländska universitet under samma
tid.* Uppsala: Academiska Bokhandeln, 1911-12.

Dissertations at universities and institutions of higher
learning in Sweden during the academic years 1890/91-
1909/10. Together with an index of the dissertations of
Swedes at foreign universities during the same time. An
author list with classified index.
Continued by:

28 Tuneld, John. *Akademiska Avhandlingar vid Sveriges Universitet och Högskolor Läsären 1910/11-1939/40: Bibliografi.* Lund: Ohlssons Boktr., 1945.

Bibliography of dissertations at universities and institutions of higher learning in Sweden during the academic
years of 1910/11-1939/40. An author list with classified
index.

29 "Forteckning över ämnen för licentiat; Och doktorsav-
handlingar i litteraturhistoria." *Samlaren,* 85
(1964), 223-233; ibid., 91 (1971), 104-19.

Index of doctoral dissertations and masters' theses
in the history of literature. Theses in language and
literature since 1935 at Swedish universities.

SWITZERLAND

30 Soret, Charles. *Catalogue des ouvrages, articles et mémoires publiés par les professeurs de l'Université
de Genève ainsi que des thèses présentées de 1873 à
1895 aux diverses Facultés pour l'obtention de grades
universitaires.* Genève: Imprimerie Rey et Malavallon,
1896.

Later vols. by different comps. and pub.: Charles
Julliard and Fernand Aubert, 1896-1907; Albert Kohler,
1908-13; Albert Roussy, 1914-26; Hermann Blanc, 1927-57;
Additional vols. in progress.

231 *Jahresverzeichnis der schweizerischen Hochschulschriften,*
     1897-/Catalogue des écrits académiques suisses,
     1897-. Basel/Bâle: Verlag der Universitatsbibliothe.
     1898-. Annual.

          Pub. varies, title varies. Arranged by name of
university. Each issue has an author index, and from 1926
a subject index.

232 Fribourg. Université. *Les Thèses de doctorat à l'Univers*
     de Fribourg depuis sa fondation en 1889 jusqu'au 1er
     mars 1936, éd. par N. Weyrich. Fribourg: Imprimerie
     St. Paul, 1936.

          Arranged by academic divisions, i.e., theology,
law, philosophy (includes literature), and science, with
authors listed alphabetically in each section. No subject
or author indexes.

UNION OF SOVIET SOCIALIST REPUBLICS

233 Moskva. Publichanaia Biblioteka. *Katalog kandidatskikh*
     i doctorskikh dissertatsii, postupivshikh v Bibliote
     imeni V. I. Lenina i Gosudarstvennuiu Tsentral'nuiu
     Nauchnuiu Meditsinskuiu Biblioteku. 1957, 2-oe
     polugodie-. Moskva, 1957-58, semiannual; 1958-,
     quarterly.

     From the Moscow Pub. Lib., principal catalog of Soviet
diss. in all fields, deposited with the Lenin Lib. and
the Central State Lib. of Medicine. M.A. and Ph.D. theses
arranged by subjects, with author and university indexes.
     Current listing of the authors' printed summaries of
15-50 pages in length is provided by *Book Chronicle,*
additional issue (*Knizhnaia letopis'; dopolnitel'nyi*
vypusk) for the years 1961-, pub. in 1964-.
     For a history of these titles and related lists see:

234 Buist, Eleanor. "Soviet Dissertation Lists since 1934."
     Library Quarterly, 33 (April 1963), 192-207.

UNITED STATES

Ph.D. Dissertations (all topics)

I. DISSERTATIONS IN PROGRESS

235 "Doctoral Dissertations in Progress." *Rackham Literary*
     Studies, No. 5 (1974), 123-32. Pub. by graduate

students in literature of the U. of Mich., Ann Arbor.

II. DISSERTATIONS ACCEPTED

(Published on microfilms by Xerox U. Microfilms, Ann Arbor, Mi.)

236 U.S. Library of Congress. Catalog Division. *List of American Doctoral Dissertations Printed in 1912-38.* 26 vols. Washington, D.C.: Gov. Printing Office, 1913-40.

      In each volume: (1) Alphabetical list of theses printed during the year; (2) Classified list, arranged under the broad classes of the L.C. scheme; (3) Index of subjects; (4) Doctors whose theses have been printed during the year, arranged by institutions.
      Lists 1 and 2 give full cataloging information and, in case of rpts., indicate the periodical or other publication in which the thesis was first printed. Includes the printed theses of about forty-five colleges and universities. No more published.

237 *Doctoral Dissertations Accepted by American Universities, 1933/34-1954/55.* Comp. for the Assn. of Research Libraries. N.Y.: Wilson, 1934-56, Nos. 1-22. Ceased publication.

      Diss. (U.S. and Canada) arranged by subject and then by university, giving for each dissertation its author, title, and--in the case of those printed--bibliographical data as to separate publication or inclusion in some periodical or collection. Alphabetical author and subject indexes.
      Continued by:

Index to American Doctoral Dissertations, 1955/56-. Comp. for the Assn. of Research Libraries. Ann Arbor, Mich.: U. Microfilms, 1957-. Annual.

      Issued annually as No. 13 of *Dissertation Abstracts*, it consolidates into one list of diss. for which doctoral degrees were granted in the U.S. and Canada during the academic year covered, as well as those available on microfilm.
      Arranged by subject classifications with author indexes. The subject classification must be used with care, as subject breakdowns are not detailed enough to make it easy to discover what has been done in a particular field.
      Preliminary tables give information on the publication and lending of dissertations, and the distribution of doctorates by university and subject field.

238 *Microfilm Abstracts. A Collection of Abstracts of Doctoral Dissertations Which Are Available in Complete Form on Microfilm.* Vols. 1-11. Ann Arbor, Mich.: U. Microfilms, 1938-1951.

Contents for each number list titles and authors under broad subject groups, i.e., under literature, without country or period subdivision. Abstracts are one to two pages long. Each vol. has a cumulative index of titles, but it is classified under subjects as above, not alphabetical.

A-Z author index covering vols. 1-11, pub. in 1956.

Of limited value because of the small number of participating universities.

Continued by:

Dissertation Abstracts: Abstracts of Dissertations and Monographs on Microfilm. Vols. 12-29. Ann Arbor, Mich.: U. Microfilms, 1952-1969. Monthly.

Subtitle varies. Coverage varies.

A compilation of abstracts of doctoral dissertations submitted to U. Microfilms, Inc., by a varying number of cooperating universities. The main list is arranged alphabetically by subject field and then by university, listing title, order number, author's name, university, date, name of supervisor, abstract, prices of microfilm and of Xerox copy, and number of pages. Each issue includes a subject index and an author index. Pt. 2 of No. 1 (June) of each year, since 1961/62, is a cumulated subject and author index for the year. This includes only the diss. abstracted and not those in the *Index to American Doctoral Dissertations.*

Continued by:

Dissertation Abstracts International. Ann Arbor, Mich.: U. Microfilms, July 1969-. Monthly.

The title changed with vol. 30, No. 1 (July 1969) in anticipation of adding more foreign diss. A keyword-in-title index replaces the subject index in monthly and annual cumulated indexes.

In Jan. 1975 the list of cooperating institutions includes about 345 universities. Except for Canada which is well covered, there are only nine foreign universities represented. The list also indicates the date service began, but due to retrospective filming, that date is not necessarily the earliest year theses were microfilmed. Moreover, some universities do not send all of their diss. and most began sending them in different years, so other sources will be necessary for a complete search.

239 *Dissertation Abstracts International. Retrospective Index vols. 1-29.* 9 vols. in 11. Ann Arbor, Mich.: Xero U. Microfilms, 1970.

Each vol. covers one or more subjects, and vol. 9 is an author index.

A subject and author index to *Microfilm Abstracts*, to *Dissertation Abstracts*, etc., 1938-68, giving a microfilm order number and reference to the original abstract (vol. and page in *Microfilm Abstracts*, etc.). The keyword-in-title system is used for subject indexing.

240   *Comprehensive Dissertation Index 1861-1972*. 37 vols. Ann Arbor, Mich.: Xerox U. Microfilms, 1973. *Supplement 1973-*, 1974-. Annual.

Coverage in early period (before 1912) was a-chieved via queries to universities from the L.S., and published lists. From 1938, *Microfilm Abstracts* and *Dissertation Abstracts* are incorporated in the index.

Each vol. covers one or more subjects (language and literature are in vols. 29 and 30). Author index (alphabetical) is in vols. 33-37.

There is a list of institutions represented (mostly of the U.S. and Canada, but including forty-three from Europe and elsewhere), and a list of the printed sources consulted.

Full information on each diss. is given, including author, title, degree, date, university, citation source and order number for microfilm (if available from Xerox U. Microfilms).

Indexing is by keywords-in-title--about six per title--arranged in alphabetical order, and executed by a computer. Many peculiarities are encountered, and the user trying a subject approach should be armed with numerous keywords. In literature, author's names are used, but only if they appear in titles, and even then some names offer difficulty. For example, for Sainte-Beuve, eighteen titles are found under Beuve, fifteen under Sainte-Beuve and two under Sainte.

The *Supplement* will include all Am. doctoral theses.

Ph.D. Dissertations in Modern Languages

241   "Doctors' Degrees in Modern Foreign Languages. 1925/26." *Modern Language Journal*. Vol. 11-, 1926/27-.

Several compilers. Title varies. Irregular. Since vol. 33 the title has been "American Doctoral Degrees Granted in the Field of Modern Languages."

242   "Dissertations in Progress." *French Review*, 1964-. Annual.

Appears generally in the Oct. issue. "By exception, the 13th listing appeared in March 1976 rather than October 1975." Pt. A is entitled "Language" and includes Linguistics, Phonetics, etc. Pt. B is entitled "Literature" and includes Culture, Literary History, and Francophonic Literatures. Part B is further divided into General, Medieval, Sixteenth Century,

Seventeenth Century, Eighteenth Century, etc.
        The diss. listed are taken from universities
belonging to the Association of American Universities and
some other leading institutions.
        The list is in two parts: "Dissertations in
Progress," and "Dissertations Defended."

Master's Theses

243 Black, Dorothy M. *Guide to Lists of Master's Theses.*
            Chicago: Am. Lib. Assn., 1965.

            U.S. and Canada through 1964. Contains general
lists, special subject field lists and those issued by
institutions.

244 *Master's Abstracts: Abstracts of Selected Master's Theses
            on Microfilm.* Ann Arbor, Mich.: U. Microfilms,
            1962-. vol. 1-.

            Vol. 1, 1962/63, semi-annual; vol. 2, 1964,
quarterly.
            Published abstracts of a selected list of
master's essays, from various universities, available on
microfilm. Classified arrangement. No indexes announced.

C. STYLE MANUALS

See Chapter 4 on reference works, nos. 103-106.

CHAPTER 8

ENCYCLOPEDIAS AND DICTIONARIES

A. ENCYCLOPEDIAS

I. HISTORY OF ENCYCLOPEDIAS

245 Collison, Robert Lewis. *Encyclopaedias, Their History throughout the Ages: A Bibliographical Guide with Extensive Historical Notes to the General Encyclopaedias Issued throughout the World from 350 B.C. to the Present Day.* N.Y.: Hafner Publishing Co., 1964; 2nd ed., 1966.

A valuable historical survey of encyclopedias from ancient times with emphasis on older works. Eight chapters; the last five covering Diderot and the *Encyclopédistes, Encyclopaedia Britannica*, Brockhaus, Nineteenth Century and Twentieth Century. French works discussed include the various Larousse publications, *La Grande Encyclopédie* and the *Encyclopédie Française*. Appendices include a general bibliography, and a list of encyclopedias not mentioned in the text (arranged by country and without commentary).

246 Walsh, S. Padraig. *General Encyclopedias in Print, 1973-74: A Comparative Analysis.* 9th ed. N.Y.: Bowker, 1973.

II. MAIN ENCYCLOPEDIAS

CANADA

247 Le Jeune, Louis-Marie. *Dictionnaire général de biographie, histoire, littérature, agriculture, commerce, industrie et des arts, sciences, moeurs, coutumes, institutions politiques et religieuses du Canada.* 2 vols. Ottawa: U. d'Ottawa, 1931.

A general, alphabetically arranged encyclopedia, mainly on French Canada. Includes many useful bibliographies with articles. Valued also for its biographies, portraits, and historical information. The only work of its kind in French.

248 *The Encyclopedia of Canada.* Ed. by W. Stewart Wallace. 6 vols. Toronto: U. Associates of Canada, 1948-49. (Previous eds. 1935-37, and 1940.)

Mostly short articles, arranged alphabetically. Some bibliographies. Includes biographical articles on writers and a fairly long article on literature (English and French Canadian). Each vol. has an index to illustrations and maps, and a list of the contributors of special articles. No general index.

249 *Encyclopedia Canadiana.* Ed. in Chief: John E. Robbins. 10 vols. Toronto: Grolier of Canada, 1972. (First published 1957; continuous revision.)

Based on the *Encyclopedia of Canada,* some articles being unchanged, others updated, and new material added, but does not entirely supersede it. Signed articles, some with bibliographies. Biographical articles on authors (including French Canadians) are numerous, and various aspects of English and French Canadian literature are covered. Vol. 10 is an atlas with gazetteer. No general index.

FRANCE

250 *Encyclopédie, ou Dictionnaire raisonné des sciences, des arts et des métiers.* . . . Mis en ordre et publié par D. Diderot, et quant à la partie mathématique, par J. d'Alembert. 35 vols. ills. P.: Briasson, 1751-80; rpt., P.: Cercle du livre précieux, 1964-65.

17 vols. of text and 11 vols. of plates. Supplements of 4 vols. of text and 1 vol. of plates. Two volumes of tables of contents. Facsimile reproduction of the 12 vols. of plates published from 1762 to 1777.
A famous encyclopedia written by Diderot and some of the most illustrious scholars of the time; strong in the arts, applied science, and technology. Philosophical concepts of the eighteenth century are reflected in this work. This *Encyclopédie* sought to summarize knowledge and to guide opinion towards political liberalism and deism.

251 *La Grande Encyclopédie, inventaire raisonné des sciences, des lettres et des arts, par une société de savants et de gens de lettres;* sous la direction de André Berthelot, et al. 32 vols. P.: Lamirault, 1886-1902.

The most important French encyclopedia of the nineteenth century. Contains authoritative articles listed alphabetically and signed. Describes the historical evolution of literature, arts and sciences through the ages and up to the time of publication. Excellent for medieval and Renaissance subjects and for biographical material on the French and other Europeans. The bibliographies appended to many subjects are still of great importance.

The Larousse Encyclopedias.
   Larousse has become a synonym for French encyclopedia
and dictionary. We have grouped here their encyclopedias
by chronological order.

252 *Grand Dictionnaire universel du XIXe siècle; français,*
        historique, géographique, mythologique, biblio-
        graphique, littéraire, artistique, scientifique,
        etc. . . . Ed. Pierre Larousse. 15 vols. P.:
        Administration du Grand Dictionnaire, 1865-76.
        Suppléments. 2 vols., 1878, 1890.

        A famous and important encyclopedia, that is a
   combination dictionary and encyclopedia. Includes articles on individual works of literature, music and songs,
   plays, poems, novels, newspapers, periodicals, etc. Very
   good for European literature, biography and history. Contains much biography not given in other general encyclopedias. Bibliographies are given for countries but not for
   writers or most other subjects.

253 *Nouveau Larousse illustré: dictionnaire universel ency-*
        clopédique. Pub. sous la direction de Claude Augé.
        7 vols. et suppl. Ills. P.: Larousse, 1897-1907.

        A concise version of the above.

254 *Larousse du XXe siècle en six volumes.* Pub. sous la di-
        rection de Claude Augé. 6 vols. P.: Larousse,
        1958. (1e éd. 1928-33).

        Both a dictionary of French and an encyclopedia.
   Each volume has about 36,000 articles. Contains maps,
   plates, and illustrations of all kinds. No bibliographical
   references, but precious as a technical and biographical
   dictionary. Gives music examples and plots of literary
   works.
        It is a modernized version of the *Grand Dicti-*
   onnaire universel du XIXe siècle.
        Larousse publishes also encyclopedias in three
   vols. classified alphabetically or by themes.

255 *Grand Larousse encyclopédique en dix volumes.* 10 vols.
        ills. et cartes. P.: Larousse, 1960-64. *1e Supplé-*
        ment, 1968. *2e Supplément*, 1975.

        Supersedes, for the most part, the two encyclo-
   pedias above.
        177,071 unsigned articles, 450,000 definitions
   of words with quotations. A completely new work. It
   aims to include a dictionary of the French language from
   the beginning of the seventeenth century, as well as an
   encyclopedia with brief articles and specific entries.
   Bibliographies (French books) are grouped at the end of

each volume. There are also references at the end of many articles. Excellent, concise, and up to date.

256 *Grande Encyclopédie (La)*. 20 vols. P.: Larousse, 1972-76. (Index vol. to come.)

The twenty basic vols. contain 12,432 pages including 15,000 illustrations. Subjects in alphabetical order are covered in 8,000 separate articles. They are made up of complete groups juxtaposing a general analysis with complementary documentation on each topic. These entries include general concepts, biographies, historical periods; philosophical, artistic, musical or literary movements; essays (scientific, technical, historico-geographical), etc. Illustrations are all in color and for the most part brand new, especially the maps, the technical diagrams, etc.

257 *Encyclopédie française*. Fondée par Anatole de Monzie; mise en oeuvre par Lucien Febvre, et par Gaston Berger. Dir. par J. Cain. 21 vols. Ills. P.: Soc. nouv. de l'Encyclopédie française, 1935-66. (Re-issued by Larousse with title: *Encyclopédie française permanente*. 22 thematic vols.)

Loose-leaf mobile binding permits the inserting of updated material sold separately by Larousse. A systematically arranged encyclopedia, the work of prominent specialists.
Although it does want to present a compendium of knowledge, there is no attempt in this work to write about everything. An important place is given to technical and practical activities of the present in comparison to speculative and theoretical activities. It takes from the past but stresses the present and even speculates on the future.
Vols. 16 and 17: "Arts et littérature," 1935-1936. Vol. 21: "Répertoire général. Index alphabétique" has separate alphabetical indexes of proper names, collaborators, places and "notions importantes."
Each vol. also has its own index and bibliographical appendix. Several vols. have been completely rewritten and issued as new editions.

258 *Clartés*. *L'Encyclopédie du présent*. 18 vols. P.: Ed. Techniques, 1948-.

Published on loose-leaf mobile binding which permits the insertion of updated material sold separately. Divided in four pts.; literature is in the *Pensée* division: t. 14, 1958; M. Brion, éd.

259 *Dictionnaire encyclopédique Quillet*. Nouv. éd. 8 vols. Ills. P.: Quillet-Flammarion, 1968-70. *Supplément,*

1971.

A dictionary and encyclopedia in alphabetical order, which seeks to limit itself to the indispensable and to be used as a quick reference work.

Definitions are concise, but give earliest meanings and brief examples or expressions. Includes synonyms, antonyms and homonyms; sometimes observations on grammar, syntax and orthographic difficulties. Not as well illustrated as comparable works by Larousse.

The encyclopedic content is general with some rather elaborate synoptic tables on the inter-relationship of subjects.

260 *Encyclopédie de la Pléiade*. Sous la dir. de Raymond Queneau. P.: Gallimard, 1955-.

Group of independent monographs, devoted each to a different field, and printed in one or more vols. Vol. 3 of *Histoire des littératures* (dir. R. Queneau. 3 vols., 1955-58) is: *Littératures françaises, connexes et marginales*. There are also: *Histoire des spectacles* (dir. Guy Dumur, 1965), and *La France et les Français* (dir. Michel François, 1972).

B. DICTIONARIES

The dictionaries devoted to linguistics, or one period, will be found in Pts. II and III.

I. BOOKS ABOUT DICTIONARIES

261 Baldinger, Kurt, et al. *Introduction aux dictionnaires les plus importants pour l'histoire du français*. Recueil d'études publié sous la direction de K. Baldinger. P.: Klincksieck, 1974.

A very useful book, written by Baldinger and several collaborators, which undertakes an explanation of the structure, purposes, and the strong and weak points of several important dictionaries. Four chs. are devoted to Wartburg's *Französisches Etymologisches Wörterbuch*, and the rest (12 chs. in all) to the dictionaries of Meyer-Lübke, Bloch-Wartburg, Dauzat-Dubois-Mitterand, Gamillscheg, Huguet, Godefroy, Tobler-Lommatzsch, and Baldinger.

262 Collison, Robert Lewis. *Dictionaries of English and Foreign Languages*. 2nd ed. N.Y.: Hafner Publishing Co., 1971.

87

This is a bibliographical guide to general and technical dictionaries with historical and explanatory notes and references.

For France: the development, main features and importance to French lexicography of the principal general dictionaries are discussed; followed by a survey of etymological and bilingual dictionaries; of synonyms, antonyms, slang and dialect dictionaries, and those relating to periods or centuries.

263 Dubois, Jean, et Dubois, Claude. *Introduction à la lexico-graphie: le dictionnaire.* P.: Larousse, 1971.

A treatise primarily on the theoretical and technical aspects of lexicography which has occasion to make frequent reference to the principal French dictionaries, often with detailed analysis of them.

264 Matoré, Georges. *Histoire des dictionnaires français.* P.: Larousse, 1968.

The first part is a chronological history of French dictionaries to the present time. The major works are described briefly (one to three pages each) with additional material on language study, encyclopedias, specialized, computer produced dictionaries, etc. The second part deals briefly with the elements of dictionaries (number and choice of words, definitions, examples, etymology, orthography, etc.), much of the work being based on the practice of various existing dictionaries.

265 Quémada, Bernard. *Les Dictionnaires du français moderne, 1539-1863. I: Etude sur leur histoire, leurs types, et leurs méthodes.* P.: Didier, 1967. (II in preparation.)

In the first part of this treatise the author classifies in detail the various types of general and special French dictionaries and discusses their history. The second part is a detailed analysis of the problems and methods of language dictionaries relating to arrangement, morphology, pronunciation, etymology, definition, etc. and extensive discussion and comparison of the more important dictionaries is brought into play.

Includes a bibliography on dictionaries, lexicography, etc., a chronological list of French dictionaries in 1539-1863, an index of authors, and an index of words cited.

II. FRENCH LANGUAGE DICTIONARIES

266 Académie Française. *Dictionnaire de l'Académie Française.* 8e éd. 2 vols. P.: Hachette, 1931-35. 1e éd. 1694; 2e, 1718; 3e, 1740; 4e, 1762; 5e, 1798, an VI; 6e, 1835; 7e, 1877. (The 6th ed. reprints the prefaces of the first five.)

A very conservative dictionary. This "official"
dictionary of the French language emphasizes literary aspects of the language and includes very few scientific or
technical terms. Contains mostly words in current use,
with examples but no quotations. No etymology.

267 Davau, Maurice. *Dictionnaire du français vivant*. Comps.
        Maurice Davau, Marcel Cohen, Maurice Lallemand. P.:
        Bordas, 1972.

        This work contains 34,000 words and 11,000 essen-
tial expressions which are indispensable. It gives origin,
if known, synonyms, pronunciation, antonyms. Each definition is preceded and illustrated by a sentence chosen from
contemporary French. Words are grouped by families, but one
finds also each word in its alphabetical place. It contains an analysis of the main difficulties of the language
and grammatical tables as well as tables of conjugations.
        Omits rarely used words and those known
only to scientists and specialists. No illustrations.

268 Hatzfeld, Adolphe, et Darmesteter, Arsène. *Dictionnaire
        général de la langue française, du commencement du
        XVIIe siècle jusqu'à nos jours précédé d'un Traité
        de la formation de la langue et contenant: 1. La
        prononciation figurée des mots; 2. Leur étymologie,
        leurs transformations successives, avec renvois aux
        chapitres du Traité qui les expliquent et l'exemple
        le plus ancien de leur emploi; 3. Leur sens propre,
        leurs sens dérivés et figurés, dans l'ordre à la
        fois historique et logique de leur développement;
        4. Des exemples tirés des meilleurs écrivains avec
        indications de la source des passages cités.* Avec
        le concours d'Antoine Thomas. 9e éd. 2 vols. P.:
        Delagrave, 1932; rpt., 1964. 1e éd. 2 vols. P.:
        Delagrave, 1890-93.

        Provides pronunciation, etymology, changes of
meaning and variant spelling. First use is documented and
dated. Usually a few examples of use by French authors,
without dates. Includes numerous words taken from other
languages. Does not replace or supersede Littré.

The Larousse Dictionaries.

        Since Larousse is probably the most famous name in
French dictionaries, a selection of the more important ones
is listed here separately.

269 *Petit Larousse en couleurs 1977*. P.: Larousse, 1976
        (Sept.).

        Petit Larousse illustré 1977. P.: Larousse, 1976 (Sept.).

In its preface, one finds its history. It was
first published as *Nouveau Dictionnaire de la langue française de P. Larousse* in 1856. It was the first French dictionary to give each definition with an example, and to de-
vote to certain words encyclopedic explanations. Added in
1876: words, works of art, and main characters in literary
works. In 1879 it adopted the list of the last *Dictionnaire
de l'Académie* (1878), and introduced illustrations for the
first time in a dictionary. The plates increased in number
subsequently. Revised, enlarged and enriched by the documentation of the *Grand Dictionnaire universel du XIXe siècle*
          In 1889, under the direction of Claude Augé, it
became *Dictionnaire complet illustré.*
          In 1906, in a new size, it received the title:
Petit Larousse illustré. It was completely redone in 1924,
and called *Nouveau Petit Larousse illustré.* The vocabulary
and the history pts. were revised in 1935 under the direction
of Paul Augé; numerous engravings and art reproductions
were added. The vocabulary and history pts. were updated
in 1948. The Fine Arts, Literatures and Sciences pts. were
totally revised in 1952. Further extensive revisions oc-
curred in 1956, 1959 and 1968, with continuous updating and
editing in every edition since then.
          Translated and adapted for various non-French-
speaking countries, the American version is: *Larousse
Illustrated, International Encyclopedia and Dictionary.*

Larousse classique, dictionnaire encyclopédique. Ed. revue
          et corrigée. P.: Larousse, 1968.

          An encyclopedic dictionary, it gives the modern
meaning of words, their "classic" meanings in the seventeenth and eighteenth centuries, etymologies, synonyms,
and antonyms. It explains the terms common to the vocabulary of each discipline, and includes charts, illustrations
and atlases.

270 *Dictionnaire du français contemporain.* Eds. Jean Dubois et
          al. Ed. rev. et corr. P.: Larousse, 1973.

          About 25,000 entry words. A dictionary of spoken
and written contemporary French used in everyday life.
This work classifies meanings of words according to grammatical constructions. It gives synonyms and antonyms, pronun-
ciations, but no etymology. It contains tables of phonetics
conjugations, a list of the main proverbs in French, etc. N
ills.

271 *Grand Larousse de la langue française.* Sous la dir. de Loui
          Guilbert, René Lagane et Georges Niobey, avec le con-
          cours de H. Bonnard, L. Casati, et A. Lerond. 5 vols
          pub. by Nov. 1976, out of the 7 announced. P.:
          Larousse, 1971-.

For each word: pronunciation, etymology, synonyms, antonyms, grammatical notes, etc., are given. Also
serves as a general encyclopedia of grammar and linguistics
explaining the diverse theories of the principal grammatical
and linguistic concepts such as accent, adjectives, adverbs,
slang, connotation, etc.

272 Littré, Emile. *Dictionnaire de la langue française contenant 1. pour la nomenclature: tous les mots qui se
trouvent dans le Dictionnaire de l'Académie française
et tous les termes usuels des sciences, des arts, des
métiers et de la vie pratique; 2. pour la grammaire:
la prononciation de chaque mot figurée, et, quand il
y a lieu, discutée; l'examen des locutions, des idio-
tismes, des exceptions et, en certains cas, de l'orthographe actuelle, avec des remarques critiques sur les
difficultés et les irrégularités de la langue; 3. pour
la signification des mots: les définitions, les diverses acceptions rangées dans leur ordre logique,
avec de nombreux exemples tirés des auteurs classiques
et autres; les synonymes principalement considérés
dans leurs relations avec les définitions; 4. pour la
partie historique: une collection des phrases appar-
tenant aux anciens écrivains depuis les premiers temps
de la langue française jusqu'au XVIe siècle et dispo-
sées dans l'ordre chronologique à la suite des mots
auxquels elles se rapportent; pour l'étymologie: la
détermination ou du moins la discussion de l'origine
de chaque mot établie par la comparaison des mêmes
formes dans le français, dans le patois et dans
l'espagnol, l'italien et le provençal ou langue d'oc.*
2 tomes en 4 vols. P.: Hachette, 1889 (1st ed. 1863-
72). Ed. intégrale, avec les différents suppléments
et additifs reclassés dans le texte selon les inten-
tions de l'auteur. 7 vols. P.: Gallimard-Hachette,
1956-58 (reprinted regularly).

Littré sought to include words in contemporary use
on a broad scale. He accepted all the entries in the
Dictionnaire de l'Académie (1835 ed.) and added seventeenth and eighteenth century words rejected by the Académie,
technical terms used in the arts and sciences, new words,
and popular and dialect words. Great care was taken to
record the primary and secondary etymology of words, but
the work is most famous for its abundance of examples, or
quotations from well-known authors since the Middle Ages.
These quotations serve both to clarify the definitions and
to illustrate historical change in meaning. Littré gives
references to sources, but no dates. Some of his etymologies
are corrected or updated by other dictionaries such as Bloch-
Wartburg and Robert; but Littré is still important for the
history, the etymology, and the usage of the French language.

_____. *Supplément renfermant un grand nombre de termes d'art, de science, d'agriculture, etc.*, et de néologismes de tous genres appuyés d'exemples et contenant la rectification de quelques définitions du Dictionnaire: l'addition de nouveaux sens, de nouveaux exemples à l'historique, enfin la correction de quelques étymologies et l'indication de l'origine précédemment inconnue de certains mots. Ce supplément est suivi d'un Dictionnaire étymologique de tous les mots d'origine orientale *par Marcel Devic. P.: Hachette, 1910. (1st ed. 1877.)

_____. *Dictionnaire de la langue française. Abrégé du Dictionnaire de E. Littré contenant tous les mots qui se trouvent dans le Dictionnaire de l'Académie française, plus un grand nombre de néologismes et de termes de science et d'art avec l'indication de la prononciation, de l'étymologie et l'explication des locutions proverbiales et des difficultés grammaticales* par A. Beaujean. P.: Hachette, 1874. Ed. rev., complétée, mise à jour sous la dir. de Géraud-Venzac, P.: Eds. Universitaires, 1950. (Rpt. under the title *Petit Littré*. P.: Gallimard-Hachette, 1959.)

273 *Dictionnaire Quillet de la langue française. Dictionnaire méthodique et pratique* rédigé sous la dir. de Raoul Mortier. 3 vols. P.: Quillet, 1946.

Latest reprint of 1963, contains a summary of the grammar of the language. It offers explanatory articles on ca. 80,000 catchwords (keywords). These articles include suggestions as to synonyms, antonyms, homonyms, lists of frequent epithets to the catchword, as well as to the grammar. The tendency of the dictionary is to be normative. Added to the text are tables of conjugations in the form of little boxes, suggestions to its uses, orthographic peculiarities, etc. There are also some sketches of technical objects with the specific terminology explained. A useful work.

Dictionnaire usuel Quillet-Flammarion, par le texte et par l'image. Rédigé sous la dir. de Pierre Gioan. 3e éd. P.: Quillet-Flammarion, 1968. Ills.

An abridgment of the *Dictionnaire encyclopédique Quillet.*
Dictionary and quick reference encyclopedia in one alphabet; about 80,000 entries, mainly words and definitions, and personal and place names. Very brief information (one to three lines). Good ills., appended atlas of colored maps.

274   Robert, Paul. *Dictionnaire alphabétique et analogique de
      la langue française. Les mots et les associations
      d'idées.* 6 vols. P.: Soc. du Nouveau Littré,
      1960-64. (Issued in fasc. 1951-64.) *Supplément,*
      1970. Rpt. with title: *Grand Robert,* 7 vols. S.N.L.
      Dictionnaire "Le Robert," 1975.

          60,000 words enlightened by the most recent find-
      ings of etymology, lexicography and semantics. A historical
      dictionary which gives etymology, derivatives, compounds,
      definitions, synonyms, antonyms, and refers to words with
      similar meanings. 200,000 quotations from Villon to con-
      temporary French writers are used to clarify usage. The
      "Robert" is the twentieth century counterpart to the "Littré,"
      which was sponsored by the Académie Française.

      _____. *Petit Robert (Le)*. *Dictionnaire alphabétique et
      analogique de la langue française.* P.: Soc. du Nou-
      veau Littré, 1967. Rpt.: *Petit Robert 1: Diction-
      naire de la langue française.* S.N.L. Dictionnaire
      "Le Robert," 1975.
      _____. *Micro Robert. Dictionnaire du français primor-
      dial.* P.: Soc. du Nouveau Littré, 1971. Rpt.,
      S.N.L. Dictionnaire "Le Robert," 1975.

275   _____. *Dictionnaire universel des noms propres.* 4 vols.
      P.: Soc. du Nouveau Littré, 1974. Rpt., S.N.L.
      Dictionnaire "Le Robert," 1975. Illustrated ed., 1976.

          It has 40,000 articles, 8,000 ills. which present
      historical and geographical proper names of the arts, letters
      and sciences.

      Petit Robert 2. Dictionnaire universel des noms propres.
      P.: SEPRET (Garnier), 1974. Rpt., S.N.L. Diction-
      naire "Le Robert," 1975.

          Contains 34,000 proper names, 2,200 ills. and 200
      maps.

276   *Trésor de la langue française. Dictionnaire de la langue du
      XIXe et du XXe siècle (1789-1960).* Pub. sous la dir.
      de P. Imbs. P.: CNRS (distributed by Klincksieck),
      1972-. (4 vols. pub. by Nov. 1976, out of the 14 vols.
      announced.)

          This work, put together with the aid of computers,
      has a synchronic classification of meanings from the seman-
      tical, stylistical and grammatical points of view. Gives
      illustrated analyses of examples in varying numbers depending
      on the importance of the word, the extent of examples, etc.
      Gives also pronunciation, a brief notice of etymology and
      history, statistical information on frequency, etc.

III. BILINGUAL DICTIONARIES

277 *Cassell's New French-English, English-French Dictionary.*
Completely rev. by Denis Girard and others. 8th ed.
London: Cassell and Co. Ltd., 1962.
Exists also in "compact" editions: *Cassell's
New Compact French-English, English-French Dictionary.*
N.Y.: Funk and Wagnall's, 1968; N.Y.: Dell, 1970.

Employs the International Phonetic Alphabet. Includes abbreviations, translations of colloquial expressions, and Canadian usage. Approximately 40,000 and 35,000
entries in the two parts. A standard, reliable work.

278 Clifton, C. Ebenezer, and Laughlin, J. *A New French-English
and English-French Dictionary.* P.: Garnier, 1970.

Earlier editions (i.e. 1904) have title: *A New
Dictionary of the French and English Languages.*

279 Dubois, Marguerite-Marie. *Dictionnaire moderne français-
anglais, anglais-français* par Marguerite-Marie Dubois
avec la collaboration de Charles Cestre, et al.
Reviseur général: William Maxwell Landers. P.:
Larousse, coll. "Jupiter," 1960.
American ed. has title: *Larousse Modern French-
English, English-French Dictionary.* N.Y.: McGraw-
Hill, 1960; rpt., 1964.

About 35,000 entries in each half, compiled by
French, English, and American collaborators. Synonyms,
idioms, usage, fine differences in meaning, pronunciation,
grammar, conjugation, and other features are contained in
this dictionary. Gives a complete and modern vocabulary,
plus colloquial and slang expressions. Ills. are often
used to associate words with visual images.

280 Guiraud, Jules. *Dictionnaire anglais-français (et français-
anglais) à l'usage des professeurs, des littéra-
teurs, des traducteurs, des commerçants, des industri-
els, des élèves, des facultés, des grandes écoles et
des classes supérieures des lycées et collèges.* . . .
3e éd. 2 vols. P.: Belin, 1947.

Contains literary and scientific words, and proper
names, in addition to general vocabulary. Indicates different meanings with many examples of usage.

281 *Harrap's Standard French and English Dictionary.* Ed. by
J. E. Mansion. 1st ed. 2 vols. London: Harrap,
1934-39.

Mansion died in 1942. The 1st part of his dictionary (French-Eng.) has been revised, reset, greatly en-

larged and pub. in 2 vols. by R. P. L. and D. M. Ledésert as *Harrap's New Standard*, 1972. Pt. 2 is being rev. American ed. is pub. by Scribner's. Abridged in 1 vol. in various sizes.

A standard work, widely recognized as the most comprehensive, up to date and authoritative work of its kind. Emphasizes twentieth century usage, including many technical and commercial terms, current idioms, new words, and slang with many examples. Names (persons, gods, places, etc.) are included if the French and English spelling differ. The International Phonetic Alphabet is used for pronunciation. No etymologies or definitions--only translations, but these include English, American, and Canadian usage. A list of common French abbreviations is found at the end of the volume.

282 Mergault, Jean. *Nouveau Larousse français-anglais*. P.: Larousse, coll. "Mars," 1971.

French-English and English-French. For each language appears pronunciation, gender of nouns, place of stress, conjugation of verbs, rules of grammar, and a conversational guide.

283 Urwin, Kenneth. *Dictionnaire français-anglais, anglais-français*. P.: Larousse, coll. "Mercure," 1974.

Excellent small dictionary, very complete for its reduced size, up to date with the modern language. Indicates clearly to what type of vocabulary (agricultural, military, judicial) the various words and idioms belong.

IV. ETYMOLOGICAL DICTIONARIES

284 Bloch, Oscar, et Wartburg, Walther von. *Dictionnaire étymologique de la langue française*. Préf. d'Antoine Meillet. 1e éd. 1932; 2e éd. refondue, 1950, par W. von Wartburg; 5e éd. revue et augmentée par W. von Wartburg. P.: PUF, 1968.

This is a scholarly etymological dictionary of ordinary contemporary French which gives the date of earliest appearance of words, their derivatives, etc.; ca. 13,000 entries. Rich in insights on the other romance languages. Words are examined only in their basic meanings.

285 Dauzat, Albert; Dubois, Jean; et Mitterand, Henri. *Nouveau Dictionnaire étymologique et historique*. 2e éd. revue et corrigée. P.: Larousse, 1971.

About 16,000 words in general current use, omitting the archaic and regional. The Larousse dictionaries are used as a base; but literary texts, the press and other sources provide new words. Attempts to give the origin and time of first use, then the principal historical changes. Strong in Greek and Latin roots, there is a separate table of them, with examples of French derivatives. Bibliography of reference works used.

286 Gamillscheg, Ernst. *Etymologisches Wörterbuch der franzö-sischen Sprache*. 2. vollst. neub. Aufl. Heidel-berg: Winter, 1966-69. (1st ed. 1928.)

This work is based on Hatzfeld's *Dictionnaire général* with a few additions. It has about 15,000 entries arranged in forty-three tables according to the original language, with an alphabetical word and subject index. German translations from the French are given. Many new etymologies and bibliographical citations.

287 Meyer-Lübke, Wilhelm. *Romanisches Etymologisches Wörter-buch*. 3. vollst. neub. Aufl. Heidelberg: Winter, 1935; rpt., 1968.

A standard etymological dictionary of all the Ro-mance languages. The main dictionary has 9,721 words, giving the basic form and various language variations. There is a separate alphabetical word index of eleven Romance languages referring to the main dictionary (337 pages), and similar short indexes for words in Albanian, Basque, German, Greek, etc.

288 Neyron, Pierre. *Nouveau Dictionnaire étymologique. Néologismes*. P.: Ed. de la Revue Moderne, 1970.

289 Picoche, Jacqueline. *Nouveau Dictionnaire étymologique du français*. P.: Hachette-Tchou, 1971.

Systematically presents word families traced his-torically, if possible, to modern French from the phonic base. One purpose is to give a history of French vocabu-lary with attention to the distinction between popular and scholarly words, and words in between. In complex families popular words are treated first. Each word is dated by century and its origin and variants are given up to modern times. Great attention is given to Latin roots and to simple, or popular French words, prefixes, suffixes, etc. A separate alphabetical index of words refers one to the basic form in the dictionary.

290 Wartburg, Walther von. *Französisches Etymologisches Wörterbuch. Eine Darstellung des galloromanischen Sprachschatzes*. Pub. by various publishers. 1922-. 1-21 and 23 have appeared, of vol. 22 only one fascicule has been published as yet. Vols. 1-3 re-vised are included in vols. 15-20; beginning of vol. 1 rev. is vols. 24 and 25.

See Baldinger (no. 261), pp. 11-92. We translate from Baldinger's Introduction:

Walther von Wartburg, deceased on 15 August 1971, left us the most important etymological dictionary of the French language which traces the history of all the families of Gallo-Romance words with all the meanings and all their derivatives from their origin up to modern French, including all the patois of Northern France (and of Walloon Belgium), Franco-Provençal (of France, Italy and French-speaking Switzerland) and *Occitan*.

V.   SPECIALIZED DICTIONARIES

a.   SLANG DICTIONARIES

1. Bibliography

91   Yve-Plessis, Robert. *Bibliographie raisonnée de l'argot et de la langue verte en France du XVe au XXe siècle.* 1e éd.   P.:   Daragon, 1901; rpt., Genève: Slatkine, 1968.

An analytical survey of about 365 sources providing information on slang, especially French criminal slang, from the thirteenth through the nineteenth century.   Writings by or about criminals are examined as well as slang glossaries, dictionaries, and works by popular authors such as Villon and Hugo.   No scholarly works are cited.   No index.

2. In French

92   Delvau, Alfred. *Dictionnaire de la langue verte.   Argots parisiens comparés.*   Nouv. éd. rev. par l'auteur, augm. d'un supp. par Gustave Fustier. P.:   Marpon et Flammarion, 1883; rpt., Genève: Slatkine, 1972.

This dictionary is a miscellaneous collection of slang words which amused the author and which he somewhat rashly classified according to social rank.   It provides the first source for many popular slang words.

93   Esnault, Gaston. *Dictionnaire historique des argots français.*   P.:   Larousse, 1965.

Includes about 10,000 words giving various meanings according to date, users, or place.   Etymology and derivations are often indicated as well as literary or other sources, which are listed with abbreviations in front of the work.   The introduction has a list, with brief commentary, of some of the more interesting works cited by Yve-Plessis (above) in chronological order.

294 Galtier-Boissière, Jean, et Devaux, Pierre. *Dictionnaire historique, étymologique et anecdotique d'argot.* Nouv. éd. augm. d'un supp. P.: *Crapouillot*, 1950.

    A separate publication of the journal *Crapouillot.* A rather unsystematic dictionary with amusing anecdotes from   literature. Good bibliography.

295 Lacassagne, Jean, et Devaux, Pierre. *L'Argot du "milieu."* Nouv. éd. P.: A. Michel, 1948.

296 La Rue, Jean. *Dictionnaire d'argot et des principales locutions populaires précédé d'une histoire de l'argot* par Clément Cascini. Nouv. éd. P.: Flammarion, 1961. (1st ed. 1894, with title: *La langue verte: Dictionnaire d'argot.*)

297 Marcillac, Jean. *Dictionnaire français-argot.* P.: Ed. de la Pensée Moderne, 1968.

298 Sandry, Géo, et Carrère, Marcel. *Dictionnaire de l'argot moderne.* 10e éd. revue, augm., et mise à jour. P.: Eds. du Dauphin, 1974.

    More than 8,000 words and expressions with most attention to current Parisian slang. Gives equivalent word or phrase in standard French. No pronunciation or etymology. Besides the general vocabulary there are several separate lists by subject or occupation, such as: aviation, cyclists, prisons, painters, theatre, military, etc.

299 Simonin, Albert. *Le Petit Simonin illustré.* Préf. de J. Cocteau. P.: Les Productions de Paris, 1958. Ills.

300 Timmermans, Adrien. *L'Argot parisien. Son vocabulaire complet, ses origines, son étymologie comparée, son esprit, ses moeurs.* P.: Victorion, 1922.

    Alphabetical dictionary.

3. In French with English Equivalents

301 Barrère, Albert Marie Victor. *Argot and Slang: A New French and English Dictionary of the Can't Words, Quaint Expressions, Slang Terms and Flash Phrases Used in the High and Low Life of Old and New Paris.* New and rev. ed. London: Whitaker, 1889.

    A dictionary of French slang culled from literary works from the sixteenth-nineteenth centuries, popular

French fiction, slang dictionaries, newspapers and conversation with criminals, soldiers, workers, etc. About 9,500 words giving designation of use (popular, thieves, college, military, etc.) followed by one or more definitions in English. No etymology is attempted. Useful for older terms.

)2   Deak, Etienne, and Deak, Simone. *A Dictionary of Colorful French Slanguage and Colloquialisms: An Up to Date Thesaurus of Modern French Slang Words and Colloquial Terms and Phrases, with their American Equivalents.* P.: Laffont, 1959. N.Y.: Dutton, 1961.

About 5,000 slang words and colloquialisms current in France. American slang equivalents are given in addition to definitions.

)3   Leitner, Moses Jonathan. *Dictionary of French and American Slang.* Ed. by M. J. Leitner and J. R. Lanen. N.Y.: Crown, 1965. Pt. 1: American-French; Pt. 2: French-American.

About 10,000 entries. Stresses spoken colloquial language and slang but includes some written figures of speech difficult to translate. Words and phrases collected via the press, radio, TV, theatre, cinema, conversation and dictionaries make up the vocabulary; words of special groups are excluded.

)4   Leroy, Olivier. *A Dictionary of French Slang.* London: Harrap, 1935.

About 2,800 French slang words from the theatre, popular speech, corrupted forms, children's expressions--in short, any word likely to puzzle an English-speaking reader. A standard English translation is given, and for most words, examples of French usage with English equivalents (including English slang).

)5   Marks, Joseph. *Harrap's French-English Dictionary of Slang and Colloquialisms.* Rev. and completed by Georgette A. Marks and Albert J. Farmer. London: Harrap, 1970.

Intended for English-speaking travelers in France and those interested in French novels, plays, and films. It includes the colloquial, the familiar, the popular and the vulgar without avoidance of "obscene" terms. English equivalents include long-standing usage as well as more recent slang. For many French slang words, ten or more different expressions are given, with English equivalents. There is also a "Table of English Slang Synonyms," to which one is often referred for more English equivalents. About 8,600 key words in the dictionary and ca. 265 in the list of synonyms.

b. DICTIONARIES OF SYNONYMS AND ANTONYMS

306 Bailly, René. *Dictionnaire des synonymes de la langue française.* 1e éd. P.: Larousse, 1946. (Frequently reprinted.)

Gives synonyms, antonyms, families of words, etc. and shows gradations of meaning, relative values and examples of usage.

307 Bar, Elvire D. *Dictionnaire des synonymes.* Nouv. éd. P.: Garnier, 1970.

Designed for quick synonym searching. Basic words are listed with a definition, followed by similar terms (adjectives, verb forms, etc.). Each entry lists one or more synonyms, or a see-reference to another basic word. About 14,000 entries.

308 Bénac, Henri. *Dictionnaire des synonymes, conforme au "Dictionnaire de l'Académie française."* P.: Hachette, 1956.

In addition to synonyms with precise meanings, also gives figurative sense. Includes "borrowed" words in current use, but excludes slang. Each synonym is followed by an example of usage. Ca. 30,000 entries.

309 Bertaud Du Chazaud, Henri. *Nouveau Dictionnaire des synonymes.* P.: Hachette-Tchou, 1971.

Synonyms are arranged in three classifications: grammatical, semantic, and alphabetical. Indication is given whether the word is used in the proper or figurative meaning, whether the sense is favorable or not, and whether the word is slang. About 20,000 entries and 200,000 synonyms. Contains a short bibliography.

310 Boussinot, Roger. *Dictionnaire des synonymes, analogies et antonymes.* P.: Bordas, 1973.

All words which have similar meanings are grouped together under headings which are arranged alphabetically. Contains also popular expressions.

311 Dupuis, Hector. *Dictionnaire des synonymes et des antonymes.* P. et Montréal: Fides, 1961; éd. rev., 1975.

In this dictionary the concept of synonyms is expanded to include analogs; antonyms are similarly broadened. Under each word a list of synonyms is given, followed by a list of antonyms. About 9,000 main words.

No definitions. Includes colloquialisms.

312 Noter, Raphaël de; Vuillermoz, P.; et Lécuyer, H.
       *Dictionnaire des synonymes. Répertoire des mots
       français usuels ayant un sens semblable, analogue
       ou approché.* 1e éd. P.: PUF, 1938; nouv. éd. 1969.

c. ANALOGICAL DICTIONARIES

313 Delas, Daniel. *Nouveau Dictionnaire analogique.* P.:
       Hachette-Tchou, 1971.

       A dictionary of association providing a means of
passing from one word or idea to another. Contains thematic tables to permit three different approaches to using
the dictionary.

314 Maquet, Charles. *Dictionnaire analogique: répertoire
       moderne des mots par les idées, des idées par les
       mots, d'après les principes de P. Boissière.* Rédigé
       sur un plan nouveau. 1e éd. P.: Larousse, 1936;
       11e éd. 1971.

       P. Boissière had published a *Dictionnaire analo-
gique de la langue française.* P.: Larousse et Boyer, 1862.
       Arranged with divided pages, the top part being
an A-Z list of words (about 25,000) referring to one or
more key words in the lower part. The key words in the
lower part are alphabetical, in bold capitals, and subdivided into different concepts, or associated ideas.
Thus, "Joie" is divided into five rubrics: "Nature
joyeuse," "Sentiments de joie," "Manifestations e:
rieures," "Donner de la joie," and "Participer à la joie."
Under each of these rubrics numerous synonyms and associated words and expressions are listed.

315 Rouaix, Paul. *Dictionnaire des idées suggérées par les
       mots, contenant tous les mots de la langue française
       groupés d'après le sens.* 30e éd. P.: Colin, 1971.

       A manual-dictionary notable for the large number
of synonyms, nuances, variant forms, etc. listed under key
words. For numerous other words one is referred to one or
more key words. Altogether about 120,000 words are listed,
but there is much less attention to expressions and phrases
than in other similar dictionaries.

d. SPECIAL DICTIONARIES

316 Dauzat, Albert. *Dictionnaire étymologique des noms de
       famille et prénoms de France.* 3e éd. P.: Larousse,
       1967.

       Gives origin, locality and date for about 24,000

101

French family names. Includes variants and meaning of
names.

317   Dauzat, Albert, et Rostaing, Charles. *Dictionnaire
           étymologique des noms de lieux en France*. P.:
           Larousse, 1963.

        About 17,000 entries, including see-references
to other names. However, for many place-names there are
numerous variants covered under a single entry. Modern
spelling of each place-name is used, giving present *Département*, followed by the oldest name and successive
names (dated), including variant spellings and forms.
Many names of persons are involved and many forms, especially Latin. For most place-names there is an indication
of the derivations or meaning, but no detailed etymology
is attempted. Gives a list of the principal authors and
sources consulted.

318   Duden français. *Dictionnaire en images*. Ed. par la ré-
           daction du Bibliographisches Institut, Mannheim,
           et la Librairie M. Didier, Paris. 2e éd. corr.
           Mannheim: Dudenverlag des Bibliographisches In-
           stitut, 1962.

        A French-French pictorial dictionary. 25,000
line-drawings; index of words. French and English indexes.

319   Gilbert, Pierre. *Dictionnaire des mots nouveaux*. P.:
           Hachette-Tchou, 1971.

        Contains about 5,500 new words from 1955 to
1971, reflecting current usage, and taken from newspapers,
magazines, books, dictionaries, etc. Includes many words
borrowed from other languages, abbreviations, prefixes,
suffixes, new combinations, old words with new meaning,
and old words revived. Pronunciation, definition, examples, explanation and sources are given (briefly cited
and keyed to the "Bibliographie des sources citées").
A very useful dictionary.

320   Juilland, Alphonse G. *Dictionnaire inverse de la langue
           française*. La Haye, P.: Mouton, 1965.

        More than 40,000 words, arranged by phonetic
ending. A-Z; thirty-two sounds form the basis. Diagrams.

321   Maloux, Maurice. *Dictionnaire des proverbes, sentences
           et maximes*. 7e éd. P.: Larousse, 1971.

        A general collection, in French, selected from
world authors and sources of all ages. Arranged alphabetically by key words and listing proverbs, etc., by
language. Sources are cited (author, title, chapter,

date, but no page). There is a "Table Analogique" referring to key words, and an alphabetical "Index des mots caractéristiques" (selected proverbs by dominant word) to facilitate search.

22   Matignon, Jeanne, et al. *Nouveau Dictionnaire de citations françaises.* Sous la dir. de Pierre Oster. P.: Hachette-Tchou, 1970.

        Arranged chronologically by authors (eleventh-twentieth centuries) including minor, seldom quoted authors, with an index of subjects. 16,241 numbered quotations; alphabetical list of authors cited.

23   Rat, Maurice. *Dictionnaire des locutions françaises.* P.: Larousse, 1957; rpt., 1973.

        An alphabetical dictionary, arranged by the dominant word, of French proverbial, literary, popular and historical expressions. In the case of simple locutions, a definition with an example or two is given with its origin. For the more complex expressions, there is considerable discussion of the probable origin, with examples of usage and meaning. Many key words have several different associated expressions, requiring extended explanation. Authors' works are quoted liberally but are not cited. Contains more than 13,000 entries with an author index and an index of words (all key words in each locution).

24   Rheims, Maurice. *Dictionnaire des mots sauvages (Ecrivains des XIXe et XXe siècles).* . . . P.: Larousse, 1969.

        Words used by French writers of the past two centuries which include coined words, revived obsolete terms, and provincialisms. Literary contexts and usage are indicated.

e. VOCABULARY RELATED TO LIBRARY SCIENCE

5   Pipics, Zoltán. *Dictionarium Bibliothecarii Practicum ad usum Internationalem XXII Linguis/The Librarian's Practical Dictionary in 22 Languages/Wörterbuch des Bibliothekars in 22 Sprachen.* 6th rev. and enl. ed. München: Verlag Dokumentation, 1974. 1st ed. 1963.

        6th ed. based on English (1st and 2nd eds. based on Hungarian; 3rd-5th on German) and covering: Serbian, French, German, Russian, Spanish, Bulgarian, Croatian, Czech, Danish, Dutch, Finnish, Greek, Hungarian, Italian, Latin, Norwegian, Polish, Portuguese, Rumanian, Slovak, and Swedish. There are 377 numbered terms with foreign equivalents. No definitions. Each foreign lan-

guage   has a separate alphabetical index giving English wor
and reference number in the table. Appendices include
terms for months, days, periodicity, numerals, and alphabets (with transliterations for the Greek and Cyrillic
alphabets).

326   Thompson, Anthony. *Vocabularium Bibliothecarii*. 2nd
        ed. P.: Unesco, 1962. 1st ed. 1953; supp. 1958.

            In English, French, German, Spanish and Russian.
This 2nd edition adds Spanish and Russian. About 2,800
terms arranged according to the U.D.C., with an alphabetical index of words in each language. Generally covers
terms in documentation, writing, bibliography, librarian-
ship, book arts, printing, booktrade, photo-reproduction,
etc. No definitions.

CHAPTER 9

BIOGRAPHICAL DICTIONARIES
(By chronological order.)

A. BIBLIOGRAPHIES OF BIOGRAPHICAL SOURCES

327 Ungherini, Aglauro. *Manuel de bibliographie biographique
     et d'iconographie des femmes célèbres.* . . . Turin:
     Roux; P.: Nilsson, 1892. *Supplément*, 1900. *2e et
     Dernier Supplément*, Rome: Roux et Viarengo, 1905;
     rpt., Naarden: Van Bekhoven, 1968.

          A useful index to material about women of all
     countries and all periods. Briefly identifies women and
     gives dates of birth and death; lists sources of biographies
     in collected works, biographical dictionaries, periodicals
     and monographs; and cites portraits, autographs, etc.
     Cumulated index.

328 Slocum, Robert B. *Biographical Dictionaries and Related
     Works. An International Bibliography of Collective
     Biographies, Biobibliographies.* . . . Detroit:
     Gale Research Co., 1967. *Supplement.* 1st-. 1972-.

          Cites several thousand biographical repertories;
     covers universal, national, regional, and professional
     dictionaries. Three indexes: subjects, authors, titles.

329 *IBN; Index Bio-Bibliographicus Notorum Hominum.* Edidit
     Jean-Pierre Lobies, François-Pierre Lobies adiuvante.
     Osnabrück: Biblio Verlag, 1973-. (Published by
     fascicules later grouped in volume; 3 vols. pub. by
     June 30, 1975.)

               General Survey of the Work:
               A. General Introduction
               B. List of the Evaluated Bio-Biographical Works
               C. Corpus Alphabeticum
               D. Supplementum
               E. General Index of References

          According to the prospectus, Pt. B is to list
     ca. 3,000 biographical dictionaries and related works plus
     a subject index. Pt. C will have an alphabetical index of
     from three to five million names from all periods and coun-
     tries. To be completed in from five to ten years.

B. RETROSPECTIVE INTERNATIONAL BIOGRAPHICAL DICTIONARIES

330 *Biographie universelle ancienne et moderne.* Nouv. éd.,
     publiée sous la direction de M. (Joseph) Michaud,

rev., corr. et considérablement augm. d'articles omis
ou nouveaux; ouvrage rédigé par une société de gens ⌀
lettres et de savants. 45 vols. P.: Mme. C.
Desplaces, 1843-65; rpt., Graz: Akad. Druck und
Verlagsanst, 1966-.

The following description is taken from Winchell,
8th ed.
Usually cited as "Michaud." The first edition,
in 84 vols. including supplements, was published in 1811-
57. Issue of the new edition, revised and enlarged, was
begun in 1843. Its publication was interrupted by a law
suit undertaken by Mme. Desplaces, its publisher, against
the firm of Didot Frères, which had started printing a
rival dictionary, edited by Hoefer (see below), which
had incorporated many articles taken in whole or in part
from "Michaud." The case was won by Mme. Desplaces, Didot
was forbidden to copy any more, and the publication of
"Michaud" was resumed.
The most important of the large dictionaries of
universal biography, still very useful. While "Michaud"
and the rival work by Hoefer cover much the same ground,
there are definite and well-recognized differences. In
spite of various inaccuracies, "Michaud" is more carefully
edited; its articles, signed with initials, are longer and
often better than those in "Hoefer"; its bibliographies
are basically better; and it contains more names in the
second half of the alphabet, N-Z. "Hoefer" contains more
names, especially minor ones, in the part A-M; has some
articles which are better than the corresponding articles
in "Michaud"; and in the bibliographies gives titles in
the original, whereas "Michaud" translates into French.

331   *Nouvelle Biographie générale depuis les temps les plus
       reculés jusqu'à nos jours.* . . . Sous la direction
       du Dr. (J. Chr. Ferdinand) Hoefer. 46 vols. P.:
       Firmin-Didot, 1853-66; rpt., Copenhague: Rosenkilde
       et Bagger, 1963.

Usually cited as "Hoefer." It planned to be more
concise and more comprehensive than "Michaud," to include
names of people then living, and to list many minor names
omitted in "Michaud." (From Winchell, 8th ed.)

332   Jal, Auguste. *Dictionnaire critique de biographie et
       d'histoire. Errata et supplément pour tous les
       dictionnaires historiques, d'après des documents
       authentiques inédits.* . . . 1e éd. P.: H. Plon,
       1867; 2e éd. corr. et augm. 2 vols. 1872; rpt.
       2 vols. Genève: Slatkine, 1970.

It supplements and corrects "Michaud" and

"Hoefer," as well as other dictionaries.   Selective, but very reliable.

333   *Galerie des hommes célèbres (La).*   P.:   Mazenod, 1947-.

> Tome 7:   *Ecrivains célèbres.*   Publiés sous la dir. de Raymond Queneau.   3 vols.   P.:   Mazenod.
> > Vol. 1.   "Antiquité, Chrétienté médiévale, Orient." 3e éd., 1966.
> > Vol. 2.   "L'Europe, la Renaissance, l'Epoque classique."   3e éd., 1966.
> > Vol. 3.   "De Goethe à Marcel Proust."   3e éd., 1966.
> > Tome 14:   *Les Ecrivains contemporains.*   Sous la dir. de Georges-Emmanuel Clancier, avec la coll. de Georges Adamovitch et al., 1965.

334   *Dizionario letterario Bompiani degli autori di tutti i tempi e di tutte le letterature.*   3 vols.   Milano: Bompiani, 1956-57.   Adapted in French:

Dictionnaire biographique des auteurs de tous les temps et de tous les pays.   2 vols.   P.:   Laffont-Bompiani, SEDE, 1957-58, 1964.

> They complement the *Dizionario. . .delle opere. . ./ Dictionnaire des oeuvres. . .,* also Laffont-Bompiani (see no. 594).
> Alphabetical classification, without contemporary authors.   However, in the *Dictionnaire des oeuvres,* these authors constitute the matter of vol. 5 and are listed separately in the Index vol.

35   Grimal, Pierre, sous la dir. de. *Dictionnaire des biographies.*   2 vols.   P.:   PUF, 1958.

> "A general biographical dictionary containing sketches of persons who have contributed to Western culture and life, from the time of the Greeks to modern times, but not including living persons.   Usually one bibliographical citation is given for each entry and often a reference to portraits."   (Winchell, 8th ed.)

C.   CURRENT INTERNATIONAL BIBLIOGRAPHICAL DICTIONARIES

See Ch. 20: nos. 1490 to 1492.

36   Vapereau, Gustave.   *Dictionnaire universel des contemporains contenant toutes les personnes notables de la France et des pays étrangers. . . .*   Ouvrage rédigé et tenu à jour avec le concours d'écrivains de tous les pays.   6e éd. entièrement refondue et considérablement augm.   P.:   Hachette, 1893.   *Supplément,* 1895.

> Covers the latter half of the nineteenth century, and includes Europe and the Americas.   Includes also names

of persons appearing in the first five editions (with
references to specific editions in each case).

337 *International Who's Who.* London: Europa, 1935-. Annual.

Contains short biographies of prominent persons
in most countries of the world. The 38th ed., *1974-75*, was
pub. in 1974. Ca. 15,000 entries and a necrology.

338 *Who's Who in Europe: dictionnaire biographique des
personnalités européennes contemporaines.* Ed. E. A.
de Maeyer. Bruxelles: Ed. de Feniks, 1965-. Bienni

Contains some 32,000 names from twenty-five countries. The Communist bloc is excluded.

D. NATIONAL BIOGRAPHICAL DICTIONARIES

BELGIUM

339 Académie Royale des Sciences, des Lettres, et des Beaux-
Arts de Belgique. *Biographie nationale.* 28 vols.
Bruxelles: Bruylant, 1866-1944.

Vols. 1-27: A-Z; vol. 28: *Table générale*; vols
29-33 (also called *Suppléments 1-5*) pub. 1957-66.
Long, signed articles by specialists, with bibliographies. Includes no living persons and, as names were
not selected for inclusion until a person had been dead
ten years, the earlier vols. contain mainly persons who
died before 1850. The supplements include both early
names, and names of the nineteenth and twentieth centuries
For names of a later date the dictionary may be supplement
usefully by the long signed obituaries, with detailed
bibliographies, often with portraits, in the *Annuaire* of
the Académie Royale. For these obituaries,
the following general indexes are helpful:

340 _____. *Annuaire: Table des notices biographiques
publiées dans l'Annuaire (1835-1914).* Bruxelles:
Hayez, 1919.

Tables included in the issue of the *Annuaire* for
81e-85e années, *1915-1919*, pp. 113-167. "Complément,
1915-1926," in *Annuaire 92e année*, *1926*, pp. 129-133.

341 _____. *Notices biographiques et bibliographiques
concernant les membres, les correspondants et les
associés.* 1e-5e éd. 5 vols. Bruxelles: Hayez,
1855-1909.

Brief biographical sketches with long bibliographies. Each edition includes some names from the pre-

108

vious edition, but also omits and adds other names.

42 _____. *Index biographique des membres, correspondants et associés. . .de 1769 à 1963.* 2e éd. Bruxelles: Palais des Académies, 1964.

Contains brief biographical information on many persons (four to five lines) plus references to entries in the *Annuaire*, and other publications of the Académie.

43 Hanlet, Camille. *Les Ecrivains belges contemporains de langue française, 1800-1946.* 2 vols. Liège: Dessain, 1946.

A biographical dictionary of Belgian authors writing in French. Includes a critical appraisal of many authors and cites bibliographies, but length of articles varies from a sentence or two to several pages.

44 *Who's Who in Belgium and Grand Duchy of Luxembourg.* 2nd ed. Ed. by F. Michielsen and Stephen S. Taylor. N.Y.: Intercontinental Book and Pub. Co.; Bruxelles: Les Editions Biographiques, 1962.

1st ed., 1957-58, had title: *Who's Who in Belgium, including the Belgian Congo. A Biographical Dictionary Containing About 7,000 Biographies of Prominent People.*

45 Dhondt, Jan, et Vervaeck, Solange. *Instruments biographiques pour l'histoire contemporaine de la Belgique.* 2e éd. Louvain: Nauwelaerts, 1964.

A partially annotated bibliography of 294 Belgian biographical sources which are regional, provincial, special, and personal. Indexes of persons, places and subjects.

CANADA

46 *Canadian Who's Who; A Handbook of Canadian Biography of Living Characters.* Vol. 1-. Toronto: Trans-Canada Pr., 1910-.

Publisher and subtitle vary. Publishing frequency varies. Vol. 2, 1936-37. Vol. 3, 1938-39. Vol. 4, 1948. Vol. 5, 1949-51. Vol. 6- triennial. Vol. 12, 1970-72, pub. 1972. Each new vol. kept up to date with additions and corrections for two years by semiannual supplements entitled: *Who's Who Biographical Service, Canada.*
In English or French. Alphabetical arrangement, with appended directory of names by profession.

47 *Who's Who in Canada: An Illustrated Biographical Record of Men and Women of the Time.* Toronto: Inter-

national Pr., 1911-. Biennial. (58th year pub.
1969/70.)

Title and subtitle vary: *Who's Who in Western
Canada*, 1911; *Who's Who and Why*. . ., 1912-1946.
About 3,000 persons with many portraits. Obituar
list. Arranged in random order with an alphabetical list
of names.

348 *The Macmillan Dictionary of Canadian Biography*. 3rd ed.
rev. and enl. London, Toronto: Macmillan; N.Y.:
St. Martin's Pr., 1963.

1st ed. 1926. Previous eds. have title: *Dictionary of Canadian Biography*.
The best general dictionary of Canadian biograph
of all periods and all classes, exclusive of living persons, i.e., Canadians who died before 1961. Contains concise biographical sketches with bibliographies. About
4,800 names in the 3rd ed.

349 *Standard Dictionary of Canadian Biography: the Canadian
Who Was Who*. 2 vols. Eds. Charles G. D. Roberts a
Arthur L. Tunnell. Toronto: Trans-Canada Pr.,
1934-38.

About 800 biographies of Canadians or foreigners
important in Canada, who died between 1875 and 1937. For
authors, a fairly complete checklist of published works i
included.

350 Sylvestre, Guy. *Ecrivains canadiens/Canadian Writers/
Un dictionnaire biographique rédigé par/A Biographi
Dictionary* ed. by Guy Sylvestre, Brandon Conron,
Carl F. Klinck./Nouv. éd. rev. et augm./New ed.
rev. and enl. Montréal: Editions HMH/Toronto:
Ryerson Pr., 1967.

1st ed. 1964; rev. and enl. ed. 1966.
Short articles on about 350 writers of all perio
giving basic biographical data, an appraisal of the autho
position in literature, list of works, and a few referenc
to biographical or critical works. In French or English.
Includes a useful chronological table of literary, histor
cal events from 1606 to 1965, and an index of titles.

351 *Dictionnaire biographique du Canada/Dictionary of Canadia
Biography*. Québec: Pr. de l'U. Laval. Toronto:
U. of Toronto Pr., 1966-. Appears in two editions,
French and English.

I: *De l'an 1600 à 1700*, 1966.
II: *1701-1740*, 1969.
III: *1741 à 1770*, 1975.

110

X: *1871 à 1880*, 1972. (Pub. out of sequence.)

The plan is to publish one vol. per year covering
Canadian biography from 1600 to the present in about
twenty vols. Each vol. covers a span of years, is arranged
by name A-Z, and contains ca. 600 biographies. Articles
are written by scholars, range in length from a half-
column to sixteen pages, and include excellent bibliographies (original writings, primary and secondary sources).
Each vol. has a long historical introduction about the
period, a list of contributors, an index of names which
includes names mentioned in the main articles, and a fine
general bibliography which includes archives and manuscript sources in Canada and England, printed primary
sources (mainly Canadian documents and newspapers), reference works, monographs, theses and journal articles.

FRANCE

52 *Dictionnaire de biographie française.* Pub. sous la dir. de
J.-C. Roman d'Amat, avec le concours de nombreux
collaborateurs. P.: Letouzey et Ané, 1933-.

Still in progress, up to "Flers" in 1975 (fasc.
78, end of Tome XIII). Editors vary.
To be completed in about twenty vols. No living
persons. Includes French persons of France and its
territories, also foreigners who played an important role
in France. Long, signed, documented articles accompanied
by excellent bibliographies. A scholarly work of importance, but one being published with agonizing slowness.

53 *Dictionnaire biographique français contemporain.* 2e éd.
P.: Pharos, 1954. *Supplément No. 1-2*, 1955-56.

Ills. 1st ed. 1950. An alphabetical dictionary
of contemporary French biography, with a classified index
by profession, etc. Bibliographies are included of works
by writers. The *Suppléments* include a few new articles,
and brief notes updating the biographies of the main work.

54 *Who's Who in France. Qui est qui en France. Dictionnaire
biographique des principales personalités de France,
des départements et territoires français d'outre-
mer, des états africains d'expression française,
des Français notables vivant à l'étranger et des
étrangers notables résidant en France.* 12e éd.
1975/76. P.: Lafitte, 1975. (Biennial.)

1st ed. *1953/54*, pub. 1953, had title: *Who's Who
in France: Paris*, and was limited to Parisians. Later
editions expanded coverage to include prominent French
persons anywhere, and notable foreigners living in France.
Typical, short biographical articles, written in French.
Authors' works are given.

111

355 *Nouveau Dictionnaire national des contemporains.* 1e-5e
      éd. 5 vols. P.: Nouveau Dictionnaire national
      des contemporains, 1961-68.

         Each new edition covers different people, about
      2,000 per vol. Short articles on prominent French people
      in a wide variety of occupations, usually with a portrait.
      Writers' works are usually given (titles only).

SWITZERLAND

356 *Dictionnaire historique et biographique de la Suisse. . .*
      7 vols. et suppls. Neuchâtel: Admin. du *Diction-
      naire historique et biographique de la Suisse*,
      1920-33. *Supplément*, Neuchâtel: Attinger, 1934.

         Ills. Contains a large amount of genealogy and
      biography, including persons still living. Covers the
      field of general, political, local, economic, and social
      history; topography; genealogy; and biography of the
      country. Signed articles, bibliographies. *Supplément*
      (1934) contains a systematic table of the 7 vols. and two
      supplements.

357 *Who's Who in Switzerland, including the Principality of
      Liechtenstein.* Genève: Nagel, 1950/51-. (Ir-
      regular.)

         Publisher varies. 1970/71 ed. pub. in 1971.
      Short biographical sketches written in English. Titles of
      writers' works are cited.

358 *Schweizer Schriftsteller der Gegenwart/Ecrivains suisses
      d'aujourd'hui/Scrittori svizzeri d'oggi/Scriptuors
      svizzers da noss dis.* Bern: Francke Verlag, 1962.

         Gives *Who's Who* type of information, including
      lists of the authors' works. Sketches are, as far as
      possible, in the language of the individual author. About
      500 entries. Edited by the Schweizer Schriftstellerverein
      (Swiss Society of Authors).

CHAPTER 10

MAIN PUBLISHERS AND COLLECTIONS (ACTIVE NOW)

See also Ronge (Ch. 2, no. 28), II, 330-56;
the catalogs of books in print (Ch. 3, nos. 69-71).

359 *Répertoire international des éditeurs et diffuseurs de
langue française.* P.: Cercle de la Librairie, 1975.

This work is composed of three parts: (1) publishers classified in alphabetical order, by country, by
specialization; (2) distributors classified in alphabetical
order, by regions for France, by countries for the rest of
the world; (3) useful addresses--unions, professional associations and their journals.

360 *Monographic Series.* Jan.-March, 1974, Washington, D.C.:
L.C., 1974-. Quarterly with annual cumulations.

It contains monographs cataloged as series,
including any item having a series statement on a catalog
card. All monographs newly cataloged in all languages are
included, popular and scholarly.

A. PUBLISHERS OF REPRINTS AND MICROFORMS

I. MAIN REPRINT AND MICROFORM PUBLISHERS

ACRPP (microfilms of periodicals, newspapers, and journals)
Burt Franklin Reprints. N.Y.
France Expansion, with the cooperation of CNRS, AUPELF, and
le Centre d'Etude du Français Moderne et Contemporain.
P. ("Archives de la Linguistique Française" on microfic
Jean-Michel Place. P.
Johnson Reprints. N.Y.
Kraus Reprint. N.Y. and Nendeln, Liechtenstein.
Laffitte Reprints. Marseille.
Maisonneuve et Larose, réimpressions. P.
Microéditions Hachette. P.
Minkoff Reprints. Genève.
Slatkine Reprints. Genève.
Xerox U. Microfilms. Ann Arbor, MI. (U.S. Ph.D. diss.)

II. BIBLIOGRAPHIES AND CATALOGS
OF REPRINTS AND MICROFORMS

361 *Bibliographia Anastatica: A Bimonthly Bibliography of
     Photo-Mechanical Reprints.* Vols. 1-10. Amsterdam,
     1964-1973. Bimonthly, with annual index.

          Indexes: vols. 1-5, 1964/68. Vols. 6-10,
     1969/73.
          About 50,000 titles are listed from European and
     American reprint publishers. Includes books, series, and
     periodicals.
          Continued by:

362 *Bulletin of Reprints.* Vol. 11-. Pullach bei München:
     Verlag Documentation, 1974-. Quarterly.

          Lists reprints published, or in preparation, in
     1973-. List of publishers and addresses.

363 *Guide to Microforms in Print 1961-.* Washington, D.C.:
     Microcard Editions, 1961-. Annual.

364 *Guide to Reprints, 1967-.* Washington, D.C.: Microcard
     Editions, 1968-. Annual.

          An alphabetical list by authors, journal and
     series titles, etc. of material which has been reprinted.
     About 255 American, Canadian, English and continental pub-
     lishers are listed with their addresses.

365 *International Microforms in Print 1974-1975: A Guide to
     Microforms of Non-United States Micropublishers.*
     Ed. by Allen B. Veaner and Alan M. Meckler. Weston,
     Conn.: Microform Review, Inc., 1974.

366 Maison des Sciences de l'Homme. Service Bibliothèque.
     *Périodiques et publications en série concernant les
     sciences sociales et humaines. Liste de reproduction
     disponibles dans le commerce (Microformes et ré-
     impressions)/Periodicals and Serials Concerning the
     Social Sciences and Humanities. Current List of
     Available Reproductions (Microforms and Reprints).*
     2 vols. P.: Maison des Sciences de l'Homme,
     Service Bibliothèque--Documentation, 1966.
     Suppléments, 1967-68, 1969-70.

          Sixty-four publishers: American, French, German,
     Austrian, Dutch, British, et al.

367 Ostwald, Renate. *Nachdruckverzeichnis von Einzelwerken,
     Serien und Zeitschriften aus allen Wissensgebieten.*
     2 vols. Wiesbaden: Nobis, 1965-69.

A list of books, series and journals reprinted by about 100 European and American reprint publishers. About 16,000 titles.

368 *Répertoire des réimpressions anastatiques d'ouvrages en langue française épuisés mentionnées dans les catalogues d'éditeurs français et étrangers, recensement de base, 1969-1970.* Etabli sous la dir. de Germaine Lebel. P.: B.N., 1972. *Supplément(s) pour 1971 et 1972, 2 vols.*

Not always clear and well classified: it lists some editors as authors, and books which were announced and never published.

B. MAIN PUBLISHERS AND COLLECTIONS OF NEW BOOKS

Some publishers do not classify their books in collections; others have so many of them that we cannot list them all.

I. MAIN PUBLISHERS OF NEW BOOKS

To this list should be added most of the university presses.

Arche (L'). P.
Argences (D'). P.
Arthaud. P.
Atelier de Reproductions des Thèses Françaises. Lille.
Athenäum. Frankfurt a/M.
Aubier. P.
Baconnière (La). Neuchâtel-Boudry.
Barron. Woodbury, N.Y.
Beauchemin. Montréal.
BELC. P.
Belin. P.
Belles Lettres (Les). P.
Berger-Levrault. P.
Bibliothèque Nationale. P.
Bibliothèque Romande. Lausanne.
Blackwell. Oxford.
Boccard, E. de. P.
Bordas. P.
Calmann-Lévy. P.
CDU et SEDES réunis. P.
Champion. P.
CLE. Yaoundé, Cameroun.
CNRS, Eds. du. P.
Cercle de la Librairie. P.
Champion, Honoré. P.
Colin, Armand. P.
Corti, José. P.
De Gruyter. Berlin.
Delagrave. P.
Del Duca. P.
Denoël. P.

Denoël-Gonthier. P.
Desclée de Brouwer. P.
Didier, Marcel. P.
Documentation Française (La). P.
Droz. Genève.
Duculot. Gembloux, Belgique.
Editeurs Français Réunis. P.
Editions Ouvrières. P.
Editions Pierre Charron. P.
Editions Sociales. P.
Editions Universitaires. P.
Encyclopédie Française (L'). P.
Fasquelle. P.
Fayard, Arthème. P.
Fides. Montréal.
Firmin-Didot. P.
Flammarion. P.
Francke. Bern-München.
Gallimard. P.
Garnier. P.
Geuthner. P.
Grasset. P.
Hachette. P.
Hamish Hamilton. London.
Harrap. London.
Hatier. P.
Hermann. P.
Herne (L'). P.
J'ai lu. P.
Jeune Afrique. P.
Julliard. P.
Klincksieck. P.
Klostermann. Frankfurt a/M.
Laffont, Robert. P.
Larousse. P.
Lettres Modernes Minard. P.
Librairie Générale Française. P.
Liguori. Napoli.
Macmillan Co. N.Y.
Maisonneuve, A., et Maisonneuve, Jean, Succ. P.
Maisonneuve, G.P., et Larose. P.
Masson. P.
McGraw-Hill Book Co. N.Y.-Toronto.
Mercure de France. P.
Michel, Albin. P.
Minuit, Eds. de. P.
Mouton. Den Haag-P.
Nathan. P.
Nijhoff, Martinus. Den Haag.
Nizet, A.-G. P.
Nouvelles Editions Africaines. Dakar, Sénégal.
Olschki, Leo S. Firenze.
Oswald, P.-J. P.
Oxford U. Pr. London-Oxford-N.Y.

Pastorelly, Eds. Monte-Carlo.
Pauvert, Jean-Jacques. P.
Pensée universelle (La). P.
Perrin. P.
Picard. P.
Plon. P.
Prentice-Hall, Inc. Englewood Cliffs, N.J.
Présence Africaine. P.
PUF. P.
Quillet. P.
Random House. N.Y.
Rencontre. Lausanne.
Rocher, Eds. du. Monaco.
Saint-Germain-des-Prés, Eds. P.
St. Martin's Pr. N.Y.
Seghers, Eds. P.
Seuil, Eds. du. P.
SEDES. See CDU.
SEVPEN. P.
Stock. P.
Table Ronde (La). P.
Twayne Publishers. N.Y.
Unesco, les Pr. de l'. P.
Union Générale d'Editions. P.
Vrin. P.

II. EDITIONS OF TEXTS

a. COLLECTED WORKS

CNRS. "Les Oeuvres intégrales."
Gallimard. "Bibliothèque de la Pléiade" (Collected works
    of one author, or collection of works in the same
    genre in one period or century. Scholarly editions).
Hermann.
Pastorelly, Eds.
Pauvert.
Rencontre.
Seuil, Eds. du. "L'Intégrale" (brief comments).

b. SCHOLARLY EDITIONS

Belles Lettres (Les).
Bibliothèque Romande (French-Swiss writers, 16th-20th
    centuries).
Champion. "Les Classiques français du Moyen Age."
Corti.
Didier. "Textes français modernes."
Droz. "Textes littéraires français," "Travaux d'Humanisme
    et Renaissance," etc.
Editions Sociales. "Classiques du peuple."
Flammarion.
Francke.

117

Gallimard NRF. "Mémoires."
Garnier. "Classiques."
Hachette.
Harrap.
Klincksieck. "Bibliothèque du XIXe siècle," "Textes du
    XXe siècle."
Lettres Modernes Minard. "Bibliothèque introuvable,"
    "Interférences," "Paralogue."
Macmillan. "Modern French Literature Series."
Nizet.
Oxford U. Pr. "Clarendon French Series."
PUF (Texts of literature and of philosophy).
Rocher, Eds. du. "Grands et Petits Chefs d'oeuvre."
Seuil, Eds. du. "Mise en scène" (Texts of plays with
    stage directions).
Vrin.

c. NON SCHOLARLY EDITIONS

They are often paperback books. See:

369 *Catalogue de livres au format de poche.* Nouv. éd. P.:
    Cercle de la Librairie, 1976. (New ed. every one
    or two years.)

Here are some publishers of these eds.:

Blackwell.
Boccard.
Bordas. "Bibliothèque Bordas."
Calmann-Lévy.
CLE.
Denoël-Gonthier.
Editions Sociales. "Classiques du peuple."
Gallimard. "Blanche," "Folio" (Literature), "Idées"
    (Philosophy), NRF, "Poésie," "Soleil" (20th century),
    "le Chemin," "Témoins."
Garnier-Flammarion (literary classics).
Grasset.
Hachette.
Hatier, "Thema anthologie" (thematic approach, selected
    excerpts with comments).
J'ai lu. (Complete texts, or excerpts.)
Jeune Afrique.
Julliard.
Librairie Générale Française. "Livre de Poche."
Marabout.
Michel.
Minuit, Eds. de.
Nouvelles Editions Africaines.
Pauvert. "Libertés."
Présence Africaine.
Rencontre. "Anthologie de la correspondance française,"
    "Anthologie de la poésie française," "Théâtre

118

classique français."
Saint-Germain-des-Prés, Eds. "Poètes contemporains."
Seghers. "Poètes d'aujourd'hui," "Ecrivains d'hier et
    d'aujourd'hui," "Philosophes de tous les temps"
    (general study and anthology of one writer).
Union Générale d'Editions. "10 X 18" (Complete or
    selected texts).

d. *PETITS CLASSIQUES*

These are small paperbacks. They contain complete
plays or excerpts of prose and poetry, with notes of a
pedagogical nature.

Bordas. "Univers des lettres."
Didier. "Classiques de la civilisation française."
Hachette. "Classiques illustrés Vaubourdolle," "Classiques
    illustrés Hachette," "Classiques France."
Hatier. "Classiques pour tous," "Nouveaux classiques
    Hatier."
Larousse. "Classiques Larousse," "Nouveaux Classiques
    Larousse" (some with a *Documentation thématique*).

III. LITERARY HISTORY AND CRITICISM

Here are some of the publishers who print books
on these topics:
Arche (L'). "Les Grands Dramaturges."
Arthaud. "Grandes Civilisations."
Atelier de Reproductions des Thèses Françaises. (Ph.D. diss.)
Baconnière (La).
Barron's Educational Series.
Belin.
Boccard.
Bordas. "Bibliothèque des connaissances essentielles,"
    "Présence littéraire" (on the writer and his works).
Buchet-Chastel.
CDU.
CNRS. "Les Voies de la création théâtrale."
Colin. "Collection U" (commented anthologies on specific
    genres or topics), "Collection U2" (studies), etc.
Corti.
Delagrave.
Del Duca.
Denoël-Gonthier. "Médiations."
Desclée de Brouwer. "Les Ecrivains devant Dieu."
Droz. "Publications Romanes et Françaises," "Travaux
    d'Humanisme et Renaissance," "Histoire des idées
    et critique littéraire," etc.
Editeurs Français Réunis.
Editions Ouvrières.
Editions Pierre Charron.
Editions Sociales.
Editions Universitaires. "Classiques du XXe siècle."

Fayard.
Firmin-Didot et Didier. "Miroir de la critique."
Flammarion. "Bibliothèque des Idées," "Bibliothèque
    Idéale," "Le Manteau d'Arlequin," "Le Point du
    Jour."
Gallimard, NRF, "Bibliothèque des idées."
Garnier. "Les Critiques de notre temps et . . ."
Grasset.
Hachette. "Faire le point," "Lire aujourd'hui" (80 to 96
    pages of comments on one 20th century literary work),
    "Poche critique" (critical studies on works of
    17th-20th centuries), "Génies et Réalités."
Hamish Hamilton.
Harrap.
Hatier. "Connaissance des lettres" (monographs on authors),
    "Profil d'une oeuvre" (brief critical analyses on
    individual works).
Herne (L').
Julliard. "Archives," etc.
Klincksieck. "Bibliothèque française et romane,"
    "Bibliothèque du XXe siècle," "Critères," etc.
Larousse. "L'Homme du XXe siècle."
Lettres Modernes Minard. "Archives des Lettres Modernes,"
    "Bibliothèque de littérature et d'histoire,"
    "Bibliothèque des Lettres Modernes," "Circé."
Liguori.
Marabout.
Masson.
McGraw-Hill. "World University Library."
Mercure de France.
Michel. "L'Evolution de l'humanité," etc.
Minuit, Eds. de.
Mouton.
Nathan. "Littérature et Langages."
Nizet.
Olschki. "Biblioteca dell'Archivum Romanicum."
Oxford U. Pr.
Pauvert.
Perrin.
Plon.
Prentice-Hall, Inc. "Confrontation Series," "French
    Literary Backgrounds Series," "Twentieth Century
    Views" (each vol. devoted to one author).
PUF. "Nouvelle Clio," "Que sais-je?" (excellent vulgari-
    sation), "SUP."
Random House.
SEDES.
Seghers. (See under editions).
Seuil, Eds. du. "Ecrivains de toujours" (studies on
    writers through excerpts of their own writings),
    "Pierres vives," "Points," "Tel Quel" (critical
    essays).
Table Ronde (La).
Twayne's "World Authors Series."

Union Générale d'Editeurs. "10X18."
Vrin.

IV. ON FRENCH LANGUAGE

BELC
Bordas
Champion
Delagrave
Didier. "Linguistique appliquée."
Droz. "Publications Romanes."
Duculot.
Francke. "Bibliotheca Romanica."
Hachette. "Collection F," "Collection Le Français
     dans le monde," etc.
Klincksieck
Larousse
Lettres Modernes Minard. "Langues et styles."
Picard
PUF. "SUP. Le Linguiste."
SEDES

V. ON BIBLIOGRAPHY

Unesco, Les Pr. de l'.

PART II

GENERAL STUDIES ON THE FRENCH LANGUAGE

CHAPTER 11

BIBLIOGRAPHIES AND GENERAL STUDIES ON THE

FRENCH LANGUAGE

See Ch. 1: Malclès, *Sources du travail biblio-graphique* (no. 8) and also her *Manuel de biblio-graphie* (no. 9); Ch. 2: *MLA Bibliography* (no. 22); Ch. 8: encyclopedias and dictionaries.

A. BIBLIOGRAPHIES ON LINGUISTICS

370 *Bulletin Signalétique 524: Sciences du Langage.* P.: CNRS, 1961-. Quarterly.

Supersedes in part *Bulletin Signalétique: Philosophie, sciences humaines*, issued 1947-60, and continues its vol. numbering.

Each issue has a list of abstracted journals, index of concepts, index of authors, detailed classifica-tion scheme, and abstracts which are brief and descriptive rather than critical. Annual cumulated index of authors and of concepts (subjects).

Selective periodical abstract tool scanning over 300 journals from many countries. Also covers publications of congresses, colloquia, vols. of *mélanges*, and diss.

Generally concerned with various concepts and aspects of interest to linguistic scholars--grammar, inscriptions, morphology, onomastics, phonetics, semantics, etc.--but indexing a substantial amount of writing on individual languages, dialects, teaching of languages, and some material relating to the analysis of literature.

371 Permanent International Committee of Linguists/Comité International Permanent des Linguistes. *Linguistic Bibliography for the Years 1939-1947./Bibliographie linguistique des années 1939-1947.* 2 vols. Utrecht: Spectrum, 1949-50. Continued by annual vols. with title: *Linguistic Bibliography for the Year (1948-) and Supplement for Previous Years/ Bibliographie linguistique de l'année (1948-) et complément des années précédentes.*

Of great importance to scholars, this is the most comprehensive current bibliography published in linguistics. International coverage of books, annuals, *Festschriften*, periodicals, etc. The 1972 annual indexes about 1,550 journals and contains 13,147 numbered citations.

Covers general linguistics, language families, individual languages and dialects. Titles of citations in lesser known languages are briefly described in a phrase, or translated into French or English. Alphabetical author index.

B. ROMANCE PHILOLOGY

See Ch. 8: "Etymological Dictionaries" (nos. 284-290).

372 Auerbach, Erich. *Introduction aux études de philologie romane*. Trad. de l'allemand. 3e éd. Frankfurt a/M.: Klostermann, 1965.

An introductory manual which provides a good survey for the beginner, and a bibliography.

373 Bal, Willy. *Introduction aux études de linguistique romane avec considération spéciale de la linguistique française*. P.: Didier, 1966.

374 Elcock, W. D. *The Romance Languages*. London: Faber and Faber, 1960.

Discusses the origins of the Romance languages.

375 Grossmann, Maria, et Mazzoni, Bruno. *Bibliographie de phonologie romane*. La Haye: Mouton, 1974.

376 Mourin, Louis, et Pohl, Jacques. *Bibliographie de linguistique romane*. 4e éd. remaniée et mise à jour. Bruxelles: Pr. univ. de Bruxelles, 1971.

A bibliography of sources used by two Belgian professors in their courses. Classified arrangement. Covers general linguistics and its parts, Romance languages, French Provençal, Occitan, Gascon, Franco-Provençal, Spanish, Catalan, Portuguese, Italian, numerous dialects, and stylistics. Most chapters include bibliography (current and retrospective) and a list of important periodicals. Includes an author index and several linguistic maps. No annotations.

377 Posner, Rebecca R. *The Romance Languages: A Linguistic Introduction*. Garden City, N.Y.: Anchor Books, 1966

A manual for the non-initiated.

C. BIBLIOGRAPHIES AND BASIC STUDIES ON THE FRENCH LANGUAGE

I. BIBLIOGRAPHIES AND GENERAL STUDIES

378 *Bulletin analytique de linguistique française*. Vol. 1, 1969. Nancy: Centre pour un Trésor de la langue française (CNRS). Vol. 2-, 1970-, P.: Didier.

(Six nos. per year.)

An excellent current bibliography with descriptive
annotations of articles, theses and books. About 100
linguistic and literary periodicals from several countries
are regularly examined. Citations to book reviews are
given. A classified bibliography with an index of authors
and anonymous titles in each issue. About 2,400 items
per year.

379 Dauzat, Albert. *Etudes de linguistique française*. P.:
d'Artrey, 1945.

Treats questions of semantics, grammar, linguistic
geography, etc. Bibliography in notes.

380 Kukenheim, Louis. *Esquisse historique de la linguistique
française et de ses rapports avec la linguistique
générale*. 2e éd. rev., corr., et augm. Leyde:
Universitaire Pers, 1966.

Discussion of French linguistic scholars and their
works.

381 Martin, Robert, et Martin, Eveline. *Guide bibliographique
de linguistique française*. P.: Klincksieck, 1973.

A selective bibliography with many annotations
covering the main divisions of linguistics, Latin, French
(by period), and bibliography. Includes a list of the
principal journals, and indexes of authors and subjects.

382 Wagner, Robert-Léon. *Introduction à la linguistique
française*. Genève: Droz, 1947. 3e tirage, 1965;
inserted at end: *Supplément bibliographique 1947-53*,
1955.

This is a basic work for French linguistics
studies. It is also an annotated bibliography.

II. HISTORIES OF THE FRENCH LANGUAGE

383 Bruneau, Charles. *Petite histoire de la langue française*.
1e éd. 2 vols. P.: Colin, 1955-58; 4e éd. rev. et
mise à jour par M. Parent et G. Moignet, 1966.

I: *Des origines à la Révolution*.
II: *De la Révolution à nos jours*.
Shows the evolution of both the spoken and
literary languages, and relates this evolution to the
literature and civilization of the times.

384 Brunot, Ferdinand. *Histoire de la langue française des
origines à nos jours*. 1e éd. 13 tomes en 21 vols.

P.: Colin, 1905-53 (Charles Bruneau wrote tomes
12 and 13). Nouv. éd. avec bibliographies mises à
jour, pub. sous la dir. de Gérald Antoine, Georges
Gougenheim et Robert Wagner. Préface de G. Antoine,
ibid., 1966-72.

The bibliographies of the new ed. have been
established by excellent specialists. G. Antoine is pre-
paring tome 14: *Fin du XIXe siècle*, and tome 15: *XXe
siècle.*
Embraces the history of the French language and
its relations with habits, customs and events. The first
vols. contain elements of phonetics, morphology, and syntax.
The following contain classic and postclassic grammar.
The final vols. deal with sociological tendencies. A
monumental work which really studies the history of France
through the language. It is also a literary history.

385   Cohen, Marcel. *Histoire d'une langue: le français (des
          lointaines origines à nos jours).* P.: Ed.
          Hier et Aujourd'hui, 1947; 3e éd. rev. et mise à
          jour. P.: Eds. Sociales, 1967; nouv. éd. 1975.

A collection of courses taught at the Université
ouvrière de Paris from 1933-1938. Meant for a vast public
which the author wishes to instruct on the formation and
development of the French language. The history of the
French language is placed in the general history of
languages starting with Indo-European. Contains a critical
bibliography. Each chapter ends with texts of the period.
Excellent for the non-specialist.

386   Pope, Mildred Katharine. *From Latin to Modern French with
          Especial Consideration of Anglo-Norman, Phonology
          and Morphology.* Manchester: U. Pr., 1934;
          2nd ed. 1952; rpt., 1961 and 1966.

The most complete and best documented work in
English on Old French, particularly Anglo-Norman.

387   Wartburg, Walther von. *Evolution et structure de la langue
          française*, 1934; 10è éd. Berne: Francke,
          1971.

A continuous history of French and a description
of its present state. This is an effort to characterize
the spirit of French at various times. Both historical
and descriptive treatment.

III.   HISTORICAL GRAMMARS

388   Brunot, Ferdinand, et Bruneau, Charles. *Précis de gram-
          maire historique de la langue française.* 3e éd.
          P.: Masson, 1969.

126

There are important bibliographies in the first
and second eds. (1887 and 1937). As of the third ed.
there are cross references to R.-L. Wagner's work mentioned
above.

89 Darmesteter, Arsène. *Cours de grammaire historique de la
      langue française*. 4 vols. P.: Delagrave, 1930-34.

> I: *Phonétique*.
> II: *Morphologie*.
> III: *Formation des mots et vie des mots*.
> IV: *Syntaxe*.
> Vols. 1-3: 14e éd., rev. et corr.; vol. 4:
12e éd., rev. et corr., 1931.
> Ed. by Léopold Sudre; vol. 3 rev. by Pierre
Laurent; vol. 1 of the 1st ed., 1891-97, was ed. by Ernest
Muret.

90 Dauzat, Albert. *Phonétique et grammaire historique de la
      langue française*. P.: Larousse, 1950.

91 Kukenheim, Louis. *Grammaire historique de la langue
      française*. Leyde: Universitaire Pers, 1967-.
      (2 vols. pub. out of the 3 planned.)

> I: *Les Parties du discours*. 1967. Table.
> II: *Les Syntagmes*. 1968. Table.
> III: *Le Phonétisme* (en préparation).

CHAPTER 12

STUDIES ON VARIOUS ASPECTS OF THE FRENCH LANGUAGE

A. GRAMMARS

392 Buyssens, Eric. *Les Catégories grammaticales du français.*
     Bruxelles: Eds. de l'U. de Bruxelles, 1975.

393 Centre d'étude du français moderne et contemporain.
     Le Français contemporain. Inventaire permanent des
     travaux inédits et des recherches en cours. I-II, P.
     Didier, 1972-75. III, P.: Klincksieck, 1976 (éd. Quér

394 Chaillet, Jean. *Etudes de grammaire et de style.* 2 vols.
     P.: Bordas, 1969.

             I: *XVIe, XVIIe, XVIIIe Siècles.*
            II: *XIXe et XXe Siècles.*
         An in-depth study of French grammar and literary
     style is presented in these vols. The author gives a
     series of literary selections drawn from the works of
     sixty great authors from the Renaissance to the twentieth
     century. He then studies and analyzes the grammatical
     points and style of the selections.

395 Chevalier, Jean-Claude; Blanche-Benveniste, Claire;
             Arrivé, Michel; et Peytard, Jean. *Grammaire*
             Larousse du français contemporain. P.: Larousse,
             1964.

             This book presents the grammatical rules of the
     French language, explains their origin, and discusses
     their validity in relationship to the contemporary language
     It gives a detailed study of the sentence, then examines
     the parts of speech. Important chapters are devoted to
     signs, sounds, vocabulary, and versification.

396 Dubois, Jean. *Grammaire structurale du français.* 3 vols.
             P.: Larousse, 1965-69.

             I: *Nom et pronom.* 1965.
            II: *Le Verbe.* 1967.
           III: *La Phrase et les transformations.* 1969.

397 Dubois, Jean, et Lagane, René. *La Nouvelle Grammaire du*
             français. P.: Larousse, 1973.

398 Galichet, Georges. *Grammaire structurale du français*
             moderne. 1e éd. P.: Charles-Lavauzelle, 1957;
             2e éd. rev. et corr. 1968.

An important vol. for the teacher of French.
It is a methodical exploration of the structures of modern
French, resulting in remarkable pedagogical applications
of the theories discussed.

99   Gougenheim, Georges. *Système grammatical de la langue
        française.* 1e éd. P.: d'Artrey, 1938; rpt.,
        1962, 1969.

        A descriptive treatise on the state of modern
French but many observations apply to older stages. An
excellent student guide for the study and teaching of
French.

00   (Académie Française, Paris.) *Grammaire de l'Académie
        Française.* P.: Firmin-Didot, 1932.

        Purist grammar.

01   Grevisse, Maurice. *Le Bon Usage: Grammaire française
        avec des remarques sur la langue française d'au-
        jourd'hui.* 9e éd. rev. Gembloux: Duculot; 10e
        éd. 1976.

        The most complete French grammar.

02   _____. *Le Français correct. Guide pratique.* Gem-
        bloux: Duculot, 1973.

        Studies difficulties of the French language in
a simple and precise manner. Good index.

03   _____. *Problèmes de langage.* 5 vols. P.: PUF,
        1961-70.

04   Mauger, Gaston. *Grammaire pratique du français d'au-
        jourd'hui, langue parlée, langue écrite.* P.:
        Hachette, 1968.

05   Wagner, Robert-Léon, et Pinchon, Jacqueline. *Grammaire du
        français classique et moderne.* 1e éd. P.: Hachette,
        1962; 2e éd. rev., 1967; éd. rev. et corr. 1973.

            B. MORPHOLOGY

06   Cohen, Marcel. *Le Subjonctif en français contemporain,
        tableau documentaire.* 2e éd. P.: SEDES, 1965.

07   Dubois, Jean. *Etude sur la dérivation suffixale en
        français moderne et contemporain; essai d'inter-
        prétation des mouvements observés dans le domaine
        de la morphologie des mots construits.* (Thèse
        complémentaire.) P.: Larousse, 1962.

408 Fouché, Pierre. *Le Verbe français, étude morpholo-*
     gique. . . . Nouv. éd. refondue et augm. P.:
     Klincksieck, 1967. (1e éd. P.: Belles Lettres,
     1931.)

409 Mok, Quirinus Ignatius Maria. *Contribution à l'étude des*
     catégories morphologiques du genre et du nombre
     dans le français parlé actuel. P.-La Haye: Mouton,
     1968.

C. PHONETICS AND PHONOLOGY

410 Bonnard, Henri. *Synopsis de phonétique historique.*
          P.: CDU-SEDES, 1975.

411 Bourciez, Edouard. *Phonétique française, étude historique*
          P.: Klincksieck, 1967.

          Revision by J. Bourciez of E. Bourciez's *Précis*
     historique de phonétique française. Ibid., 9e éd. 1958.

412 Carton, Fernand. *Introduction à la phonétique du français*
          P.: Bordas, 1974.

          An intensive analysis of French phonetics is
     given in this study, which deals with the spoken language.
     It tells of the various theories prevailing today, and
     serves as an orientation for the reader.

413 Fouché, Pierre. *Etudes de phonétique générale (syllabe,*
          diphtongaison, consonnes additionnelles). P.:
          Belles Lettres, 1927.

414 _____. *Phonétique historique du français.* 3 vols.
          P.: Klincksieck, 1952-69.
          1: *Introduction.*
          2: *Les Voyelles.* 2e éd. rev. et corr. 1969.
          3: *Les Consonnes et index général.* 2e éd.
             rev. et corr. 1966.

          Basic book.

415 _____. *Traité de prononciation française.* P.:
          Klincksieck, 1956; 2e éd. 1959.

416 Haudricourt, André, et Juilland, Alphonse. *Essai pour une*
          histoire structurale du phonétisme français. P.:
          Klincksieck, 1949.

417 Malmberg, Bertil. *La Phonétique.* 7e éd. P.: PUF,
          "Que sais-je?" 1968. English translation: *Phonetic*
          N.Y.: Dover, 1963.

          A good general introduction to phonetics.

.8   Martinet, André, et Walter, Henriette. *Dictionnaire de la prononciation française dans son usage réel.* P.: France Expansion, 1973.

.9   Rochette, Claude E. *Les Groupes de consonnes en français.* 2 vols. P.: Klincksieck, 1973.

      I: *L'Enchaînement articulatoire à l'aide de la radiocinématographie et de l'oscillographie.*
      II: *Documents.* 137 ills. et tables.

'0   Straka, Georges. *Album phonétique.* Québec: Les Pr. de l'U. Laval, 1965.

      An experimental treatise on French phonetics.

'1   Troubetskoy, Nicolaj Sergejevič. *Principes de phonologie.* Trad. de l'allemand par J. Cantineau. P.: Klincksieck, 1949; rpt., 1957, 1967.
Trubetskoi, Nikolai Sergeievich. *Principles of Phonology.* Trans. by Christiane Baltaxe. Berkeley: U. of California Pr., 1969.

2   Warnant, Léon. *Dictionnaire de la prononciation française.* I: 1962; 2e éd. 1964; 3e éd. rev. et corr. Gembloux: Duculot, 1968. II: *Noms propres.* Ibid., 1966.

      More than 55,000 words. Gives the pronunciation in International Phonetic Alphabet. More than twenty tables of concordance for each of today's modern languages.

D.   SYNTAX

3   Boer, Cornelis de. *Syntaxe du français moderne.* Leyde: Universitaire Pers, 1947; 2e éd. entièrement rev. 1954.

4   Chevalier, Jean-Claude. *Histoire de la syntaxe. Naissance de la notion de complément dans la grammaire française (1530-1750).* P.: Editions Sociales, 1954; Genève: Droz, 1968.

5   Deloffre, Frédéric. *La Phrase française.* P.: CDU-SEDES, 1967. 3e éd. 1975.

6   Dubois, Jean, et Dubois-Charlier, Françoise. *Eléments de linguistique française. Syntaxe.* P.: Larousse, 1970.

7   Gross, Maurice. *Grammaire transformationnelle du français. Syntaxe du verbe.* P.: Larousse, 1968.

428 Guiraud, Pierre. *La Syntaxe du français*. 5e éd. P.:
PUF, "Que sais-je?" 1970.

429 Kayne, Richard S. *French Syntax: The Transformational
Cycle*. Cambridge, Mass.: M.I.T. Pr., 1975.

430 Le Bidois, Georges et Robert. *Syntaxe du français modern
ses fondements historiques et psychologiques*.
2 vols. P.: Picard, 1935-38; 2e éd. rev. et complétée, 1968.

I: Prolégomènes. Les Articles. Les Pronoms.
Théorie générale du verbe: les voix, les temps, les
modes.
II: L'Ordre des mots dans la phrase. L'Accord.
Syntaxe des propositions. Les Propositions subor-
données. Les Mots-outils. Paragrammaticales.

431 Wartburg, Walther von, et Zumthor, Paul. *Précis de
syntaxe du français contemporain*. Berne: Francke,
1947; 2e éd. ent. remaniée 1958.

E. SEMANTICS

432 Darmesteter, Arsène. *La Vie des mots étudiés dans leurs
significations*. P.: Delagrave, 1886; rpt., 19e
éd. 1937.

433 Guiraud, Pierre. *La Sémantique*. P.: PUF, "Que sais-je?
8e éd. mise à jour, 1975.

434 Huguet, Edmond. *L'Evolution du sens des mots depuis le
XVIe siècle*. P.: Droz, 1934; 2e tirage, 1967.

435 Tutescu, Mariana. *Précis de sémantique française*. P.:
Klincksieck, 1975.

436 Ullmann, Stephen. *Précis de sémantique française*. Berne
Francke, 1952; 4e éd. 1969; 5e éd. (conforme à la 4e),

F. LEXICOLOGY AND ETYMOLOGY

437 Gougenheim, Georges. *Les Mots français dans l'histoire
et dans la vie*. 3 vols. P.: Picard, 1962-75.

438 Guiraud, Pierre. *Structures étymologiques du lexique
français*. P.: Larousse, 1967.

439 Huguet, Edmond. *Mots disparus ou vieillis depuis le
XVIe siècle*. P.: Droz, 1935.

440 Mitterand, Henri. *Les Mots français*. P.: PUF, "Que
sais-je?" 4e éd. 1972; 5e éd. mise à jour, 1976.

Clear exposé of the principles of the new lexicology: word is considered not in itself but in a structure of forms and usages.

1 Quémada, Bernard. *Matériaux pour l'histoire du vocabulaire français; datations et documents lexicographiques.* 1e sér., vols. 1-3, A-C. Besançon: Centre d'étude du vocabulaire français, 1959-65. 2e sér., vols. 1-6. P.: Didier, 1970-75 (each vol. A-Z). (In progress.)

Presents for each word an assembly of dates, meanings, bibliographical citations in books, articles, dictionaries, etc. Intended to complement the etymological dictionaries.

2 Wagner, Robert-Léon. *Les Vocabulaires français.* 2 vols. I: *Définition. Les Dictionnaires.* II: *Les Tâches de la lexicologie synchronique. Glossaires et dépouillements. Analyse lexicale.* P.: Didier, 1967-70.

G. SPELLING

3 Bavart, Paul, et Didier, M. *Guide pratique d'orthographe.* P.: Bordas, 1965.

4 Beaulieux, Charles. *Histoire de l'orthographe française.* 2 vols. P.: Champion, 1927; nouv. tirage, 1967.

    I: *Formation de l'orthographe, des origines au milieu du XVIe siècle.* (See Catach, no. 770.)
    II: *Les Accents et autres signes auxiliaires dans la langue française, suivi de: La Briefve Doctrine, par Montflory, et: Les Accents, par Dolet.*

5 Grevisse, Maurice. *Code de l'orthographe française.* 4e éd. Bruxelles: Baude, 1965; Amiens: Les Eds. Scientifiques et littéraires, 1965.

6 Sève, André. *Ortho. Dictionnaire orthographique et grammatical.* Avec la collaboration de Jean Perrot. Nice: G. Boyer, 1946; 18e éd.: *Ortho vert.* . . . . P.: Eds. Sociales, 1976.

7 Thimonnier, René. *Code orthographique et grammatical.* Préf. de Georges Matoré. P.: Hatier, 1970.

Awarded the Académie Française Prize for 1971. Excellent.

8 _____. *Le Système graphique du français. Introduction à une pédagogie rationnelle de l'orthographe.* Préf.

d'Etiemble.   P.:   Plon, 1967.

H.   STYLISTICS

449   Bally, Charles. *Traité de stylistique française.* 2 vols
      1e éd. 1902.   2e éd.   Heidelberg: Winter, 1908-09.
      13e éd. 2 vols. in 1.   P.:   Klincksieck, 1951.

450   Cressot, Marcel. *Le Style et ses techniques. Précis
      d'analyse stylistique.* 1e éd.   P.:   PUF, 1947;
      8e éd. mise à jour par Laurence James, 1974.

      Important bibliography.

451   Hatzfeld, Helmut Anthony. *A Critical Bibliography of the
      New Stylistics Applied to the Romance Literatures
      1900-1952.* Chapel Hill, North Carolina: U. of
      North Carolina Pr., 1953.

           . Ibid. *1953-1965.* Chapel Hill, North Carolina
      U. of North Carolina Pr., 1966.

      The 1900-1952 volume is a bibliographical histor
of the development of trends and schools in stylistics
during the period, arranged in eleven chapters and taking
the form of a running commentary on the 1,600 scholarly
books and articles included (international coverage).
The second work for 1953-65 lists 1,900 titles with
annotations on theory, explanation of texts, parallels,
style and structure of literary works (divided by century
and by country), and such elements of style as grammar,
rhetoric, rhythm, motive and language.   Both works includ
studies of individual authors and literary works.   Indexe
of writers, authors, titles and terms.   A very important
critical bibliography.

452   Hatzfeld, Helmut Anthony, et Le Hir, Yves. *Essai de
      bibliographie critique de stylistique française et
      romane (1955-1960).* P.:   PUF, 1961.   (Supplements
      Hatzfeld's bibliography above.)

453   Le Hir, Yves. *Analyses stylistiques.* P.:   Colin, 1965.

454   Marouzeau, Jules. *Précis de stylistique française.* 3e
      éd. rev. et augm.   P.:   Masson, 1950; 5e éd. 1965;
      rpt., 1969.

      Chapters on sounds, grammatical categories,
sentence construction, etc.   Contains a short bibliograph

455   Sumpf, Joseph. *Introduction à la stylistique du françai*
      P.:   Larousse, 1971.

I. VERSIFICATION

56 Deloffre, Frédéric. *Stylistique et poétique françaises.*
2e éd. rev. et corr. P.: CDU-SEDES, 1974.

57 Elwert, W. Theodor. *Traité de versification française des
origines à nos jours.* (Translated from German.)
P.: Klincksieck, 1965.

58 Gauthier, Michel. *Système euphonique et rythmique du vers
français.* P.: Klincksieck, 1974.

59 Grammont, Maurice. *Essai de psychologie linguistique,
style et poésie.* P.: Delagrave, 1950.

> Most of his theories on the French verse are
considered erroneous by Yves Le Hir in his *Analyses
stylistiques* (see no. 453).

60 Guiraud, Pierre. *La Versification.* 1e éd. P.: PUF,
"Que sais-je?" 1970. 2e éd. 1973.

61 Lote, Georges. *Histoire du vers français.* 3 vols. P.:
Boivin et Hatier, 1949-55.

> I, ptie 1: *Le Moyen Age. I. Les Origines du
> vers français. Les éléments consti-
> tutifs du vers: la césure; la rime;
> le numérisme et le rythme.* Boivin, 1949.
> II, ptie 1: *Le Moyen Age. II. La Déclamation.
> Art et versification. Les formes
> lyriques.* Boivin, 1951.
> III, ptie 1: *Le Moyen Age. III. La Poétique.
> Le vers et la langue.* Hatier, 1955.
> This work will be in twelve vols. It will include
the history of French verse from its origins to the beginning of the twentieth century. Interrupted by the death
of G. Lote, it is continued by Ch. Rostaing.

62 Mazaleyrat, Jean. *Eléments de métrique française.* P.:
Colin, 1974.

J. SLANG

See Ch. 8: Dictionaries of Slang.

63 Dauzat, Albert. *Les Argots. Caractères, évolution, influence.* 1e éd. P.: Delagrave, 1929; rpt., 1946,
1956.

> On the different French slangs and their evolution,
changes in meanings, penetration of slang into French, etc.
Bibliography.

PART III

BIBLIOGRAPHIES AND STUDIES OF

LITERATURE

CHAPTER 13

SURVEYS, ANTHOLOGIES AND GENERAL STUDIES
OF THE LITERATURE OF FRANCE

We place in this chapter only general surveys,
anthologies, and studies on the literature of France.
Works concerning one particular period of French
literature, or the literature written in French
outside of France will be found in the chapters
devoted to them.

A. SURVEYS OF FRENCH LITERATURE

In the case of a multivolume survey of French
literature, if the authors are responsible for the
whole publication, we describe it here. If each
volume of a series is prepared by a different author,
we give here only the title of the series, and we
mention in the proper chapter the individual author
and the title of his book.

I. HISTORIES

See in Ch. 8 nos. 258 and 260.

64 Adam, Antoine; Lerminier, Georges; et Morot-Sir, Edouard,
sous la dir. de. *Littérature française*. 2 vols.
P.: Larousse, 1967-68.

> I: *Des origines à la fin du XVIIIe siècle.*
> II: *XIXe et XXe siècles.*

65 Bédier, Joseph, et Hazard, Paul. *Littérature française.*
Nouv. éd. ref. et augm. sous la dir. de Pierre
Martino. 2 vols. P.: Larousse, 1948-49. (1st ed.
entitled: *Histoire de la littérature française
illustrée.* 2 vols. P.: Larousse, 1923.)

> I: *Moyen Age, XVIe, XVIIe siècles.* 1948.
> II: *XVIIIe, XIXe siècles et époque contemporaine.*
>   1949.

66 *Histoire de la littérature française*, sous la dir. de
Jean Calvet. 1e éd. 10 vols. P.: de Gigord, 1931;
nouv. éd. P.: del Duca, 1955-64.

Each vol. is written by one or two specialists
(see following chs.). Covers Middle Ages through twentieth
century.

467 Jasinski, René. *Histoire de la littérature française.*
1e éd. 2 vols. P.: Hatier; nouv. éd. rev. et
compl. par Robert Bossuat, René Fromilhague, René
Pomeau, et Jacques Robichez, 2 vols. P.: Nizet,
1965.

468 *Literary History of France (A).* Ed. P. Charvet. 5 tomes ⅰ
6 vols. London: Benn; N.Y.: Barnes and Noble, 19⬤

Covers Middle Ages through 1940. See following ⬤

469 *Littérature française.* Ed. Claude Pichois. P.: Arthaud⬛
1968-.

16 vols. announced, each done by one or more
specialists, see following chs. Covers Middle Ages throug⬤
twentieth century.

470 Nitze, William A., and Dargan, E. Preston. *A History of
French Literature from the Earliest Times to the
Present.* 1st ed. N.Y.: Holt, 1938; 3rd ed. 1958.

471 Roger, Jacques, et Payen, Jean-Charles, éds. *Histoire de
la littérature française.* 2 vols. P.: Colin,
1969-70.

I: *Du Moyen Age à la fin du XVIIe siècle.* 1969
II: *Du XVIIIe siècle à nos jours.* 1970.

II. MANUALS

472 Abraham, Pierre, et Desné, Roland, sous la dir. de.
Manuel d'histoire littéraire de la France. 6 tomes
en 7 vols. P.: Eds. Sociales, 1965-.

I: *Des origines à 1600.* 1965.
II: *De 1600 à 1715.* 1966.
III: *De 1715 à 1789.* 1969.
IV: *De 1789 à 1848, 1e partie.* 1972.
IV: *De 1789 à 1848, 2e partie.* 1973.
V: *De 1848 à 1917.* (En préparation.)
VI: *De 1917 à nos jours.* (En préparation.)
Published by the Centre of Marxist Studies and Re
search. Collective work undertaken by some hundred par-
ticipants.

473 Calvet, Jean. *Manuel illustré d'histoire de la litté
rature française.* P.: de Gigord, 1966.

474 Castex, Pierre-Georges, et Surer, Paul. *Manuel des études
littéraires françaises.* 6 vols. P.: Hachette,
1946-67. (Periodically rev. and reprinted.)

One volume per period. Covers Middle Ages throug⬤
twentieth century.

Castex, Pierre-Georges; Surer, Paul; et Becker, Georges. *Histoire de la littérature française*. Ibid., 1974.

The above 6 vols. are here grouped in one, updated and enlarged.

75 Cazamian, Louis. *A History of French Literature*. London: Clarendon Pr., 1955; rpt. with corrections, London: Oxford U. Pr., 1959, 1960.

76 Charlton, Donald Geoffrey, ed. *France: A Companion to French Studies*. London: Methuen, 1972.

77 Cruickshank, John, ed. *French Literature and Its Background*. 6 vols. London: Oxford U. Pr., 1968-70.

Each vol. contains studies of the major authors by mostly English scholars. Covers Renaissance to present.

78 Lanson, Gustave. *Manuel illustré d'histoire de la littérature française*. Ed. complétée pour la période 1919-1950 par Paul Tuffrau. P.: Hachette, 1953.

79 Salomon, Pierre. *Précis d'histoire de la littérature française*. 2e éd. rev. et complétée. P.: Masson, 1964.

III. DICTIONARIES

80 Braun, Sidney. *Dictionary of French Literature*. N.Y.: Philosophical Lib., 1958.

Definitions of literary terms with entries for titles, genres and literary movements. For authors there are brief biographical sketches, capsule evaluations of principal works and a few references to writings about them.

81 *Dictionnaire des auteurs français*. Nouv. ed. P.: Seghers, 1961; rpt., 1972.

Gives dates, principal works and a summary of the literary importance of writers, historians, critics, scholars, etc. from early times to the present. This ed. adds a supplement and a short section describing the main literary schools.

82 *Dictionnaire des oeuvres érotiques: domaine français*. P.: Mercure de France, 1971.

Discusses the publication, content and effect of a large number of erotic works in French literature--essays, drama, poetry, novels, memoirs, etc. Arranged by title with tables for variant titles and for authors. List of thirty-eight collaborators. Piquant illustrations.

483   Grente, Georges, éd. *Dictionnaire des lettres françaises.*
      5 tomes en 7 vols. P.: Fayard, 1951-1973.

      I: *Le Moyen Age.* 1964.
      II: *Le XVIe siècle.* 1951.
      III: *Le XVIIe siècle.* 1954.
      IV: *Le XVIIIe siècle.* 2 vols. 1959-60.
      V: *Le XIXe siècle.* 2 vols. 1972-73.

An important scholarly dictionary. Each vol. begins with a general article and bibliography of the period
concerned. Major authors are treated at length in a detailed biographical and critical account followed by bibliographical information on best editions, separate works and
works to consult about them. Secondary authors are also
included and there are articles on literary forms, themes
and elements, on anonymous titles, and on general topics.

484   Malignon, Jean. *Dictionnaire des écrivains français des
      troubadours à Sartre.* P.: Eds. du Seuil, 1971.

485   Nathan, Jacques. *Encyclopédie de la littérature française.*
      P.: Nathan, 1952.

     B. ANTHOLOGIES CONCERNING MORE THAN ONE PERIOD

         I. GENERAL ANTHOLOGIES

486   Chassang, Arsène, et Senninger, Charles. *Recueil de textes
      littéraires français.* 5 vols. P.: Hachette,
      1966-70.

      I: *XVIe Siècle.*
      II: *XVIIe Siècle.*
      III: *XVIIIe Siècle.*
      IV: *XIXe Siècle.*
      V: *XXe Siècle.*

Accompanied by vols. (for teachers only) offering
a documentation on the texts.
    The following vols. have appeared:
XVIe Siècle. Points de vue et références. 2 vols. Ibid.,
1968-1969.
XVIIIe Siècle. Points de vue et références. Ibid., 1966.

487   Lagarde, André, et Michard, Laurent, et al. *Les Grands
      Auteurs français du programme.* Textes et littérature
      6 vols. Ills. P.: Bordas, 1959. (Reprinted often.)

      I: *Moyen Age.*
      II: *XVIe Siècle.*
      III: *XVIIe Siècle.*
      IV: *XVIIIe Siècle.*
      V: *XIXe Siècle.*
      VI: *XXe Siècle.* Nouv. éd. mise à jour, remaniée
           et augm. 1972.

A condensed version is also pub. under the same title.

For the sixteenth, seventeenth, eighteenth, and nineteenth centuries, there exists a collection of documents for teachers.

II. BY GENRES

a. POETRY

488 *Anthologie poétique française.* Choix, introduction et
     notices par André Mary et Maurice Allem. 7 vols. P.:
     Garnier-Flammarion, 1965-67.

> *Moyen Age.* Préf. par A. Mary. 2 vols. 1967.
> *XVIe Siècle.* Préf. par M. Allem. 2 vols. 1965.
> *XVIIe Siècle.* Préf. par M. Allem. 2 vols. 1965-66.
> *XVIIIe Siècle.* Préf. par M. Allem. 1 vol. 1966.

489 Boase, Alan Martin, ed. *The Poetry of France. An Anthology.*
     4 vols. London: Methuen, 1964-73.

> I: *1400-1600.*   1964.
> II: *1600-1800.*   1973.
> III: *1800-1900.*   2nd ed. 1967.
> IV: *1900-1965.*   1969.

490 Bonnefoy, Claude. *La Poésie française des origines à nos
     jours.* P.: Eds. du Seuil, 1975.

491 Chapelan, Maurice. *Anthologie du poème en prose.* P.:
     Grasset, 1959.

492 Clancier, Georges-Emmanuel. *Panorama de la poésie fran-
     çaise de Chénier à Baudelaire.* P.: Seghers, 1970.

493 _____. *Panorama de la poésie française de Rimbaud au
     surréalisme.* P.: Seghers, 1970.

494 Kanters, Robert, et Nadeau, Maurice. *Anthologie de la
     poésie française.* 12 vols. Lausanne: Rencontre,
     1966-67.

495 Mansell Jones, P., ed. *Oxford Book of French Verse (The).*
     XIIIth Century-XXth Century. Chosen by St. John
     Lucas. 1st ed. Oxford: Clarendon Pr., 1907;
     2nd ed. 1957; rpt., 1959.

496 Moulin, Jeanine, éd. *La Poésie féminine.* 2 vols. P.:
     Seghers, 1963-66. Rpt. under a different title:
     Huit Siècles de poésie française. P.: Seghers,
     1975.

Anthology of about one hundred *poétesses* notably:

Louise Labé, Marceline Desbordes-Valmore, Anna de Noailles.

497 *Penguin Book of French Verse (The)*. With plain prose
      translations of each poem. 4 vols. Baltimore, Md.:
      Penguin Books, 1958-61.

> I: *To the Fifteenth Century*. Introduced and
>   edited by Brian Woledge. 1st ed. 1961; rpt.
>   1966, 1968.
> II: *Sixteenth to Eighteenth Centuries*. Intro-
>   duced and edited by Geoffrey Brereton, 1958.
> III: *Nineteenth Century*. Ed. by Anthony Hartley.
>   1st ed. 1957; rpt. with revisions 1958-1968.
> IV: *Twentieth Century*. Introduced and edited
>   by Anthony Hartley. 1st ed. 1959; rpt.,
>   1963; rpt., with additional poems, 1966.

498 Seghers, Pierre, éd. *Livre d'or de la poésie française
      des origines à 1940 (Le)*. Verviers: Gérard, 1961.

499 _____. *Livre d'or de la poésie française contemporaine.
      1940-1960 (Le)*. 2 vols. Verviers: Gérard, 1969.

b. PROSE

500 Arland, Marcel. *La Prose française, anthologie, histoire
      et critique d'un art*. P.: Stock, 1951.

501 Castex, Pierre-Georges. *Anthologie du conte fantastique
      français*. 1e éd. P.: José Corti, 1947; 2e éd. 1963

c. THEATRE

502 Fournier, Edouard, éd. *Le Théâtre français au XVIe et au
      XVIIe siècle; ou choix des comédies les plus remar-
      quables antérieures à Molière*, avec une introduction
      et une notice sur chaque auteur. 2 vols. P.: La
      Place, s.d. (1874).

503 _____. *Le Théâtre français avant la Renaissance
      (1450-1550); mystères, moralités et farces*, précédé
      d'une introduction et accompagné de notes pour l'in-
      telligence du texte. P.: La Place, Sanchez et
      Cie, 1873.

504 Picot, Emile, et Nyrop, Christophe, éds. *Nouveau Recueil
      de farces françaises des XVe et XVIe siècles*.
      P.: Morgand et Fatout, 1880.

505 Viollet-le-Duc, Emmanuel Louis Nicolas. *Ancien Théâtre
      français ou collection des ouvrages dramatiques les
      plus remarquables, depuis les mystères jusqu'à
      Corneille*, pub. avec des notes et éclaircissements.
      10 vols. P.: Jannet, 1854-57.

C. GENERAL STUDIES

I. STUDIES CONCERNING MORE THAN ONE PERIOD

506   Derche, Roland. *Etudes de textes français.* Nouv. sér.
         6 vols. P.: CDU-SEDES, 1964-68.
         I: *Moyen Age.* 1964.
         II: *XVIe Siècle.* 1965.
         III: *XVIIe Siècle.* 1964.
         IV: *XVIIIe Siècle.* 1968.
         V: *XIXe Siècle.* (Up to Victor Hugo.) 1966.
         VI: *XIXe et XXe Siècles.* (From Baudelaire to
                Giraudoux.) 1966.

507   Van Tieghem, Philippe. *Les Grandes Doctrines littéraires
         en France de la Pléiade au surréalisme.* 8e éd.
         P.: PUF, 1968.

a. POETRY

1. Poetry in Verse

508   Béguin, Albert. *Poésie de la présence, de Chrétien de
         Troyes à Pierre Emmanuel.* Neuchâtel: La Baconnière,
         1957.

509   Citron, Pierre. *La Poésie de Paris dans la littérature
         française de Rousseau à Baudelaire.* 2 vols. P.:
         Eds. de Minuit, 1961.

510   Dubruck, Edelgard. *The Theme of Death in French Poetry
         of the Middle Ages and the Renaissance.* P.-The Hague:
         Mouton, 1964.

511   Jasinski, Max. *Histoire du sonnet en France.* Douai, 1903;
         rpt., Genève: Slatkine, 1970.

512   Lebègue, Raymond. *La Poésie française de 1560 à 1630.*
         2 tomes en 1 vol. P.: SEDES, 1951.

513   Lemaître, Henri. *La Poésie depuis Baudelaire.* P.:
         Colin, 1965.

514   Patterson, Warner Forrest. *Three Centuries of French
         Poetic Theory; A Critical History of the Chief Arts
         of Poetry in France (1328-1630).* 2 vols. Ann Arbor:
         U. of Michigan Pr., 1935; rpt., N.Y.: Russell and
         Russell, 1966.

515   Payen, Jean-Charles, et Chauveau, Jean-Pierre. *La Poésie
         des origines à 1715.* P.: Colin, 1968.

516   Richard, Jean-Pierre. *Poésie et profondeur.* P.: Eds.
         du Seuil, 1955, 1976.

517 Sabatier, Robert, éd. *Histoire de la poésie française.*
P.: Michel, 1975-.
I: *La Poésie du Moyen Age.* 1975.
II: *La Poésie du XVIe siècle.* 1975.
III: *La Poésie du XVIIe siècle.* 1975.
IV: *La Poésie du XVIIIe siècle.* 1975.
V: *La Poésie du XIXe siècle* (in preparation).
VI: *La Poésie contemporaine* (in preparation).

2. *Prose Poetry*

518 Bernard, Suzanne. *Le Poème en prose de Baudelaire jusqu'à
nos jours.* P.: Nizet, 1959.

519 Moreau, Pierre. *La Tradition française du poème en prose
avant Baudelaire, suivi de Anti-roman et poème en
prose.* 2e éd. augm. P.: Lettres Modernes Minard,
1969 (1e éd. 1959).

520 Parent, Monique. *Saint-John Perse et quelques devanciers.
Etudes sur le poème en prose.* P.: Klincksieck, 196

b. PROSE

1. *Novel and Short Story*

521 Coulet, Henri. *Le Roman jusqu'à la Révolution.* 2 vols.
P.: Colin; N.Y.: McGraw-Hill, 1967-68.

522 Démoris, René. *Le Roman à la première personne. Du
Classicisme aux Lumières.* P.: Colin, 1975.

523 Doutrepont, Georges. *Les Mises en prose des épopées et
des romans chevaleresques du XIVe au XVIe siècle.*
Bruxelles: Palais des Académies, 1939.

524 Godenne, René. *La Nouvelle française.* P.: PUF, 1974.

525 Merlant, Joachim. *Le Roman personnel, de Rousseau à
Fromentin.* 1e éd. P.: Hachette, 1905; rpt.,
Genève: Slatkine, 1970.

526 Raimond, Michel. *Le Roman depuis la Révolution.* P.:
Colin; N.Y.: McGraw-Hill, 1967.

527 Showalter, English. *The Evolution of the French Novel.*
Princeton: Princeton U. Pr., 1972.

2. *Autobiography*

528 Lejeune, Philippe. *L'Autobiographie en France.* P.:
Colin, 1971.

529 Leleu, Michèle. *Les Journaux intimes.* P.: PUF, 1952.

3. Oratory

30 Rambaud, Louis. *L'Eloquence française. La chaire, le barreau, la tribune.* 2 vols. P.: Vitte, 1948.

31 Senger, Jules. *L'Art oratoire.* 4e éd. P.: PUF, "Que sais-je?" 1967.

c. THEATRE

532 "Bibliographie," in *Revue d'Histoire du Théâtre*, 1948-.

    It was first a small part of each issue; since 1966 a whole number is devoted to it (no. 3 in 1966, no. 4 since).

33 Brereton, Geoffrey. *French Tragic Drama in the Sixteenth and Seventeenth Centuries.* London: Methuen, 1973.

34 Cohen, Gustave. *Etudes d'histoire du théâtre en France au Moyen Age et à la Renaissance.* P.: Gallimard, 1956.

35 Daniel, George Bernard. *The Development of the tragédie nationale in France from 1552-1880.* Chapel Hill: U. of North Carolina Pr., 1964.

36 Forsyth, Elliott. *La Tragédie française de Jodelle à Corneille, 1533-1640; le thème de la vengeance.* P.: Nizet, 1962.

37 Gaiffe, Félix. *Le Rire et la scène française.* P.: Boivin, 1931; rpt., Genève: Slatkine, 1970.

38 Garapon, Robert. *La Fantaisie verbale et le comique dans le théâtre français du Moyen Age à la fin du XVIIe siècle.* P.: Colin, 1957.

39 Girdlestone, Cuthbert. *La Tragédie en musique, considérée comme genre littéraire (1673-1750).* Genève: Droz, 1972.

40 Knowles, Dorothy. *La Réaction idéaliste au théâtre depuis 1890.* P.: Droz, 1934; rpt., Genève: Slatkine, 1974.

41 Lebègue, Raymond. *Le Théâtre comique en France de Pathelin à Mélite.* P.: Hatier, 1972.

42 Lewicka, Halina. *Bibliographie du théâtre profane français des XVe et XVIe siècles.* Neuilly: Institut de Recherche et d'histoire des textes, 1972.

43 _____. *La Langue et le style du théâtre comique français des XVe et XVIe siècles.* 2 vols. P.: Klincksieck, 1960-68.

I: *Les Dérivations.*
II: *Les Composés.*

544 Lioure, Michel. *Le Drame de Diderot à Ionesco.* P.:
Colin, 1973 (rev. version of *Le Drame en France,* 1963)

545 Marsan, Jules. *La Pastorale dramatique en France à la fin
du XVIe et au commencement du XVIIe siècle.* P.:
Hachette, 1905 . (Thèse.)

546 Morel, Jacques. *La Tragédie.* P.: Colin, 1964. 3e éd.
rev. 1968.

547 Petit de Julleville, Louis. *Le Théâtre en France, histoire
de la littérature dramatique,depuis ses origines
jusqu'à nos jours.* 1e éd. P.: Colin, 1889;
2e éd. 1894; rpt., 1923; nouv. éd. 1927.

548 Ribaric, Maria Demers. *Le Valet et la soubrette: de
Molière à la Révolution.* P.: Nizet, 1970.

549 Sakharoff, Micheline. *Le héros, sa liberté et son effica-
cité, de Garnier à Rotrou.* P.: Nizet, 1967.

550 Voltz, Pierre. *La Comédie.* P.: Colin, 1964.

551 Wiley, William Leon. *The Early Public Theatre in France
(1580-1630).* Cambridge, Mass.: Harvard U. Pr.,
1960.

II. TYPES, THEMES AND MYTHS

See above: POETRY and THEATRE.

552 Albouy, Pierre. *Mythes et mythologies dans la littérature
française.* P.: Colin, 1969.

553 Bouty, Michel. *Dictionnaire des oeuvres et des thèmes de
la littérature française.* P.: Hachette, 1972.

554 Calvet, Jean. *L'Enfant dans la littérature française.*
2 vols. P.: Lanore, 1931.
I: *Des origines à 1870.*
II: *De 1870 à nos jours.*

555 Chinard, Gilbert. *L'Amérique et le rêve exotique dans la
littérature française au XVIIe et au XVIIIe siècles.*
1e éd. P.: Hachette, 1913; rpt., Genève: Slatkine,
1970.

556 Cruchet, René. *La Médecine et les médecins dans la littérature française.* Baton Rouge: Louisiana State U.
Pr., 1939.

557 Dédéyan, Charles. *Le Nouveau Mal du siècle, de Baudelaire à nos jours.* 2 vols. P.: CDU-SEDES, 1968-72.

558 Derche, Roland. *Quatre Mythes poétiques. Oedipe, Narcisse, Psyché, Lorelei.* P.: SEDES, 1962.

559 Doutrepont, Georges. *Les Types populaires dans la littérature française.* 2 vols. Bruxelles: Lamertin, 1926-28.

560 Jourda, Pierre. *L'Exotisme dans la littérature française depuis Chateaubriand. I: Le Romantisme.* P.: Boivin, 1938. *II: Du romantisme à 1939.* P.: PUF, 1956.

561 Marquiset, Jean. *Les Gens de justice dans la littérature française.* P.: Librairie gén. de droit et de jurispr., 1967.

562 Martino, Pierre. *L'Orient dans la littérature française au XVIIe et au XVIIIe siècles.* 2e éd. P.: Droz, 1934.

563 Milner, Max. *Le Diable dans la littérature française de Cazotte à Baudelaire. 1772-1861.* (Thèse.) 2 vols. P.: J. Corti, 1960.

564 Mortier, Roland. *La Poétique des ruines en France. Ses origines, ses variations de la Renaissance à Victor Hugo.* Genève: Droz, 1974.

565 Newton, Winifred. *Le Thème de Phèdre et d'Hippolyte dans la littérature française.* P.: Droz, 1939.

566 Paribatra, Marsi, princesse. *Le Romantisme contemporain. Essai sur l'inquiétude et l'évasion dans les lettres françaises de 1850 à 1950.* P.: Les Eds. Polyglottes, 1954.

567 Turbet-Delof, Guy. *L'Afrique barbaresque dans la littérature française aux 16e et 17e siècles.* Genève: Droz, 1973.

568 Vovard, André. *Les Turqueries dans la litterature française. Le cycle barbaresque.* Toulouse: Privat, 1959.

569 Weinstein, Leo. *The Metamorphoses of Don Juan. . . Catalogue of Don Juan Versions. . .III. France and Versions in French. . . .* Stanford, Calif.: Stanford U. Pr., 1959.

III. CRITICISM

570 Allemand, André. *Nouvelle Critique, nouvelle perspective.* Neuchâtel: La Baconnière, 1967.

571   Doubrovsky, Serge. *Pourquoi la nouvelle critique.*
      Critique et objectivité. 1e éd. P.: Mercure de
      France, 1966; nouv. éd. P.: Denoël-Gonthier, 1972.

      _____ . *The New Criticism in France.* Tr. by Derek
      Coltman. Chicago: U. of Chicago Pr., 1973.

572   Fayolle, Roger. *La Critique littéraire.* 1e éd. P.:
      Colin, 1964.

573   Jones, Robert Emmet. *Panorama de la nouvelle critique en*
      France de Gaston Bachelard à Jean-Paul Weber. P.:
      SEDES, 1968.

          On Bachelard, Poulet, Richard, Sartre, Starobinski
      Mauron, Goldmann, Barthes, J.-P. Weber. Bibliography.

574   LeSage, Laurent, et Yon, André. *Dictionnaire des critique*
      littéraires: guide de la critique française du XXe
      siècle. University Park: Pennsylvania State U. Pr.,
      1969.

          Gathers information on 119 French critics. Sub-
      stantial Introduction and Bibliography.

575   Moreau, Pierre. *La Critique littéraire en France.* P.:
      Colin, 1960.

576   Rousset, Jean. *Forme et signification. Essai sur les*
      structures littéraires de Corneille à Claudel.
      1e éd. P.: J. Corti, 1962; rpt., 1969.

577   Sartre, Jean-Paul. *Qu'est-ce que la littérature?* 1e éd.
      P.: Gallimard, 1948; rpt., Gallimard, "Idées,"
      1957.

578   Starobinski, Jean. *L'Oeil écoute.* P.: Gallimard, 1961.

579   Wellek, René, and Warren, Austin. *Theory of Literature.*
      1st ed. N.Y.: Harcourt, Brace and World, 1949;
      3rd rev. ed. London: Cape, 1966.

      Has been translated in many languages.

IV. HISTORY AND CIVILIZATION

580   *Nouvelle Histoire de France.* Pub. sous la dir. de Julien
      Cain. 37 vols. et un index général. P.: Tallandier
      1965-1968.

          French history from Celtic time to 1958, in
      chronological order.

581   Duby, Georges, sous la dir. de. *Histoire de la France.*

3 vols. P.: Larousse, 1970-72.
  I: *Naissance d'une nation des origines à 1348.*
  II: *Dynasties et révolutions de 1348 à 1852.*
  III: *Les Temps nouveaux de 1852 à nos jours.*

Undertaken by a team of young university professors, who aim at giving a new explanation of French history, through history of the French nation. Intelligent survey.

582 Duby, Georges, et Mandrou, Robert. *Histoire de la civilisation française.* 5e éd. 2 vols. P.: Colin, 1972.

583 Gaxotte, Pierre. *Histoire des Français.* P.: Flammarion, 1957. Ills.

584 Lenoble, Robert. *Esquisse d'une histoire de l'idée de nature.* Textes réunis et présentés par le Père Joseph Beaude, Oratorien. P.: A. Michel, 1968.

585 Sée, Henri. *Histoire économique de la France.* 2 vols. P.: Colin, 1948-51.

V. PHILOSOPHY

586 Daval, Roger. *Histoire des idées en France.* P.: PUF, "Que sais-je?" 1953.

587 *Histoire de la philosophie,* sous la dir. de Brice Parain et Yvon Belaval (in *Encyclopédie de la Pléiade*). 3 vols. P.: Gallimard, 1969-74.

  I: *Orient, Antiquité, Moyen Age.* 1969.
  II: *De la Renaissance à la révolution kantienne.* 1973.
  III: *Du XIXe siècle à nos jours.* 1974.

588 Robinet, André. *La Philosophie française.* 2e éd. P.: PUF, "Que sais-je?" 1969.

589 Wahl, Jean-André. *Tableau de la philosophie française.* 1e éd. P.: Fontaine, 1946; nouv. éd. mise à jour, Gallimard, 1962.

VI. EDUCATION

590 Léon, Antoine. *Histoire de l'enseignement en France.* P.: PUF, "Que sais-je?" 1967.

591 Prost, Antoine. *Histoire de l'enseignement en France (1800-1967).* P.: Colin, 1968.

D. COMPARATIVE LITERATURE

See Bibliographies (Ch. 2, nos. 36-39), Journals

(no. 187), and *Encyclopédie de la Pléiade* (no. 260).

592 Bies, Jean. *Littérature française et pensée hindoue, des origines à 1950.* P.: Klincksieck, 1974.

593 Clarac, Pierre, éd. *Dictionnaire universel des lettres.* P.: SEDES, 1961.

594 *Dizionario letterario Bompiani delle opere e dei personaggi di tutti i tempi e di tutte le letterature.* 1a ed. 9 vols. Milano: Bompiani, 1947-57; 2a ed. 1960-61. Vols. 1-7: *Opere*; vol. 8: *Personaggi*; vol. 9: *Indici.*

Dizionario letterario Bompiani delle opere. 2 vols. Ibid., 1964-66: *Appendice, Indici.*

The *Dizionario*, 1st ed., has been translated in two parts in French:

Dictionnaire des oeuvres de tous les temps et de tous les pays. Littérature, philosophie, musique, sciences. 5 vols. et 1 index. P.: Laffont-Bompiani, SEDE, 1952-67.

Dictionnaire des personnages littéraires et dramatiques de tous les temps et de tous les pays. Poésie, théâtre, roman, musique. P.: Laffont-Bompiani, SEDE, 1964.

In the French edition one finds not only the translation of the Italian book but a development of the part concerning French literature.

595 *Enciclopedia dello spettacolo.* 9 vols. Roma: Casa editrice Le Maschere, 1954-62. *Aggiornamento 1955-65.* Roma: Unione editoriale, 1966. *Indice, Repertorio.* Roma: Unione editoriale, 1968.

596 Eppelsheimer, Hans Wilhelm. *Handbuch der Weltliteratur von den Anfängen bis zur Gegenwart.* 3., neubearb. und erg. Auflage Frankfurt, a/M.: Klostermann, 1960. (1st ed. 1937.)

Geographical divisions: China, Japan, Indian culture, ancient Orient, Islam, classical antiquity, and the West. These are followed by chronologies, texts, selected bibliographies.

597 Escarpit, Robert. *Dictionnaire international des termes littéraires,* sous la dir. de Robert Escarpit. P.-La Haye: Mouton, 1973. (Sponsored by the Association Internationale de Littérature Comparée.)

598   Guyard, Marius-François. *La Littérature comparée.* P.:
         PUF, "Que sais-je?" 1951.

599   Hargreaves-Mawdsley, W. N. *Everyman's Dictionary of
         European Writers.* London: Dent, 1968.

         More than 2,000 entries for European, non-English
authors from more than twenty countries, tenth century to
date. Bibliographical data include titles and dates of
English translations, and books for further reading.

600   *Histoire générale des littératures.* 3 vols. P.:   Quillet,
         1961.

601   Pichois, Claude, et Rousseau, André-Marie. *La Littérature
         comparée.* P.: Colin, 1967.

602   Sainz de Robles, Federico Carlos. *Ensayo de un diccionario
         de la literatura.* (1a ed. 1949-50.) 3a ed. corr.
         y aumentada, 3 vols. Madrid: Aguilar, 1964-67.

603   Van Tieghem, Paul. *Histoire littéraire de l'Europe et de
         l'Amérique, de la Renaissance à nos jours.* 3e
         éd. P.: Colin, 1951. (1e éd. 1941.)

         French literature and its links with other
literatures.

604   _____, éd. *Répertoire chronologique des littératures
         modernes.* P.: Droz, 1935. (Pub. par la Commission
         internationale d'histoire litt. moderne.)

605   Van Tieghem, Philippe. *Dictionnaire des littératures.*
         Avec la collab. de Pierre Josserand. 3 vols.
         P.: PUF, 1968.

         Considered by the authors to be a new "Vapereau,"
20,000 writers all over the world are listed by alphabetical order.

606   _____. *Influences étrangères sur la littérature
         française, 1550-1880 (Les).* P.: PUF, 1961.

CHAPTER 14

MEDIEVAL LANGUAGE AND LITERATURE
See Ch. 13.

A. WORKS CONCERNING THE ENTIRE MEDIEVAL PERIOD

I. BIBLIOGRAPHIES

See Chs. 2 and 3, especially in Ch. 2 the retrospective bibliography of Cabeen, vol. I, 1952 (no.
13); the current bibliographies of: Klapp, 1960-
(no. 17), *MLA Bibliography*, 1921-(no. 22), Rancoeur,
1953-(no. 26), and *Year's Work in Modern Language
Studies*, 1931-(no. 34).

607 Bossuat, Robert. *Manuel bibliographique de la littérature
     française du Moyen Age*. Melun: Librairie d'Argences,
     1951. *Supplément 1949-53*, avec le concours de Jacques
     Monfrin, 1955. *Second Supplément 1954-60*, 1961.

          Important bibliography of over 8,000 items.
     Includes principal editions, translations, adaptations and
     critical works (books and articles). Index of authors and
     titles.

608 Rouse, Richard H.; Clayton, J. H.; and Metager, M. O.
     Serial Bibliographies for Medieval Studies. Berkeley:
     U. of California Pr., 1969.

          Annotated list of 283 bibliographies useful for
     medieval studies grouped by areas of interest. Includes
     periodicals, annuals, national and regional bibliographies.

a. POETRY

609 Jeanroy, Alfred. *Bibliographie sommaire des chansonniers
     français du Moyen Age (manuscrits et éditions)*.
     P.: Champion, 1918; nouv. tirage P.: Champion, 1974.

          "Appendice" contains additions and corrections to
     G. Raynaud (below).

610 Raynaud, Gaston. *Bibliographie des chansonniers français
     des XIIIe et XIVe siècles, comprenant la description
     de tous les manuscrits, la table des chansons
     classées par ordre alphabétique de rimes et la liste
     des trouvères*. 2 vols. P.: Vieweg, 1884; rpt.,
     N.Y.: Franklin, 1972.

b. PROSE

611 Woledge, Brian. *Bibliographie des romans et nouvelles en prose française antérieurs à 1500.* Genève: Droz, 1954; rpt., 1975. *Supplément.* . . , 1975.

c. THEATRE

612 Henshaw, Millett. "A Survey of Studies in Medieval Drama, 1933-50." *Progress of Medieval and Renaissance Studies in the U.S. and Canada,* 21 (1951), 7-35.

613 Rolland, Joachim. *Essai paléographique et bibliographique sur le théâtre profane en France avant le XVe siècle.* P.: Bibliothèque d'histoire littéraire, 1945.

614 Stratman, Carl Joseph. *Bibliography of Medieval Drama.* Berkeley: U. of California Pr., 1954; 2nd ed. rev. and enl. 2 vols. N.Y.: Ungar, 1972.

II. JOURNALS

See Ch. 6. See Bossuat (no. 607), pp. xix-xxiv. We list hereafter periodicals which deal predominantly with medieval studies (some are no longer published).

Bibliographical Bulletin of the International Arthurian Society/Bulletin Bibliographique de la Société Internationale Arthurienne. Hull: Hull Printers Ltd.
Bibliothèque de l'Ecole des Chartes. Genève: Droz.
Bulletin Bibliographique de la Société Roncesvals. P.: Nizet.
Cahiers de Civilisation Médiévale (Xe-XIIe siècles). Poitiers: Centre d'étude sup. de civ. médiévales.
Medieval Studies. Toronto.
Medievalia et Humanistica. Boulder, Colorado.
Medium Aevum. Oxford: Blackwell.
Moyen Age (Le), Revue d'histoire et de philologie. Bruxelles: La Renaissance du livre.
Nottingham Mediaeval Studies. Nottingham.
Progress of Medieval and Renaissance Studies in the U.S. and Canada. Boulder, Colorado.
Revue de Philologie Française et de Littérature. P.

Romania. P.
Romanische Forschungen. Frankfurt a/M.: Klostermann.
Scriptorum. Revue Internationale des Etudes Relatives aux Manuscrits. Anvers/Bruxelles.
Speculum. A Journal of Mediaeval Studies. The Mediaeval Academy of America. Cambridge, Mass.
Zeitschrift für Romanische Philologie. Tübingen: Max Niemeyer Verlag.

III. DICTIONARIES OF OLD FRENCH

See also our Ch. 8 for etymological dictionaries.

615   Godefroy, Frédéric Eugène. *Dictionnaire de l'ancienne
      langue française et de tous les dialectes du IXe au
      XVe siècle.* 10 vols. P.: Vieweg, 1881-1902;
      rpt., N.Y.: Kraus, 1961.

616   Grandsaignes d'Hauterive, Robert. *Dictionnaire d'ancien
      français. Moyen Age et Renaissance.* P.: Larousse,
      1947.

617   Greimas, Algirdas Julien. *Dictionnaire de l'ancien français
      jusqu'au milieu du XIVe siècle.* P.: Larousse, 1968.

618   Tobler, Adolf, und Lommatzsch, Erhard. *Tobler-Lommatzsch,
      Altfranzösisches Wörterbuch.* Wiesbaden: Steiner,
      1925- (in progress; 9 vols. in 1974, to "top").

IV. STUDIES ON OLD FRENCH

See Ch. 11, II: "Histories of the French Language," and III: "Historical Grammars."

a. GENERALITIES

619   Raynaud de Lage, Guy. *Introduction à l'ancien français.*
      9e éd. P.: CDU-SEDES, 1975.

620   Rohlfs, Gerhard. *From Vulgar Latin to Old French. An
      Introduction to the Study of the Old French Lan-
      guage.* Tr. from the German by Vincent Almazan and
      Lillian McCarthy. Detroit: Wayne State U. Pr.,
      1970.

621   Wagner, Robert-Léon. *L'Ancien français. Points de vue.
      Programmes.* P.: Larousse, 1974.

b. GRAMMARS

622   Anglade, Joseph. *Grammaire élémentaire de l'ancien fran-
      çais.* Nouv. éd. P.: Colin, 1968.

623   Faral, Edmond. *Petite Grammaire de l'ancien français.*
      (XIIe-XIIIe siècles.) P.: Hachette, 1941; rpt.,
      1968.

624   Moignet, Gérard. *Grammaire de l'ancien français.* P.:
      Klincksieck, 1973; 2e éd. rev., 1976: *De l'ancien fra*

c. SYNTAX

625   Foulet, Lucien. *Petite Syntaxe de l'ancien français.*

3e éd. rev.   P.:   Champion, 1958.   (Reprinted
regularly.)

d.   PHONETICS AND VOCABULARY

526   La Chaussée, François de.   *Initiation à la phonétique
historique de l'ancien français*.   P.:   Klincksieck,
1974.

527   Burgess, Glyn Sheridan.   *Contribution à l'étude du vocabulaire précourtois*.   Genève: Droz, 1970.

V.   HISTORY, CIVILIZATION, PHILOSOPHY

528   Duby, Georges.   *Hommes et structures du Moyen Age,
recueil d'articles*.   P.-La Haye: Mouton, 1973.

629   Lemarignier, Jean-François.   *La France médiévale*.   P.:
Colin, 1970.

630   Vignaux, Paul.   *La Philosophie au Moyen Age*.   P.:   Colin,
1958.

B.   MEDIEVAL LITERATURE

I.   MEDIEVAL LITERATURE IN GENERAL

a.   CHRONOLOGY

631   Lévy, Raphaël.   *Chronologie approximative de la littérature
française du Moyen Age*.   Tübingen: Niemeyer, 1957.

b.   LITERARY HISTORIES

632   Bossuat, Robert.   *Le Moyen Age*.   (*Histoire de la littérature
française*, éd. par J. Calvet, vol. I.)   P.:   Gigord,
1931; nouv. éd.   P.:   del Duca, 1955.

633   Demats, Paule.   *Fabula.   Trois Etudes de mythographie
antique et médiévale*.   Genève: Droz, 1973.

634   *Dictionnaire des lettres françaises.   (I)   Le Moyen Age*.
P.:   Fayard, 1964.

635   Faral, Edmond.   *Les Jongleurs en France au Moyen Age*.
P.:   Champion, 1910; 2e éd. 1964.

636   Fox, John Howard.   *The Middle Ages*.   (*A Literary History of
France*, ed. by Patrick Charvet, vol. I, Pt. 1.)
London: Benn; N.Y.:   Barnes and Noble, 1974.

637   *Histoire littéraire de la France où l'on traite de
l'origine et du progrès, de la décadence et du ré-
tablissement des sciences parmi les Gaulois et les*

Français. Ouvrage commencé par les Bénédictins de la Congrégation de Saint-Maur. 12 vols., 1733-63. Continué à partir du vol. 13 (1814) par L'Académie des Inscriptions et Belles-Lettres. P.: Imprimerie Nationale (etc.). (40 vols. pub. by 1974.)

638 Kukenheim, Louis, et Roussel, Henri. *Guide de la littérature française du Moyen Age*. Leyde: Universitaire Pers, 1957; 3e éd. 1963.

639 Le Gentil, Pierre. *La Littérature française du Moyen Age*. P.: Colin, 1963; 2e éd. 1966.

640 *Moyen Age (Le)*. (*Littérature française*, éd. par Claude Pichois, vols. 1, 2.) P.: Arthaud, 1970-71.
    Vol. 1: *Des origines à 1300*, par Jean-Charles Payen, 1970.
    Vol. 2: *1300-1480*, par Daniel Poirion, 1971.

641 Owen, Douglas David Roy. *The Vision of Hell: Infernal Journeys in Medieval French Literature*. Edinburg: Scottish Academic Pr., 1970.

642 Pauphilet, Albert. *Le Moyen Age*. P.: Delalain, 1937.

643 Ryding, William W. *Structure in Medieval Narrative*. P.-The Hague: Mouton, 1971.

c. GENERAL ANTHOLOGIES

644 Batany, Jean. *Français médiéval: textes choisis, commentaires linguistiques, commentaires littéraires, chronologie phonétique*. P.: Bordas, 1972.

645 Galliot, Marcel. *Etudes d'ancien français. Moyen Age et XVIe siècle*. P.: Didier, 1967.

646 Groult, Pierre, et Edmond, V. *Anthologie de la littérature française du Moyen Age*. 2 vols. 3e éd. renouv. par Guy Muraille. Gembloux: Duculot, 1964-67.

647 Henry, Albert, éd. *Chrestomathie de la littérature en ancien français. I: Textes, II: Notes, glossaire, table des noms propres*. 2 tomes en un vol. Berne: Francke, 1953; 4e éd. 1967.

648 Wagner, Robert-Léon, éd. *Textes d'étude (ancien et moyen français)*. Lille: Giard, 1949; rpt., Genève: Droz, 1964.

d. ANTHOLOGIES AND STUDIES BY GENRES

See Ch. 13, and above in this Ch.: Bibliographies and Medieval Literature.

1. Poetry and Romances

649 Clédat, Léon. *La Poésie lyrique et satirique en France au Moyen Age*. P.: Lecène, Oudin, 1893.

650 Guiette, Robert. *D'une poésie formelle en France au Moyen Age*. P.: Nizet, 1972.

651 Jeanroy, Alfred. *Les Origines de la poésie lyrique en France au Moyen Age. Etudes de littérature française et comparée, suivies de textes inédits.* 4e éd., avec additions et un appendice bibliographique. P.: Champion, 1965.

652 Jung, Marc-René. *Etudes sur le poème allégorique en France au Moyen Age*. Berne: Francke, 1971.

653 Neff, Théodore Lee. *La Satire des femmes dans la poésie lyrique française du Moyen Age*. P.: Giard et Brière, 1900; rpt., Genève: Slatkine, 1975.

654 Pauphilet, Albert, éd. *Poètes et romanciers du Moyen Age*. P.: Gallimard, "Bibliothèque de la Pléiade," 1951, 1958.

655 Porter, Lambert C. *La Fatrasie et le fatras; essai sur la poésie irrationnelle en France au Moyen Age*. Genève: Droz, 1960.

656 Vinaver, Eugène. *A la recherche d'une poétique médiévale*. P.: Nizet, 1970.

657 Zink, Michel. *La Pastourelle. Poésie et folklore au Moyen Age*. P.: Bordas, 1972.

   2. Narrative Literature: Fables, "Fabliaux," etc.

658 Bastin, Julia, éd. *Recueil général des Isopets*. 2 vols. P.: Champion, 1929-30.

659 Bédier, Joseph. *Les Fabliaux. Etudes de littérature populaire et d'histoire littéraire du Moyen Age*. 6e éd. P.: Champion, 1969.

660 Johnston, Ronald Carlyle, and Owens, D. D. R., eds. *Fabliaux*. Oxford: Blackwell, 1957.

661 Méon, Dominique Martin, éd. *Nouveau Recueil de fabliaux et contes inédits, des poètes français des XIIe, XIIIe, XIVe et XVe siècles*. 2 vols. P.: Chasseriau, 1823; rpt., Genève: Slatkine, 1976.

662 Montaiglon, Anatole de Courde, éd. *Recueil général et complet des fabliaux des XIIIe et XIVe siècles*. 6 vols. P.: Librairie des bibliophiles, 1872-90.

663 Nykrog, Per. *Les Fabliaux*. Copenhague: Munksgaard, 1957; nouv. éd. Genève: Droz, 1973.

664 Rychner, Jean. *Contributions à l'étude des fabliaux: variantes, remaniements, dégradations*. 2 vols. Genève: Droz, 1960, 1974.

        With the texts of seventeen fabliaux.

665 Walters-Gehrig, Martha, éd. *Trois Fabliaux: Saint Pierre et le jongleur, De Haimet et de Barat et Travers, Estula*. Tübingen: Niemeyer, 1961.

3. Chronicles

666 Archambault, Paul. *Seven French Chroniclers: Witnesses to History*. Syracuse, N.Y.: Syracuse U. Pr., 1974.

667 Pauphilet, Albert, éd. *Historiens et chroniqueurs du Moyen Age: Robert de Clari, Villehardouin, Joinville Froissart, Commynes*. P.: Gallimard, "Bibliothèque de la Pléiade," 1952. Nouv. éd. 1963.

4. Théâtre

668 Aebischer, Paul. *Neuf Etudes sur le théâtre médiéval*. Genève: Droz, 1972.

669 Chevallier, Claude Alain. *Théâtre comique du Moyen Age*. P.: Union Générale d'Editions, 1973.

670 Cohen, Gustave. *Anthologie du drame liturgique en France au Moyen Age. Textes originaux accompagnés de traductions*. P.: Cerf, 1955.

671   . *Le Théâtre en France au Moyen Age*. 2 vols. P.: Rieder, 1929-31; nouv. éd. P.: PUF, 1948. I: *Le Théâtre religieux*, 1929. II: *Le Théâtre profane*, 1931. Ills.

672 Frank, Grace. *The Medieval French Drama*. N.Y.: Oxford U. Pr., 1954.

673 Frappier, Jean. *Le Théâtre profane en France au Moyen Age, XIIIe et XIVe siècles*. P.: CDU-SEDES, 1960.

674 Jeanroy, Alfred. *Le Théâtre religieux en langue française jusqu'à la fin du XIVe siècle*. P.: Imp. Nat., 1959.

675 Lewicka, Halina. *Etudes sur l'ancienne farce française*. P.: Klincksieck, 1974.

676 Pauphilet, Albert, éd. *Jeux et sapience du Moyen Age.*
P.: Gallimard, "Bibliothèque de la Pléiade," 1941,
1960.

677 Rolland, Joachim. *Le Théâtre comique en France avant le
XVe siècle; essai bibliographique.* P.: Eds. de
La Revue des Etudes littéraires, 1926.

II. MEDIEVAL LITERATURE UP TO THE END OF
THE THIRTEENTH CENTURY

a. REPERTORY AND STUDIES

678 Moore, John Clare. *Love in Twelfth Century France.*
Philadelphia: U. of Pennsylvania Pr., 1972.

679 Payen, Jean-Charles. *Le Motif du repentir dans la littérature française médiévale (des origines à 1230).*
Genève: Droz, 1968.

680 Woledge, Brian, et Clive, H. P. *Répertoire des plus anciens
textes en prose française depuis 842 jusqu'aux pre-
mières années du XIIIe siècle.* Genève: Droz, 1964.

b. FIRST TEXTS, BIBLICAL AND HAGIOGRAPHIC LITERATURE

681 Bowen, Willis Hubert. "Present Status of Studies in
Saints' Lives in Old French Verse." *Symposium,* I,
no. 2 (May 1947), 82-86.

682 Meyer, Paul. "Légendes hagiographiques en français,"
in *Histoire Littéraire de la France,* 33 (1906),
328-458.

683 Tintignac, Claude. *Le Thème du renoncement dans "La Vie
de Saint Alexis" et sa permanence dans les lettres
françaises.* P.: Nizet, 1973.

684 Zaal, Johannes W. B. *"A lei francesca" (Sainte Foy,
v. 20): étude sur les chansons de saints gallo-
romanes du XIe siècle.* Leiden: Brill, 1962.

c. EPIC LITERATURE (*LES CHANSONS DE GESTE*)

1. *Bibliographies, General Studies, Anthologies*

See *Bulletin Bibliographique de la Société
Roncesvals.*

Bibliographies

685 Gautier, Léon. *Bibliographie des chansons de geste.
(Complément des Epopées françaises.)* P.: Welter,
1897; rpt., Osnabrück: Zeller, 1966.

General Studies and Anthologies

686 Aebischer, Paul. *Des Annales carolingiennes à Doon de Mayence.* Genève: Droz, 1975.

687 Bédier, Joseph. *Les Légendes épiques. Recherches sur la formation des chansons de geste.* 4 vols. P.: Champion, 1908-13; 3e éd. 4 vols. 1926-66.

688 Jonin, Pierre. *Pages épiques du Moyen Age français, textes, traductions nouvelles, documents. Le Cycle du roi.* 2 vols. P.: CDU-SEDES, 1963, 1970-72.

689 Riquer, Martin de, éd. *Les Chansons de geste françaises.* 2e éd. P.: Nizet, 1957.

690 Siciliano, Italo. *Les Chansons de geste et l'épopée. Mythes. Histoire. Poèmes.* Torino: Società Editrice Internazionale, 1968.

2. *The Cycle of Charlemagne ("La Geste du Roi")*

691 Aebischer, Paul. *Rolandiana et Oliveriana. Recueil d'études sur les Chansons de geste.* Genève: Droz, 1967.

692 Mandach, André de. *Naissance et développement de la chanson de geste en Europe.* 3 vols. Genève: Droz, 1961-75. I: *La Geste de Charlemagne et de Roland.* II: *La Chronique de Turpin.* III: *La Chanson d'Aspremont.*

3. *The Cycle of Garin de Monglane (Central Figure: Guillaume d'Orange)*

693 Frappier, Jean. *Les Chansons de geste du cycle de Guillaume d'Orange.* 2 vols. P.: CDU-SEDES, 1955-67.

4. *The Cycle of Doon de Mayence*

694 Calin, William C. *The Old French Epic of Revolt: Raoul de Cambrai, Renaud de Montauban, Gormond et Isembard* Genève: Droz, 1962.

d. THE ANTIQUITY ROMANCES

695 Cormier, Raymond J. *One Heart One Mind. The Rebirth of Virgil's Hero in Medieval French Romance.* Universit Miss.: Romance Monographs, Inc., 1973.

696 Jones, Rosemarie. *The Theme of Love in the Romans d'Antiquité.* London: Modern Humanities Research Assn., 1972.

e. COURTLY LITERATURE, ARTHURIAN ROMANCES,
   NARRATIVE *LAIS*

See *Bibliographical Bulletin of the International Arthurian Society.*

97 Barteau, Françoise. *Les Romans de Tristan et Iseut: Introduction à une lecture plurielle.* P.: Larousse, 1972.

98 Bezzola, Reto Roberto. *Les Origines et la formation de la littérature courtoise en Occident (500-1200).* 3 parties en 4 vols. P.: Champion, 1944-63; rpt., 3 parties en 5 vols. 1966-68.

I. *La Tradition impériale, de la fin de l'antiquité au XIe siècle,* 1968. II. *La Société féodale et la transformation de la littérature de cour,* 1966. III. *La Société courtoise: littérature de cour et littérature courtoise,* 1967.

99 Brault, Gérard J. *Early Blazon: Heraldic Terminology in the Twelfth and Thirteenth Centuries with Special Reference to Arthurian Literature.* Oxford: Clarendon Pr., 1972.

00 Cohen, Gustave. *Le Roman courtois au XIIe siècle; les origines du roman; les lais de Marie de France.* P.: CDU, 1949.

01 Curtis, Renée L. *Tristan Studies.* Munich: Fink, 1969.

02 Donovan, Mortimer J. *The Breton Lay: A Guide to Varieties.* Notre Dame, Indiana: U. of Notre Dame Pr., 1969.

03 Frappier, Jean. *Amour courtois et Table Ronde.* Genève: Droz, 1973.

04 _____. *Chrétien de Troyes et le mythe du Graal. Etude sur "Perceval ou le conte du Graal."* P.: CDU-SEDES, 1972.

05 _____. *Le Roman Breton.* (4 vols. in 1.) P.: CDU-SEDES, 1952-58; rpt., 1966.

06 Lazar, Moshé. *Amour courtois et "Fin Amors" dans la littérature du XIIe siècle.* P.: Klincksieck, 1964.

07 Luttrell, Claude. *The Creation of the First Arthurian Romance: A Quest.* Evanston: Northwestern U. Pr., 1974.

08 Martin, June Hall. *Love's Fools: Aucassin, Troilus, Calisto, and the Parody of the Courtly Lover.* London: Tamesis, 1972.

709 Marx, Jean. *La Légende arthurienne et le Graal.* P.:
     PUF, 1952.

710 _____. *Nouvelles Recherches sur la littérature arthuri*
     ne. P.: Klincksieck, 1965.

711 Ménard, Philippe. *Le Rire et le sourire dans le roman*
     courtois en France au Moyen Age (1150-1250).
     Genève: Droz, 1969.

712 Payen, M. *Les Origines de la courtoisie dans la litté-*
     rature française médiévale. 2 vols. P.: CDU-SEDES,
     1967-68.

713 Pelan, Margaret. *L'Influence du Brut de Wace sur les*
     romanciers français de son temps. P.: Droz, 1931;
     rpt., Genève: Slatkine, 1974.

714 Roulleau, Gabriel. *Etude chronologique de quelques thèmes*
     narratifs des romans courtois. Avant-propos de
     Jean Frappier. P.: Champion, 1966.

715 Stevens, John E. *Medieval Romance. Themes and Approaches*
     London: Hutchinson, 1973.

716 Vinaver, Eugène. *The Rise of Romance.* Oxford: Claren-
     don, 1971.

     f. POETRY: LYRIC, SATIRICAL, ETC.

717 Boogaard, Nico H. J. van den, comp. *Rondeaux et refrains*
     du XIIe siècle au début du XIVe. Collationnement,
     intr. et notes de Nico H. J. van den Boogaard. P.:
     Klincksieck, 1969.

718 Fauchet, Claude. *Recueil de l'origine de la langue et*
     poésie françoise: Ryme et romans plus les noms et
     sommaire des oeuvres de CXXVII poètes françois,
     vivants avant l'an MCCC. P.: Patisson, 1581;
     Genève: Slatkine, 1972.

719 Frappier, Jean. *La Poésie lyrique française aux XIIe*
     et XIIIe siècles. P.: CDU-SEDES, 1949; rpt., 1963

720 Jeanroy, Alfred, et Långfors, A., éds. *Chansons satirique*
     et bachiques du 13e siècle. P.: Champion, 1921.

721 Klein, Karen Wilk. *The Partisan Voice: A Study of the*
     Political Lyric in France and Germany, 1180-1230.
     P.-The Hague: Mouton, 1971.

722 Rivière, Jean-Claude, éd. *Pastourelles des XIIe et XIIIe*
     siècles. Ed. crit. par J.-C. Rivière. 3 vols. Genève
     Droz. I: 1974-76.

162

723 Uitti, Karl D. *Story, Myth and Celebration in Old French
Narrative Poetry, 1050-1200*. Princeton: Princeton
U. Pr., 1973.

724 Zumthor, Paul. *Langue et techniques poétiques à l'époque
romane (XIe-XIIIe siècles)*. P.: Klincksieck, 1963.

g. *ROMAN DE RENART*

725 Flinn, John. *Le Roman de Renart dans la littérature
française et dans les littératures étrangères au
Moyen Age*. P.: PUF, 1963.

h. DIDACTIC LITERATURE: *LE ROMAN DE LA ROSE*, ETC.

726 Fleming, John V. *The Roman de la Rose: A Study in Alle-
gory and Iconography*. Princeton: Princeton U. Pr.,
1969.

727 Hentsch, Alice-Adèle. *De la littérature didactique du
Moyen Age s'adressant spécialement aux femmes*.
Cahors: Coueslant, 1903; rpt., Genève: Slatkine,
1975.

728 Lecoy de La Marche, Albert. *La Chaire française au Moyen
Age spécialement au 13e siècle, d'après les manuscrits
contemporains*. 2e éd. P.: Renouard, 1886; rpt.,
Genève: Slatkine, 1974.

729 Louis, René. *Le Roman de la Rose. Essai d'interprétation
de l'allégorisme érotique*. P.: Champion, 1974.

730 Welter, J.-Th. *L'Exemplum dans la littérature religieuse
et didactique du Moyen Age. La Tabula exemplorum
secondum ordinem alphabeti*. Recueil d'exempla com-
pilé en France à la fin du XIIIe siècle. 2 vols.
P.: Occitania, 1927; rpt., 2 vols. Genève: Slatkine,
1973.

i. CHRONICLES

731 Dufournet, Jean. *Les Ecrivains de la IVe Croisade:
Villehardouin et Clari*. 2 vols. P.: CDU-SEDES,
1973.

732 Paris, Gaston. "Joinville," in *Histoire littéraire de la
France*, XXXII (1898), 291-459. (See no. 637.)

j. THE EARLY DRAMA: *JEU, MIRACLE*

733 Marichal, Robert, éd. *Le Théâtre en France au Moyen Age;
textes choisis*. 2 vols. P.: CDU-SEDES, 1958-61.

Vol. I: *Drames liturgiques et théâtre religieux*

du XIIe et du XIIIe siècles.
Vol. II: *Le Théâtre comique au XIIIe siècle.*

III.   THE FOURTEENTH AND FIFTEENTH CENTURIES:
THE MIDDLE FRENCH PERIOD

See also those works in Pt. A which pertain to
this period.

a.   GENERAL WORKS

734   Coville, Alfred. *Recherches sur quelques écrivains du
XIVe et du XVe siècles.* P.:   Droz, 1935.

735   Des Garets, Marie-Louise de Garnier. *Un artisan de la
Renaissance française au XVe siècle, le roi René,
1409-1480.* P.:   La Table Ronde, 1946.

736   Huizinga, Johan. *L'Automne du Moyen Age.* Tr. du hollandais
par J. Bastin. P.:   Payot, 1975. (Ed. previously
under title *Le Déclin du Moyen Age*, 1961.)

737   Lagarde, Georges de. *La Naissance de l'esprit laïque au
déclin du Moyen Age.* Nouv. éd. 5 vols. Louvain:
Nauwelaerts, 1956-70.

738   Schmidt, Albert-Marie. *Les XIVe et XVe siècles français,
les sources de l'humanisme.* P.:   Seghers, 1964.

739   Soleil, Félix. *Les Heures gothiques et la littérature
pieuse aux XVe et XVIe siècles.* Rouen: Augé,
1882; rpt., Genève: Slatkine, 1965.

740   Utley, Francis Lee, ed. *The Forward Movement of the Fourteenth Century.* Columbus: Ohio State U. Pr., 1961.

b.   POETRY

741   Champion, Pierre. *Histoire poétique du quinzième siècle.*
2 vols. P.:   Champion, 1923. Nouveau tirage 1966.

742   Chatelain, Henri-Louis. *Recherches sur les vers français
au XVe siècle; rimes, mètres et strophes.* P.:
Champion, 1908; rpt., Genève: Slatkine, 1974.

743   Poirion, Daniel. *Le Poète et le prince. L'Evolution du
lyrisme courtois de Guillaume de Machaut à Charles
d'Orléans.* P.:   PUF, 1965.

744   Seaton, Ethel. *Studies in Villon, Vaillant and Charles
d'Orléans.* Oxford: Blackwell, 1957.

c.   ROMANCES AND TALES

Anthologies

45 Cholakian, Patricia Frances, and Rouben, Charles, eds. and
       trs. *The Early French Novella: An Anthology of
       Fifteenth and Sixteenth Century Tales.* Albany: SUNY
       Pr., 1972.

46 Dubuis, Roger. *Les Cent Nouvelles Nouvelles, et la tradi-
       tion de la nouvelle en France au Moyen Age.* Gre-
       noble: Pr. Universitaires de Grenoble, 1973.

47 Ferrier, Janet Mackay. *French Prose Writers of the Four-
       teenth and Fifteenth Centuries.* Oxford: Pergamon,
       1966.

48 Rasmussen, Jens. *La Prose narrative française du XVe
       siècle. Etude esthétique et stylistique.* Copen-
       hague: Munksgaard, 1958.

49 Soederhjelm, Werner. *La Nouvelle française au XVe siècle.*
       P.: Champion, 1910; rpt., Genève: Slatkine, 1973.

                    d. CHRONICLES

50 Dufournet, Jean. *La Destruction des mythes dans les
       "Mémoires" de Philippe de Commynes.* Genève: Droz,
       1966.

                e. DRAMATIC LITERATURE

51 Chassang, Alexis. *Des essais dramatiques imités de
       l'Antiquité au XIVe et au XVe siècle.* P.: Durand,
       1852; rpt., Genève: Slatkine, 1974.

52 Rey-Flaud, Henri. *Le Cercle magique. Essai sur le théâtre
       en rond à la fin du Moyen Age.* P.: Gallimard, 1973.

1. Religious Theatre

Anthologies

           See Ch. 13, nos. 503 and 505.

Studies

53 McKean, Mary Faith. *The Interplay of Realistic and
       Flamboyant Art Elements in the French Mystères.*
       Washington, D.C.: Catholic U. of Am. Pr., 1959;
       rpt., N.Y.: AMS, 1969.

54 Petit de Julleville, Louis. *Histoire du théâtre en
       France au Moyen Age. Les Mystères.* 2 vols. P.:
       Hachette, 1880; rpt., Genève: Slatkine, 1968.

55 Roy, Emile. *Etudes sur le théâtre français du XIVe
       siècle. La Comédie sans titre. . .et les
       miracles de Notre-Dame par personnages.* Dijon:

Damidot, 1902; rpt.,N.Y.: Franklin, 1971; Genève: Slatkine, 1975.

756 _____. *Le Mystère de la Passion en France du XIVe au XVIe siècle*. Etude sur les sources et le classement des mystères de la Passion, accompagnée de textes inédits: La Passion d'Autun, La Passion bourgui-gnonne de Semur, La Passion d'Auvergne, La Passion *Secundum legem debet mori*. 2 vols. Dijon: Damidot 1904; rpt., Genève: Slatkine (in press).

2. *Non Religious Theatre*

Anthologies

757 Balmas, Enea, éd. *Comédies du XVe siècle*. "La Trésorière par J. Grévin; "La Reconnue" par Rémy Belleau; "Les Napolitains" par François d'Ambroise; "La Nouvelle Tragicomique" par Marc Papillon*. P.: Nize 1967.

758 Bossuat, André et Robert. *Deux Moralités inédites composées et représentées en 1427 et 1428 au collège de Navarre*. P.: Lib. d'Argences, 1955.

759 Cohen, Gustave, éd. *Recueil de farces françaises inédites du XVe siècle*. 2 vols. Cambridge, Mass.: Medieval Academy of America, 1949.

760 Droz, Eugénie, et Lewicka, Halina, éds. *Le Recueil Treppe* 2 vols. P.-Genève: Droz, 1935-61.
    I: *Les Sotties*. Ed. E. Droz. P.: Droz, 1935; rpt., Genève: Slatkine, 1974.
    II: *Les Farces*. Eds. E. Droz et H. Lewicka. Genève: Droz

761 Lacroix, Paul, éd. *Recueil de farces, soties et moralités du quinzième siècle* réunies. . .par P. L. Jacob (pseud.). P.: Delahaye, 1859, 1876. Rpt. of 1876 ed., Genève: Slatkine (in press).

762 Picot, Emile. *Recueil général des sotties*. 3 vols. P.: Champion, 1902-12.

Studies

763 Cohen, Gustave. *Le Théâtre comique au XVe siècle*. P.: CDU, 1938; Tournier et Constans, 1940.

CHAPTER 15

SIXTEENTH CENTURY

A. GENERAL WORKS

See Ch. 13.

I. BIBLIOGRAPHIES

See Chs. 2 and 3, especially in Ch. 2 the retrospective
bibliographies of Cabeen, vol. II, 1966 (no. 13), Ciora-
nescu (vol. I), 1959 (no. 14), Lanson 1931 (no. 18), and
Giraud, 1939-70 (no. 19); the current bibliographies of
Klapp, 1960-(no. 17), *MLA Bibliography*, 1921-(no. 22),
Rancoeur, 1953-(no. 26), and *The Year's Work in Modern
Language Studies*, 1931-(no. 34).

764   *Bibliothèque d'Humanisme et Renaissance.* Genève: Droz.

Contains an annual bibliography only for 1956-64
(published in 1958-65). Since 1966, the bibliography has
been published separately in:
*Bibliographie internationale de l'Humanisme et de la
    Renaissance 1965-.* Genève: Droz, 1966-. Yearly.

765   "Literature of the Renaissance. . .a Bibliography."
        Studies in Philology. 1917-. Annual.

First confined to Great Britain, since 1939 covers
also Western Europe Renaissance. The title has varied.

II. JOURNALS

See Ch. 6.

Amis de Rabelais et de la Devinière (Les). Tours.
Bibliothèque d'Humanisme et Renaissance. Genève: Droz,
    1941-. Rpt. years 1941-62, Genève: Slatkine, 1973.
Bulletin de la Société des Amis de Montaigne, later
    Bulletin des Amis de Montaigne. P.: 1913-21,
    1937-. Rpt. Nos. pub. in 1913-64, Genève: Slatkine,
    1970-74.
Etudes Rabelaisiennes. Genève: Droz, 1956-. (Pub. at
    various intervals.)
Humanisme et Renaissance. Genève: Droz, 1934-40. *Table*,
    1956. Became: *Bibliothèque d'Humanisme et Re-
    naissance.*
Revue de la Renaissance. Organe international des Amis du
    XVIe siècle et de la Pléiade. 14 vols. 1901-13.
    Rpt., Genève: Slatkine, 1968.

Revue des Etudes Rabelaisiennes. 10 vols. P.: Champion,
1903-12. *Table* par Clouzot et Martin, 1924. Rpt.,
Genève: Slatkine, 1974. Continued by:
Revue du Seizième Siècle. 19 vols. P.: Champion, 1913-
33. *Table* par Jeanne Marie, Genève: Droz, 1959.
Rpt., Genève: Slatkine, 1974.

III. DICTIONARIES

See Chs. 8 and 14.

766 Cotgrave, Randle. *A Dictionarie of the French and English
Tongues.* 1st ed. London: Islip, 1611; rpt.,
Columbia, S.C.: U. of South Carolina Pr., 1950;
Menston, Yorkshire: Scolar Pr., 1968; Genève:
Slatkine, 1971.

767 Estienne, Robert. *Dictionnaire françois-latin, autrement
dict, les mots françois, avec les manieres d'user
d'iceulx, tournez en latin.* 1e éd. P.: R. Estienne,
1539; 2e éd. corr. et augm. 1549; rpt. (2nd ed.),
Genève: Slatkine, 1972.

768 Huguet, Edmond. *Dictionnaire de la langue française du
seizième siècle.* 7 vols. Vols. I-II, P.: Champion;
vols. III-VII, Didier, 1925-67.

769 Nicot, Jean. *Thresor de la langue francoyse tant ancienne
que moderne, auquel entre autres choses sont les mots
propres de marine, venerie et faulconnerie, cy-devant
ramassez par Aimar de Ranconnet.* Reveu et augmenté er
ceste dernière impression de plus de la moitié par
Jean Nicot. P.: Douceur, 1606, 1621; rpt., P.:
Picard, 1960; Genève: Slatkine, 1971.

IV. STUDIES ON THE LANGUAGE OF THE SIXTEENTH CENTURY

See Chs. 11 and 12.

770 Catach, Nina. *L'Orthographe française à l'époque de la
Renaissance (auteurs, imprimeurs, ateliers d'imprimerie).* Genève: Droz, 1968.

771 Dubois, Claude-Gilbert. *Mythe et langage au XVIe siècle.*
Bordeaux: Ducros, 1970.

772 Gougenheim, Georges. *Grammaire de la langue française du
seizième siècle.* Lyon: I.A.C., 1951; nouv. éd.
refondue, P.: Picard, 1974.

773 Livet, Charles-Louis. *La Grammaire française et les grammairiens du XVIe siècle.* P.: Didier, 1859; rpt.,
Genève: Slatkine, 1967.

4   Lorian, Alexandre. *Tendances stylistiques dans la prose narrative française du XVIe siècle.* P.: Klinck-sieck, 1973.

5   Rickard, Peter. *La Langue française au seizième siècle. Etude suivie de textes.* Cambridge: U. Pr., 1968.

6   Starnes, Dewitt Talmage. *Robert Estienne's Influence on Lexicography.* Austin: U. of Texas Pr., 1963.

V.   HISTORY, CIVILIZATION

See Ch. 13.

7   Babelon, Jean. *La Civilisation française de la Renaissance.* P.: Casterman, 1961.

8   Bennassar, Bartholomé, et Jacquart, Jean. *Le XVIe siècle.* P.: Colin, 1972.

9   Denieul-Cormier, Anne. *La France de la Renaissance, 1488-1559.* Grenoble: Arthaud, 1962.

0   Doucet, Roger. *Les Institutions de la France au XVIe siècle.* 2 vols. P.: Picard, 1948.

1   Ferguson, Wallace Klippert. *The Renaissance in Historical Thought. Five Centuries of Interpretation.* Boston: Houghton-Mifflin, 1948. Tr. in French: *La Renaissance dans la pensée historique.* P.: Payot, 1950.

2   France. Ministère de l'Education Nationale. *Répertoire des ouvrages pédagogiques du XVIe siècle.* (Biblio-thèques de Paris et des départements.) P., 1886; rpt. Nieuwkoop: B. de Graaf, 1962.

3   Gaufrès, Mathieu-Jules. *Claude Baduel et la réforme des études au XVIe siècle.* 1e éd. P.: Hachette, 1880; rpt., Genève: Slatkine, 1969.

4   Haydn, Hiram Collins. *The Counter-Renaissance.* N.Y.: Scribner, 1950.

5   Lévis-Mirepoix, Antoine, duc de. *Les Guerres de religion. 1559-1610.* P.: Fayard, 1950.

6   Mandrou, Robert. *Introduction à la France moderne, 1500-1640. Essai de psychologie historique.* P.: A. Michel, 1961.

VI.   RELIGION

7   Busson, Henri. *La Pensée religieuse française de Charron à Pascal.* P.: Vrin, 1933.

788 Febvre, Lucien. *Au coeur religieux du XVIe siècle*. P.: SEVPEN, 1957. 2e éd. 1968.

789 _____. *Le Problème de l'incroyance au XVIe siècle. La religion de Rabelais*. P.: A. Michel, 1942, 1968.

790 Zeller, Gaston. *La Réforme*. P.: CDU-SEDES, 1973.

VII. PHILOSOPHY

791 Busson, Henri. *Le Rationalisme dans la littérature française de la Renaissance (1533-1601)*. P.: Vrin, 1922; nouv. éd. rev. et augm., 1957.

792 Mesnard, Pierre. *L'Essor de la philosophie politique au XVIe siècle*. 2e éd. P.: Vrin, 1952; 3e éd. 1969.

793 Védrine, Hélène. *Les Philosophies de la Renaissance*. P.: PUF, "Que sais-je?" 1971.

VIII. HUMANISM

794 Bady, René. *Humanisme chrétien dans les lettres françaises: XVIe-XVIIe siècles*. P.: Fayard, 1972.

795 Toffanin, Giuseppe. *History of Humanism*. Eng. tr. by E. Gianturco. N.Y.: Las Americas Pub. Co., 1954.

IX. INFLUENCE OF ANTIQUITY

(See also the rest of this Ch.)

796 Fraisse, Simone. *L'Influence de Lucrèce en France au seizième siècle: Une conquête du rationalisme*. P.: Nizet, 1962.

X. ITALIAN INFLUENCE

797 Festugière, André-Marie-Jean. *La Philosophie de l'amour de Marcile Ficin et son influence sur la littérature française au XVIe siècle*. P.: Vrin, 1941.

798 Gambier, H. *Italie et Renaissance poétique en France*. Padoue: Cedam, 1936.

799 Vianey, Joseph. *Le Pétrarquisme en France au XVIe siècle*. 1e éd. Montpellier: Coulet et fils, 1909; rpt., Genève: Slatkine, 1969.

B. LITERATURE

I. LITERARY HISTORIES AND GENERAL STUDIES

See Ch. 13.

300 Chinard, Gilbert. *L'Exotisme américain dans la littérature française au XVIe siècle, d'après Rabelais, Ronsard, Montaigne.* . . . P.: Hachette, 1911; rpt., Genève: Slatkine, 1970.

301 *Dictionnaire des lettres françaises. (II) Le Seizième siècle.* P.: Fayard, 1951.

302 Jung, Marc-René. *Hercule dans la littérature française du XVIe siècle: de l'Hercule courtois à l'Hercule baroque.* Genève: Droz, 1966.

303 McFarlane, Ian Dalrymple. *Renaissance France, 1470-1589. (A Literary History of France,* ed. by Patrick E. Charvet, vol. 1, pt. 2.) London: Benn; N.Y.: Barnes and Noble, 1974.

304 Ménager, Daniel. *Introduction à la vie littéraire du XVIe siècle.* P.: Bordas, 1968, 1976.

305 Michel, Pierre. *Continuité de la sagesse française: Rabelais, Montaigne, La Fontaine.* P.: CDU-SEDES, 1965.

306 Morçay, Raoul, et Müller, Armand. *La Renaissance. (Histoire de la littérature française,* éd. J. Calvet, vol. II.) 2e éd. rev. par A. Müller. P.: del Duca, 1960.

307 Payen, Jean-Charles. *Les Origines de la Renaissance.* P.: CDU-SEDES, 1969.

308 Plattard, Jean. *La Renaissance des lettres en France, de Louis XII à Henri IV.* P.: Colin, 1967.

309 *Renaissance (La). (Littérature française,* éd. par Claude Pichois, vols. 3, 4, 5.) P.: Arthaud, 1972-74.
      Vol. 1: *1480-1548,* par Yves Giraud et Marc-René Jung, 1972.
      Vol. 2: *1548-1570,* par Enea Balmas, 1974.
      Vol. 3: *1570-1624,* par Jacques Morel, 1973.

310 Saulnier, Verdun-Louis. *La Littérature française de la Renaissance (1500-1610).* 9e éd. P.: PUF, "Que sais-je?" 1969.

311 Schmidt, Albert-Marie. *Etudes sur le XVIe siècle.* P.: A. Michel, 1967.

312 Simone, Franco. *Il rinascimento francese. Studi e ricerche.* Torino: Società Editrice Internazionale, 1961.
      _____. *The French Renaissance. Medieval Tradition and Italian Influence in Shaping the Renaissance in*

France. Tr., abridged and annotated by Gaston Hall.
London: Macmillan, 1969.

813 Stone, Donald, Jr. *France in the Sixteenth Century; a Medieval Society Transformed.* Englewood Cliffs, N.J.: Prentice-Hall, 1969.

II. ANTHOLOGIES AND STUDIES BY GENRES

a. POETRY

Anthologies

814 Cave, Terence C., et Jeanneret, Michel, éds. *Métamorphoses spirituelles. Anthologie de la poésie religieuse française, 1570-1630.* P.: J. Corti, 1972.

815 Defaut, Maurice, et Salomon, Pierre. *Les Poètes du XVIe siècle.* P.: Masson, 1970.

816 Graham, Victor Ernest, ed. *Sixteenth-Century French Poetry.* Toronto: U. of Toronto Pr., 1964.

817 Gray, Floyd Francis. *Anthologie de la poésie française du XVIe siècle.* N.Y.: Appleton-Century-Crofts, 1967

818 Schmidt, Albert-Marie, éd. *Poètes du XVIe siècle.* P.: Gallimard, "Bibliothèque de la Pléiade," 1953.

819 Weinberg, Bernard, ed. *French Poetry of the Renaissance.* N.Y.: Harper, 1954.

820 Wilson, Dudley Butler, ed. *French Renaissance Scientific Poetry.* London: U. of London, The Athlone Pr., 1974.

Studies

821 Cave, Terence C. *Devotional Poetry in France c. 1570-1613.* London: Cambridge U. Pr., 1969.

822 Guy, Henry. *Histoire de la poésie française au XVIe siècle* I: *L'Ecole des Rhétoriqueurs.* II: *Clément Marot et son école.* 2 vols. P.: Champion, 1910-26; rpt., 1968.

823 Hagiwara, Michio P. *French Epic Poetry in the Sixteenth Century. Theory and Practice.* P.-The Hague: Mouton, 1972.

824 Harvey, Lawrence E. *The Aesthetics of the Renaissance Love Sonnet; an Essay on the Art of the Sonnet in the Poetry of Louise Labé.* Genève: Droz, 1962.

825 Holyoake, Sidney John. *An Introduction to French Sixteenth Century Poetic Theory. Texts and Commentary.* N.Y.: Barnes and Noble, 1972.

172

826 Hulubei, Alice. *L'Eglogue en France au XVIe siècle,
époque des Valois (1515-1589)*. P.: Droz, 1938.
(Thèse.)

827 Jeanneret, Michel. *Poésie et tradition biblique au XVIe
siècle. Recherches stylistiques sur les para-
phrases des "Psaumes" de Marot à Malherbe*. P.:
J. Corti, 1969.

828 Joukovsky-Micha, Françoise. *La Gloire dans la poésie
française et néo-latine du XVIe siècle (des Rhétoriqueurs à Agrippa d'Aubigné)*. Genève: Droz, 1969.

829 _____. *Orphée et ses disciples dans la poésie française
et néo-latine du XVIe siècle*. Genève: Droz, 1970.

830 _____. *Poésie et mythologie au XVIe siècle: quelques
mythes de l'inspiration chez les poètes de la
Renaissance*. P.: Nizet, 1969.

831 Merrill, Robert Valentine, and Clements, Robert John.
Platonism in French Renaissance Poetry. N.Y.:
N.Y. U. Pr., 1957.

832 Müller, Armand. *La Poésie religieuse catholique de Marot
à Malherbe*. P.: Foulon, 1950. (Thèse.)

833 Naïs, Hélène. *Les Animaux dans la poésie française de la
Renaissance; science, symbolique, poésie*. P.:
Didier, 1961. (Thèse.)

834 Richter, Mario. *La poesia lirica in Francia nel secolo
XVI*. Milano-Varese: Istituto editoriale cisalpino,
1971.

835 Schmidt, Albert-Marie. *La Poésie scientifique en France
au seizième siècle: Peletier, Ronsard, Scève, Baïf,
Belleau, du Bartas, les cosmologues, les hermé-
tistes. . . .* P.: Michel, 1939; rpt., Lausanne:
Rencontre, 1970.

836 Scollen, Christine M. *The Birth of the Elegy in France,
1500-1550*. Genève: Droz, 1967.

837 Weber, Henri. *La Création poétique au XVIe siècle en
France de Maurice Scève à Agrippa d'Aubigné*. 1e
éd. 2 vols. P.: Nizet, 1956; 2e éd. 1 vol. 1969.

838 Wilson, Dudley Butler. *Descriptive Poetry in France from
Blason to Baroque*. Manchester: Manchester U. Pr.,
1967.

b. PROSE

1. Prose-Writers in General

173

839 Vianey, Joseph, éd. *Les Prosateurs du XVIe siècle.*
     P.: Hatier, 1939.

2. *Novel and Short Story*
Anthologies
840 Jourda, Pierre, éd. *Conteurs français du XVIe siècle.*
     P.: Gallimard, "Bibliothèque de la Pléiade," 1965.

     Short stories by Bonaventure Des Périers, Noël Du
Fail, Marguerite de Navarre, B. Poissenot, J. Yver.

841 Krailsheimer, A. J., ed. *Three Sixteenth-Century Conteurs.*
     London: Oxford U. Pr., 1966.

     Short stories by Bonaventure Des Périers, Noël Du
Fail, Marguerite de Navarre.

Studies
842 De Jongh, William Frederick Jekel. *A Bibliography of the
     Novel and Short Story in French from the Beginning of
     Printing till 1600.* Albuquerque: U. of New Mexico
     Pr., 1944.

843 Reynier, Gustave. *Les Origines du roman réaliste.* P.:
     Hachette, 1912.

844 _____. *Le Roman sentimental avant l'Astrée.* P.: Colin
     1908.

845 Stone, Donald, Jr. *From Tales to Truths. Essays on French
     Fiction in the Sixteenth Century.* Frankfurt a/M.:
     Klostermann, 1973.

3. *Essay*
846 Atkinson, Geoffroy. "La Forme de l'essai avant Montaigne."
     Bibliothèque d'Humanisme et Renaissance, VIII
     (1946), 129-36.

847 Bady, René. *L'Homme et son "Institution" de Montaigne à
     Bérulle.* P.: Les Belles Lettres, 1964.

4. *Historical Writings*
848 Bates, Blanchard Wesley. *Literary Portraiture in the
     Historical Narrative of the French Renaissance.*
     N.Y.: Stechert, 1945. (Diss., Princeton.)

849 Huppert, George. *The Idea of Perfect History. Historical
     Erudition and Historical Philosophy in Renaissance
     France.* Urbana: U. of Illinois Pr., 1970.

     On E. Pasquier, L. Le Roy, N. Vignier, La Pope-
linière.

c. SATIRE

Anthology
850 Fleuret, Fernand, et Perceau, Louis, éds. *Les Satires françaises du XVIe siècle*, recueillies et publiées, avec une préface, des notices et un glossaire. 2 vols. P.: Garnier, 1922.

Studies
851 Lenient, Charles. *La Satire en France ou la littérature militante au XVIe siècle*. P.: Hachette, 1886.

852 Rossettini, Olga Trtnik. *Les Influences anciennes et italiennes sur la satire en France au XVIe siècle*. Firenze: Sansoni, 1958. (Thèse.)

d. THEATRE

Anthology
853 Stone, Donald, Jr., ed. *Four Renaissance Tragedies*. Cambridge, Mass.: Harvard U. Pr., 1966.

Studies
854 Boughner, Daniel Cliness. *The Braggart in Renaissance Comedy: A Study in Comparative Drama from Aristophanes to Shakespeare*. Minneapolis: The U. of Minnesota Pr., 1954.

   Including French comedy from Grévin to Molière.

855 Bowen, Barbara. *Les Caractéristiques essentielles de la farce française et leur survivance dans les années 1550-1620*. Urbana: U. of Illinois Pr., 1964.

856 Feldman, Sylvia D. *The Morality Patterned Comedy of the Renaissance*. P.-The Hague: Mouton, 1971.

857 Jacquot, Jean, éd. *Les Tragédies de Sénèque et le théâtre de la Renaissance*. P.: CNRS, 1964.

858 Jeffery, Brian. *French Renaissance Comedy. 1552-1630*. Oxford: Clarendon Pr., 1969.

859 Lebègue, Raymond. "Tableau de la comédie française de la Renaissance." *Bibliothèque d'Humanisme et Renaissance*, VIII (1946), 278-344.

860 _____. *La Tragédie française de la Renaissance*. 1e éd. Bruxelles: Office de Publicité, 1944; 2e éd. rev. et augm., 1954.

861 _____. *La Tragédie religieuse en France. Les débuts (1514-1573)*. P.: Champion, 1919; rpt., Genève: Slatkine, 1975.

862 Leblanc, Paulette. *Les Ecrits théoriques et critiques*
français des années 1540-1561 sur la tragédie.
P.: Nizet, 1972.

863 Le Hir, Yves. *Les Drames bibliques de 1541 à 1600.*
Etudes de langue, de style, et de versification.
Grenoble: Pr. Universitaires de Grenoble, 1974.

864 Stone, Donald, Jr. *French Humanist Tragedy: A Reassess-*
ment. Manchester: Manchester U. Pr., 1974.

C. ANTHOLOGIES AND STUDIES ON LITERARY MOVEMENTS

See Ch. 13, and Ch. 15, Pts. A and B.

I. WRITERS OF THE FIRST HALF OF THE SIXTEENTH
CENTURY

865 Bowen, Barbara. *The Age of Bluff: Paradox and Ambiguity*
in Rabelais and Montaigne. Urbana: U. of Illinois
Pr., 1972.

866 Trofimoff, André. *Poètes français avant Ronsard (Au*
jardin des Muses françaises). P.: Marin, 1950.

a. *LES RHETORIQUEURS*

See in particular H. Guy (no. 822).

b. THE POETS OF LYONS

Anthologies
867 Aynard, Joseph, éd. *Les Poètes lyonnais précurseurs de*
la Pléiade: Maurice Scève, Louise Labé, Pernette
du Guillet. Intr. et notes. P.: Bossard, 1924.

868 *Maurice Scève et l'Ecole lyonnaise.* Extraits présentés
et commentés par Antoinette Roubichou-Stretz.
P.: Bordas, 1973.

Studies
869 Baur, Albert. *Maurice Scève et la Renaissance lyonnaise.*
Etude d'histoire littéraire. 1906; rpt., Genève:
Slatkine, 1969.

870 Giudici, Enzo. *Louise Labé e l'école lyonnaise. Studi*
e ricerche, con documenti inediti. Napoli: Liguori,
1964.

871 Schmidt, Albert-Marie. "Poètes lyonnais du XVIe siècle."
Information Littéraire, vol. 4, no. 3 (mai-juin
1952), pp. 90-95; vol. 4, no. 4 (sept.-oct. 1952),
pp. 127-131.

II. WRITERS OF THE SECOND HALF OF THE
SIXTEENTH CENTURY

872 Mathieu-Castellani, Gisèle. *Les Thèmes amoureux dans la
poésie française (1570-1600)*. P.: Klincksieck,
1975.

a. THE *PLEIADE*

See Pts. A. and B.

Collective Editions
873 Formont, Maxime, éd. *Choix de poésies par Joachim Du
Bellay, Pontus de Tyard, Rémy Belleau, Jodelle,
J. A. de Baïf*. Notice par Maxime Formont. P.:
Lemerre, 1931.

874 Marty-Laveaux, Charles-Joseph, éd. *La Pléiade française.*
20 vols. P.: Lemerre, 1866-98; rpt., Genève: Slatkine,
1965. (Contains the works of all the *Pléiade* writers,
and an Appendix in 2 vols by the editor: *La Langue de la
Pléiade.)*

Studies
875 Bonnot, Jacques. *Humanisme et Pléiade*, présenté par Jacques
Bonnot. P.: Hachette, 1959, 1974.

876 Cameron, Alice Virginia. *The Influence of Arioste's Epic
and Lyric Poetry on Ronsard and his Group*. Baltimore: Johns Hopkins Pr., 1930.

877 Castor, Grahame. *Pléiade Poetics. A Study in Sixteenth
Century Thought and Terminology*. Cambridge: Cambridge U. Pr., 1964.

878 Chamard, Henri. *Histoire de la Pléiade*. 4 vols. P.:
Didier, 1939-40; nouv. éd. 1963.

879 Clements, Robert John. *Critical Theory and Practice of the
Pléiade*. Cambridge, Mass.: Harvard U. Pr., 1942.

880 Demerson, Guy. *La Mythologie classique dans l'oeuvre
lyrique de la Pléiade*. Genève: Droz, 1972.

881 Roubichou-Stretz, Antoinette. *La Vision de l'histoire dans
l'oeuvre de la Pléiade. Thèmes et structures*.
P.: Nizet, 1973.

882 Silver, Isidore. *Ronsard and the Hellenic Renaissance in
France*. Saint Louis, Missouri: Washington U. Pr.,
1961.

b. THE LITERATURE AND THE RELIGIOUS WARS

883 Charbonnier, F. *La Poésie française et les guerres de religion (1560-1574). Etude historique et littéraire sur la poésie militante depuis la conjuration d'Amboise jusqu'à la mort de Charles IX.* P.: *Revue des Oeuvres Nouvelles,* 1919; rpt., Genève: Slatkine, 197

884 Delumeau, Jean. *La Réforme et la littérature française.* Carrières-sous-Poissy: "La Cause," 1972.

885 Garnier, Armand. *Agrippa d'Aubigné et le parti protestant.* 3 vols. P.: Fischbacher, 1928.

886 Pineaux, Jacques. *La Poésie des protestants de langue française du premier synode national à la proclamation de l'Edit de Nantes, 1559-1598.* P.: Klincksieck, 1971.

C. *MANIERISME* AND *BAROQUE*

As this movement develops mainly in the Seventeenth Century, it will be found in next chapter.

CHAPTER 16

SEVENTEENTH CENTURY

A. GENERAL WORKS

See Ch. 13.

I. BIBLIOGRAPHIES

See Chs. 2 and 3, especially in Ch. 2 the retrospective
bibliographies of Cabeen, vol. III, 1961 (no. 13), Ciora-
nescu (vol. II), 1965-67 (no. 14), Lanson, 1931 (no. 18),
Giraud, 1939-70 (no. 19); the current bibliographies of
Klapp, 1960-(no. 17), *MLA Bibliography*, 1921-(no. 22),
Rancoeur, 1953-(no. 26), and *The Year's Work in Modern
Language Studies*, 1931-(no. 34).

887 Baldner, Ralph Willis. *Bibliography of Seventeenth-Century
        French Prose Fiction*. N.Y. Printed for the Index
        Committee of the MLA by the Columbia U. Pr., 1967.

888 British Museum. Dept. of Printed Books. *Short Title
        Catalogue of French Books, 1601-1700 in the Library
        of the British Museum*, by V. F. Goldsmith. London:
        Dawsons, 1969-73.

889 Lachèvre, Frédéric. *Bibliographie des recueils collectifs
        de poésies publiés de 1597 à 1700*. 4 vols. P.:
        Leclerc, 1901-05; rpt., Genève: Slatkine, 1967.

II. JOURNALS

See Ch. 6.

Amis de Bossuet (Les). Meaux.
Association des amis de Maynard. Bulletin. P.
Baroque. Centre International de synthèse du baroque.
      Montauban.
Cahiers Raciniens. Neuilly-sur-Seine.
Cahiers Saint-Simon. P.
Chroniques de Port-Royal. P.
XVIIe Siècle. P. "Tables décennales de la revue *XVIIe
      Siècle*," in *XVIIe Siècle*, 89 (1970), 59-74.
Jeunesse de Racine. P.

III. DICTIONARIES

See Ch. 8.

See Ch. 15: Cotgrave (no. 766).

890 Cayrou, Gaston. *Le François classique. Lexique de la langue du dix-septième siècle expliquant d'après les dictionnaires du temps et les remarques des grammairiens le sens et l'usage des mots aujourd'hui vieillis ou différemment employés.* 6e éd. rev. et corr. P.: Didier, 1948. (1e éd. 1923.)

891 Dubois, Jean, et Lagane, R. *Dictionnaire de la langue française classique.* Préf. de P. Clarac. P.: E. Belin, 1960.

892 Furetière, Antoine. *Dictionnaire universel contenant généralement tous les mots françois tant vieux que modernes et les termes de toutes les sciences et les arts.* 2 vols. La Haye, Rotterdam: Arnout et Reiner Leers, 1690. (1e éd. *Essai d'un dictionnaire universel. . . .* Amsterdam: Desbordes, 1685.) Rpt. of 1690 ed., Genève: Slatkine, 1970.

893 Huguet, Edmond. *Petit Glossaire des classiques français du dix-septième siècle, contenant les mots et locutions qui ont vieilli ou dont le sens s'est modifié.* 7e éd. P.: Hachette, 1936. (1e éd. 1907.)

894 Richelet, Pierre. *Dictionnaire de la langue française ancienne et moderne.* Nouv. éd. augm. d'un très grand nombre d'articles par l'abbé Claude Pierre Goujet. 3 vols. Lyon: J. M. Bruyset, 1759. (1e éd. Genève: Widerhold, 1680.) Rpt. of 1680 ed., 2 vols. Genève: Slatkine, 1970, with title: *Dictionnaire françois contenant les mots et les choses. . . .*

895 Somaize, Antoine Baudeau, sieur de. *Le Grand Dictionnaire des prétieuses. Historique, poétique, géographique, cosmographique, chronologique et armoirique, où l'on verra leur antiquité, coustumes, devises, éloges, études, guerres, hérésies, jeux, lois, langage, moeurs, mariage. Avec la clef du grand dictionnaire des prétieuses.* P., 1661; nouv. éd. augm. . . . d'une clef historique et anecdotique par Ch.-L. Livet, 2 vols. P.: Jannet, 1856; rpt., Genève: Slatkine, 1972 (1661 ed.).

IV. STUDIES ON THE LANGUAGE OF THE SEVENTEENTH CENTURY

See Chs. 11 and 12.

896 Blégny, Etienne de. *L'Ortografe française.* P., 1667; rpt. Genève: Slatkine, 1972.

897 Boysen, Gerhard. *Précis de syntaxe française du dix-septième siècle.* Odense: Odense U. Pr., 1973.

898   Cornelius, Paul. *Languages in Seventeenth and Early Eighteenth Century Imaginary Voyages.* Geneva: Droz, 1965.

899   Donzé, Roland. *La Grammaire générale et raisonnée de Port-Royal: Contribution à l'histoire des idées grammaticales en France.* Berne: Francke, 1967.

900   Dumonceaux, Pierre. *Langue et sensibilité au XVIIe siècle, l'évolution du vocabulaire affectif.* Genève: Droz, 1975.

901   Haase, A. *Syntaxe française du XVIIe siècle.* Nouv. éd. trad. et remaniée par M. Obert. P.: Delagrave, 1935; rpt., 1965.

V.   HISTORY AND CIVILIZATION

902   Darle, Françoise. *Marly, ou la vie de cour sous Louis XIV.* P.: Fernand Lanore, 1959.

903   Erlanger, Philippe. *Louis XIV.* P.: Fayard, 1965. *Louis XIV.* Tr. by Stephen Cox. N.Y.: Praeger, 1970.

904   Goubert, Pierre. *Louis XIV et vingt millions de Français.* P.: Fayard, 1966. Am. ed. *Louis XIV and Twenty Million Frenchmen.* Tr. by Anne Carter. N.Y.: Pantheon, 1970.

905   Grand-Mesnil, Marie-Noëlle. *Mazarin, la Fronde et la Presse, 1647-1649.* P.: Colin, 1967.

906   Lough, John. *An Introduction to Seventeenth Century France.* London: Longmans, 1954; 6th impression 1964.

907   Maland, David. *Culture and Society in Seventeenth Century France.* N.Y.: Scribner, 1970.

908   Mandrou, Robert. *Louis XIV en son temps.* P.: PUF, 1973.

909   Martin, Henri-Jean. *Livre, pouvoirs et société à Paris au 17e siècle (1598-1701).* 2 vols. Genève: Droz, 1969.

910   Méthivier, Hubert. *Le Siècle de Louis XIV.* 7e éd. mise à jour. P.: PUF, 1972.

911   Ranum, Orest. *Paris in the Age of Absolutism; an essay.* N.Y.: Wiley, 1968.

912   Roger, Jacques. *XVIIe siècle français: Le Grand siècle.* P.: Seghers, 1962.

913 Saint-Germain, Jacques. *Louis XIV secret.* P.: Hachette, 1970.

914 Treasure, Geoffrey Russell Richards. *Cardinal Richelieu and the Development of Absolutism.* London: A. and C. Black, 1972.

VI. RELIGION AND *LIBERTINAGE*

a. RELIGION

915 Adam, Antoine. *Du mysticisme à la révolte. Les Jansénistes du XVIIe siècle.* P.: Fayard, 1968.

916 Ceyssens, Lucien, et Legrand, A. *La Fin de la première période du jansénisme: sources des années 1654-60.* 2 vols. Bruxelles: Institut Historique Belge de Rome, 1963-65.

917 Christoflour, Raymond, éd. *Spirituels et mystiques du Grand Siècle.* P.: Fayard, 1961.

918 Cognet, Louis. *Le Jansénisme.* Nouv. éd. rev. P.: PUF, 1964.

919 Delassault, Geneviève. *La Pensée janséniste en dehors de Pascal.* P.: Buchet-Chastel, 1963.

920 Escholier, Marc. *Port-Royal.* P.: Laffont, 1965.

921 Goldmann, Lucien. *Le Dieu caché. Etude sur la vision tragique dans les Pensées de Pascal et dans le théâtre de Racine.* P.: Gallimard, 1956.

922 Jansen, Paule. *Le Cardinal Mazarin et le mouvement janséniste français, 1653-1659.* P.: Vrin, 1967.

923 Kirkinen, Heikki. *Les Origines de la conception moderne de l'homme machine. Le problème de l'âme en France à la fin du règne de Louis XIV (1670-1715).* Helsinki: Suomalainen Tiedeakatemia, 1960.

924 Marin, Louis. *La Critique du discours. Sur la "logique de Port-Royal" et les "Pensées" de Pascal.* P.: Eds. de Minuit, 1975.

925 Stankiewicz, W. J. *Politics and Religion in Seventeenth Century France: A Study of Political Ideas from the Monarchomachs to Bayle, as Reflected in the Toleration Controversy.* Berkeley: U. of California Pr., 1960.

926 Taveneaux, René. *Jansénisme et politique.* P.: Colin, 1966

927 _____. *La Vie quotidienne des jansénistes aux XVIIe et XVIIIe siècles.* P.: Hachette, 1973.

182

928   Thomas, Jacques-François. *Le Problème moral à Port-Royal.*
       P.: Eds. Latines, 1963.

b. *LIBERTINAGE*

929   Adam, Antoine. *Les Libertins au XVIIe siècle.* P.:
       Buchet-Chastel, 1964.

930   Pintard, René. *Le Libertinage érudit dans la première
       moitié du XVIIe siècle.* 2 vols. P.: Boivin, 1943.

931   Spink, John Stephenson. *French Free-Thought from Gassendi
       to Voltaire.* London: U. of London, Athlone Pr.,
       1960. Tr. into French: *La Libre-pensée française
       de Gassendi à Voltaire.* Traduit par Paul
       Meier. P.: Eds. Sociales, 1966.

B. LITERATURE

I. LITERARY HISTORIES AND GENERAL ANTHOLOGIES

See Ch. 13.

a. LITERARY HISTORIES

932   Adam, Antoine. *Histoire de la littérature française au
       XVIIe siècle.* 5 vols. P.: Domat, 1948-56; del Duca,
       1962.

933   *Age Classique (L').* (*Littérature française*, éd. par Claude
       Pichois vols. 6, 7, 8.) 3 vols. P.: Arthaud,
       1968-71.
       Vol. I: *1624-1660*, par Antoine Adam, 1968.
       Vol. II: *1660-1680*, par Pierre Clarac, 1969.
       Vol. III: *1680-1720*, par René Pomeau, 1971.

934   Calvet,   Jean. *La Littérature religieuse de François
       de Sales à Fénelon.* (*Histoire de la littérature
       française*, éd. J. Calvet, vol. V.) P.: del Duca,
       1956.

935   *Dictionnaire des lettres françaises.* (III) *Le Dix-
       septième siècle.* P.: Fayard, 1954.

936   Gaillard de Champris, Henri. *Les Ecrivains classiques.*
       Mis au point par H. Berthaut et Jean Calvet.
       (*Histoire de la littérature française*, éd. J. Calvet,
       vol. IV.) P.: del Duca, 1960.

937   Sage, Pierre. *Le Préclassicisme*, d'après Raoul Morçay.
       (*Histoire de la littérature française*, éd. J.
       Calvet, vol. III, rev.) P.: del Duca, 1962.

938   Saulnier, Verdun-Louis. *La Littérature française du siècle
       classique.* P.: PUF, "Que sais-je?" 1943; 8e éd. 1970.

939 Yarrow, Philip John. *The Seventeenth Century, 1600-1715.*
     (*A Literary History of France*, ed. by Patrick E.
     Charvet, vol. II.) London: Benn; N.Y.: Barnes and
     Noble, 1967.

b. GENERAL ANTHOLOGIES

940 Eustis, Alvin Allen. *Seventeenth Century French Literature:*
     Poetry, Theater, Novel: a Critical Anthology. N.Y.:
     McGraw-Hill, 1969.

941 Peyre, Henri, and Grant, Elliott M., eds. *Seventeenth*
     Century French Prose and Poetry. Boston: D. C.
     Heath, 1937.

II. GENERAL STUDIES

See Ch. 13.

942 Abraham, Claude Kurt. *Gaston d'Orléans et sa cour: Etude*
     littéraire. Chapel Hill, N.C.: U. of North Caro-
     lina Pr., 1963.

943 Bénichou, Paul. *Morales du Grand Siècle.* P.: Gallimard,
     1948; rpt., 1967.

944 Conlon, Pierre. *Prélude au Siècle des Lumières en France.*
     Répertoire chronologique de 1680 à 1715. 6 vols.
     Genève: Droz, 1970-75.

945 François, Carlo. *La Notion de l'absurde dans la littéra-*
     ture française du XVIIe siècle. P.: Klincksieck,
     1973.

946 Hepp, Noémie. *Homère en France au XVIIe siècle.* P.:
     Klincksieck, 1968.

947 Krailsheimer, Alban J. *Studies in Self-Interest: from*
     Descartes to La Bruyère. London: Oxford U. Pr.,
     1962.

948 Lebois, André. *XVIIe siècle. Recherches et portraits.*
     P.: Denoël, 1966.

949 Litman, Théodore A. *Le Sublime en France (1660-1714).*
     P.: Nizet, 1971.

950 Marmier, Jean. *Horace en France au XVIIe siècle.* P.:
     PUF, 1962.

951 Praz, Mario. *Studies in Seventeenth Century Imagery.*
     2nd ed. Rome: Ed. di storia e letteratura, 1964.

952 Rigault, Hippolyte. *Histoire de la Querelle des Anciens et des Modernes*. P.: Hachette, 1856; rpt., N.Y.: Burt Franklin, 1963.

953 Rousset, Jean. *L'Intérieur et l'extérieur. Essais sur la poésie et sur le théâtre au XVIIe siècle*. P.: J. Corti, 1968.

954 Société Française de Littérature Comparée. *L'Italianisme en France au 17e siècle*. Turin: Soc. ed. int., 1968.

955 Tournand, Jean-Claude. *Introduction à la vie littéraire du XVIIe siècle*. P.: Bordas, 1970.

III. ANTHOLOGIES AND STUDIES BY GENRES
a. POETRY

Anthology
956 Mourgues, Odette de, ed. *An Anthology of French Seventeenth Century Lyric Poetry*. London: Oxford U. Pr., 1966.

Studies
957 Fukui, Y. *Raffinement précieux dans la poésie française du XVIIe siècle*. P.: Nizet, 1964.

958 Picard, Raymond. *La Poésie française de 1640 à 1680*. I: *Poésie religieuse, épopée, lyrisme officiel*. II: *Satire, épître, burlesque, poésie galante*. P.: CDU-SEDES, 1964-69.

b. PROSE

1. *"Epistoliers"*
    Anthology
959 Lanson, Gustave, éd. *Choix de lettres du dix-septième siècle*. P.: Hachette, s.d.

    Studies
960 Bray, Bernard. *L'Art de la lettre amoureuse, des manuels aux romans (1550-1700)*. P.-La Haye: Mouton, 1966.

961 Vigouroux, Monique. *Le Thème de la retraite et de la solitude chez quelques épistoliers du XVIIe siècle*. P.: Nizet, 1972.

2. *Novel and Short Story*
    Anthology
962 *Romanciers du XVIIe siècle*. Ed. Antoine Adam. P.: Gallimard, "Bibliothèque de la Pléiade," 1958.

    Studies
963 Deloffre, Frédéric. *La Nouvelle en France à l'âge classique*. P.: Didier, 1967.

964 Reynier, Gustave. *Le Roman réaliste au XVIIe siècle*. P.: Hachette, 1914; rpt., Genève: Slatkine, 1971.

c. THEATRE

Anthologies
965 Peyre, Henri, and Seronde, Joseph, eds. *Nine Classic French Plays: Corneille, Molière, Racine.* Boston: D. C. Heath, 1936; rev. ed. 1974.

966 Scherer, Jacques, éd. *Théâtre du XVIIe siècle.* Textes choisis, établis, présentés et annotés par Jacques Scherer. I, P.: Gallimard, "B. de la Pléiade," 1975.

Studies
967 Adam, Antoine. *Le Théâtre classique.* P.: PUF, "Que sais-je?" 1970.

968 Barnwell, Henry Thomas. *The Tragic in French Tragedy.* Belfast: Queen's U., 1966.

969 Deierkauf-Holsboer, Sophie Wilma. *Le Théâtre de l'Hôtel de Bourgogne.* 2 vols. P.: Nizet, 1968-70. I: *1548-1635. Documents inédits.* II: *Le Théâtre de la Troupe Royale 1635-80.*

970 _____. *Histoire de la mise en scène dans le théâtre français à Paris de 1600 à 1673.* P.: Nizet, 1960.

971 Guichemerre, Roger. *La Comédie avant Molière. 1640-1660.* P.: Colin, 1972.

972 Lancaster, Henry Carrington. *A History of French Dramatic Literature in the Seventeenth Century.* 5 vols. in 9. N.Y.: Gordian Pr., 1966. (1st ed. 5 parts in 9 vols. Baltimore: Johns Hopkins U. Pr.; P.: PUF, 1929-42.)

973 Lockert, Lacy. *Studies in French Classical Tragedy.* Nashville, Tennessee: The Vanderbilt U. Pr., 1958.

974 Mongrédien, Georges, et Robert, Jean. *Dictionnaire biographique des comédiens français du XVIIe siècle; suivi d'un inventaire des troupes (1590-1710) d'après des documents inédits.* P.: CNRS, 1961. *Supplément.* 1972.

975 Moore, Will Grayburn. *The Classical Drama of France.* London: Oxford U. Pr., 1971.

976 Scherer, Jacques. *La Dramaturgie classique en France.* P.: Nizet, 1950.

977 Turnell, Martin. *The Classical Moment: Studies of Corneille, Molière, and Racine.* London: Hamish Hamilton, 1947; rpt., Wesport, Conn.: Greenwood, 1971.

C. ANTHOLOGIES AND STUDIES ON LITERARY MOVEMENTS

I. *MANIERISME*, *BAROQUE*, AND *PRECIOSITE*

Anthologies

978 Blanchard, André, éd. *Trésor de la poésie baroque et précieuse.* P.: Seghers, 1969.

979 Raymond, Marcel, éd. *La Poésie française et le maniérisme, 1546-1610.* Textes choisis et présentés par M. Raymond. Notes et index bibliographique par A. J. Steele. Genève: Droz, 1971.

980 Rousset, Jean, éd. *Anthologie de la poésie baroque française.* 2 vols. in 1. P.: Colin, 1961.

Studies

981 Backer, Dorothy A. L. *Precious Women: A Feminist Phenomenon in the Age of Louis XIV.* N.Y.: Basic Books, 1974.

982 Charpentrat, Pierre. *Le Mirage baroque.* P.: Eds. de Minuit, 1967.

983 Debu Bridel, Jacques. *La Préciosité: Conception héroïque de la vie.* Bologne: R. Patron, 1965.

984 Delley, Gilbert. *L'Assomption de la nature dans la lyrique française de l'âge baroque.* Berne: Lang, 1969.

985 Dubois, Claude-Gilbert. *Le Baroque, profondeurs de l'apparence.* P.: Larousse, 1973.

986 Lathuillère, Roger. *La Préciosité: Etude historique et linguistique. Tome I: Position du problème: Les origines.* Genève: Droz, 1966.

987 Maillard, Jean-François. *Essai sur l'esprit du "héros baroque," 1580-1640. Le même et l'autre.* P.: Nizet, 1973.

988 Mongrédien, Georges, éd. *Les Précieux et les précieuses.* P.: Mercure de France, "Les Plus Belles Pages," 1963.

989 Rousset, Jean. *La Littérature de l'âge baroque en France. Circé et le paon.* P.: J. Corti, 1953; rpt., 1970.

990 Tapié, Victor-Lucien. *Le Baroque.* 3e éd. mise à jour. PUF, "Que sais-je?" 1968.

II. THE CLASSICAL MOVEMENT

991 Bénac, Henri. *Le Classicisme. La Doctrine par les textes.* P.: Hachette, 1949; rpt., 1968.

992 Bray, René. *La Formation de la doctrine classique en France.* P.: Hachette, 1927; rpt., P.: Nizet, 1966.

993 Brody, Jules, ed. *French Classicism. A Critical Miscellany.* Englewood Cliffs, N.J.: Prentice-Hall, 1966.

994 Emery, Léon. *L'Age classique.* Lyon: Cahiers Libres, 1967

995 Moore, Will Grayburn. *French Classical Literature: An Essay.* London: Oxford U. Pr., 1961.

996 Nurse, Peter H. *Classical Voices: Studies of Corneille, Racine, Molière, Madame de Lafayette.* Totowa, N.J.: Rowman and Littlefield, 1971.

997 Peyre, Henri. *Qu'est-ce que le classicisme?* Ed. rev. et augm. P.: Nizet, 1965.

998 Saisselin, Rémy G. *The Rule of Reason and the Ruses of the Heart: A Philosophical Dictionary of Classical French Criticism, Critics, and Aesthetic Issues.* Cleveland: Case Western Reserve U. Pr., 1970.

999 Zuber, Roger. *Les "Belles Infidèles" et la formation du goût classique.* P.: Colin, 1968.

III. MORALISTS

1000 Levi, Anthony. *French Moralists: The Theory of the Passions, 1585 to 1649.* Oxford: Clarendon Pr., 1964.

IV. BURLESQUE

1001 Bar, Francis. *Le Genre burlesque en France au XVIIe siècle. Etude de style.* P.: d'Artrey, 1960.

CHAPTER 17

EIGHTEENTH CENTURY

A. GENERAL WORKS

See Ch. 13.

I. BIBLIOGRAPHIES

See Chs. 2 and 3; especially in Ch. 2 the retrospective bibliographies of: Cabeen, vol. IV, 1951, and *Supplement*, 1968(no. 13), Cioranescu (vol. III), 1969(no. 14), Lanson, 1931(no. 18), Giraud, 1939-70(no. 19); the current bibliographies of: Klapp, 1960-(no. 17), *MLA Bibliography*, 1921-(no. 22), Rancoeur, 1953-(no. 26), and *The Year's Work in Modern Language Studies*, 1931-(no. 34).

II. JOURNALS

See Ch. 6.

Annales de la Société Jean-Jacques Rousseau. Genève.
Annales Historiques de la Révolution Française. P.
*Association des Amis de Jean-Jacques Rousseau, Bulletin
    d'Information*. Neuchâtel.
Casanova Gleanings. Nice.
Diderot Studies. Geneva.
XVIIIe Siècle. Revue annuelle pluridisciplinaire pub. par la
    Soc. française d'étude du XVIIIe siècle. P.
Eighteenth Century Studies, an interdisciplinary journal,
    Dept. of English. Davis, California.
Studies on Voltaire and the Eighteenth Century. Banbury,
    Oxfordshire.

III. DICTIONARIES

See Chs. 8 and 16.

1002 Alletz, Pons-Auguste. *Dictionnaire des richesses de la
    langue française et du néologisme qui s'y est intro-
    duit; contenant les termes nouveaux et reçus, les
    nouvelles locutions, les tours figurés et brillants,
    les expressions de génie, les grâces et les délica-
    tesses dont la langue a été ornée et enrichie depuis
    le commencement du XVIIIe siècle*. P., 1770; rpt.,
    Genève: Slatkine, 1968.

IV. STUDIES ON THE LANGUAGE OF THE EIGHTEENTH CENTURY

See Chs. 11 and 12.

1003 François, Alexis. *La Grammaire du purisme et l'Académie française au XVIIIe siècle. Introduction à l'étude des commentaires grammaticaux d'auteurs classiques: les origines lyriques de la phrase moderne. Etude sur la prose cadencée dans la littérature française au XVIIIe siècle.* 2 vols. P.: Soc. nouv. de librairie et d'édition, 1905. (Thèse.) Rpt., 2 vols. Genève: Slatkine, 1973.

1004 Gohin, Ferdinand. *Les Transformations de la langue française pendant la deuxième moitié du XVIIIe siècle (1740-1789).* P.: Belin, 1903; rpt., Genève: Slatkine, 1970.

1005 Seguin, Jean-Pierre. *La Langue française au XVIIIe siècle.* P.: Bordas, 1972.

1006 Stewart, Philip. *Le Masque et la parole: Le langage de l'amour au XVIIIe siècle.* P.: J. Corti, 1973.

V. HISTORY, CIVILIZATION

See Ch. 13.

1007 Aubertin, Charles. *L'Esprit public au XVIIIe siècle. Etude sur les Mémoires et les correspondances politiques des contemporains (1715-1789).* 2e éd. P.: Didier, 1873; rpt., Genève: Slatkine, 1968.

1008 Barni, Jules. *Histoire des idées morales et politiques en France au dix-huitième siècle.* 2 vols. P., 1865; rpt., Genève: Slatkine, 1967.

1009 Bluche, François. *La Vie quotidienne de la noblesse française au XVIIIe siècle.* P.: Hachette, 1973.

1010 Daumard, Adeline, et Furet, François. *Structures et relations sociales à Paris au XVIIIe siècle.* P.: Colin, 1961.

1011 Gaxotte, Pierre. *Le Siècle de Louis XV.* P.: Fayard, 1933; rpt., 1974.

1012 Gerson, Frédéric. *L'Amitié au XVIIIe siècle.* P.: Pensée Universelle, 1974.

1013 Gowan, Christopher D'Olier. *France from the Regent to the Romantics.* London: Harrap, 1961.

1014 Kunstler, Charles. *La Vie quotidienne sous la Régence.*
P.: Hachette, 1960.

1015 _____. *La Vie quotidienne sous Louis XV.* P.: Hachette,
1953.

1016 Levron, Jacques. *Louis le Bien-Aimé.* P.: Perrin, 1965.

1017 Lough, John. *An Introduction to Eighteenth Century France.*
London: Longmans, 1960.

1018 Manuel, Frank Edward. *The Eighteenth Century Confronts
the Gods.* Cambridge, Mass.: Harvard U. Pr., 1959.

1019 Martin, Kingsley. *French Liberal Thought in the Eighteenth
Century: A Study of Political Ideas from Bayle to
Condorcet.* Ed. J. P. Mayer. London: Phoenix
House, 1962. (Previous ed. Boston: Little, Brown,
1929.)

1020 Plongeron, Bernard. *Théologie et politique au Siècle des
Lumières. 1770-1820.* Genève: Droz, 1973.

1021 Poitrineau, Abel. *Le Premier XVIIIe siècle, 1680-1750.*
P.: Masson, 1971.

VI. *LE MOUVEMENT PHILOSOPHIQUE* AND THE
ENCYCLOPEDIE

a. *LE MOUVEMENT PHILOSOPHIQUE*

1022 Adam, Antoine. *Le Mouvement philosophique dans la première moitié du XVIIIe siècle.* P.: CDU-SEDES,
1967.

1023 Anchor, Robert. *The Enlightenment Tradition.* N.Y.:
Harper and Row, 1967.

1024 Brumfitt, J. H. *The French Enlightenment.* London:
Macmillan, 1972.

1025 Coleman, Francis X. J. *The Aesthetic Thought of the
French Enlightenment.* Pittsburg: Pittsburg U.
Pr., 1971.

1026 Crocker, Lester G. *An Age of Crisis: Man and World in
Eighteenth Century French Thought.* Baltimore: Johns
Hopkins Pr., 1959.

1027 _____. *Nature and Culture: Ethical Thought in the
French Enlightenment.* Baltimore: Johns Hopkins
Pr., 1963.

1028 Desné, Roland. *Les Matérialistes français de 1750 à 1800.*
P.: Buchet-Chastel, 1965.

1029 Ehrard, Jean. *L'Idée de nature en France dans la première moitié du XVIIIe siècle.* 2 vols. P.: SEVPEN, 1963.

1030 Gay, Peter. *The Enlightenment. An Interpretation.* 2 vols. N.Y.: Knopf, 1966-69.

1031 Goulemot, Jean-Marie, et Launay, Michel. *Le Siècle des Lumières.* P.: Eds. du Seuil, 1968.

1032 Goyard-Fabre, Simone. *La Philosophie des Lumières en France.* Préf. de Pierre Chaunu. P.: Klincksieck, 1972.

1033 Mauzi, Robert. *L'Idée de bonheur dans la littérature et la pensée françaises au XVIIIe siècle.* P.: Colin, 1960.

1034 Mousnier, Roland. *Progrès scientifique et technique au XVIIIe siècle.* P.: Plon, 1958.

1035 Nicolson, Sir Harold George. *The Age of Reason.* London: Constable, 1960.

1036 O'Keefe, Cyril B. *Contemporary Reactions to the Enlightenment (1728-1762). A Study of Three Critical Journals: the Jesuit Journal de Trévoux, the Jansenist Nouvelles Ecclésiastiques, and the Secular Journal des Savants.* P.: Champion, 1974. (Thesis, Ph.D. U. of Toronto, 1959.)

1037 Palmer, Robert Roswell. *Catholics and Unbelievers in Eighteenth Century France.* Princeton: Princeton U. Pr., 1939; 2nd ed. 1961.

1038 Perkins, Jean Ashmead. *The Concept of the Self in the French Enlightenment.* Geneva: Droz, 1969.

1039 Pomeau, René. *L'Europe des Lumières. Cosmopolitisme et unité européenne au XVIIIe siècle.* P.: Stock, 1966.

1040 Roger, Jacques. *Les Sciences de la vie dans la pensée française du XVIIIe siècle. La Génération des animaux de Descartes à l'Encyclopédie.* P.: Colin, 1963.

1041 Vereker, Charles. *Eighteenth Century Optimism: A Study of the Interrelations of Moral and Social Theory in English and French Thought between 1689 and 1789.* Liverpool: Liverpool U. Pr., 1967.

1042 Vyverberg, Henry. *Historical Pessimism in the French Enlightenment.* Cambridge, Mass.: Harvard U. Pr., 1958.

043 Wade, Ira Owen. *The Intellectual Origins of the French Enlightenment.* Princeton: Princeton U. Pr., 1971.

b. THE *ENCYCLOPEDIE*

044 Lough, John. *The Contributors to the Encyclopedia.* London: Grant and Cutler, 1973.

045 _____. *L'Encyclopédie.* London: Longmans, 1971.

046 Proust, Jacques. *Diderot et l'Encyclopédie.* P.: Colin, 1962.

047 Schwab, Richard Nahum. *Inventory of Diderot's Encyclopédie,* by R. N. Schwab, W. E. Rex, and J. Lough. Geneva: Institut et Musée Voltaire, 1971-.

B. LITERATURE

I. LITERARY HISTORIES AND GENERAL ANTHOLOGIES

See Ch. 13.

a. LITERARY HISTORIES

048 Berthaut, Henri. *De "Candide" à "Atala."* (*Histoire de la littérature française,* éd. J. Calvet, vol. VII.) P.: del Duca, 1958.

049 Chérel, Albert. *De "Télémaque" à "Candide."* (*Histoire de la littérature française,* éd. J. Calvet, vol. VI.) P.: del Duca, 1958.

050 *Dictionnaire des lettres françaises.* (IV) *Le Dix-huitième siècle.* P.: Fayard, 1959-60.

051 *Dix-huitième Siècle (Le).* (*Littérature française,* éd. par Claude Pichois, vols. 9, 10, 11.) P.: Arthaud, 1974-76.
Vol. I: *1720-1750,* par Jean Ehrard, 1974.
Vol. II: *1750-1778,* par Robert Mauzi et Sylvain Menant, 1976.
Vol. III: *1778-1820,* par Béatrice Didier, 1976.

052 Niklaus, Robert. *The Eighteenth Century, 1715-1789.* (*A Literary History of France,* ed. by Patrick E. Charvet, vol. III.) London: Benn; N.Y.: Barnes and Noble, 1970.

053 Saulnier, Verdun-Louis. *La Littérature française du siècle philosophique.* 7e éd. rev. P.: PUF, "Que sais-je?" 1967; 10e éd. mise à jour, 1976.

193

b. GENERAL ANTHOLOGIES

1054 Bousquet, Jacques, éd. *Anthologie du XVIIIe siècle romantique.* P.: Pauvert, 1972.

1055 Crocker, Lester G., éd. *Anthologie de la littérature française du XVIIIe siècle.* N.Y.: Holt, Rinehart, and Winston, 1972.

1056 Fellows, Otis Edward, and Torrey, Norman L. *The Age of Enlightenment: An Anthology of Eighteenth Century French Literature.* 2nd ed. N.Y.: Appleton-Century-Crofts, 1971; rpt., Prentice-Hall.

1057 Francastel, Pierre, éd. *Utopie et institutions du XVIIIe siècle. Le Pragmatisme des Lumières.* Textes recueillis par P. Francastel. P.-La Haye: Mouton, 1963.

1058 Saisselin, Rémy. *Le Dix-huitième Siècle: goût, lumières,* Englewood Cliffs, N.J.: Prentice-Hall, 1973.

II. GENERAL STUDIES

1059 Atkinson, Geoffroy, and Keller, Abraham C. *Prelude to the Enlightenment: French Literature, 1690-1740.* Seattle: U. of Washington Pr., 1970.

1060 Atkinson, Geoffroy. *The Sentimental Revolution: French Writers of 1690-1740.* Ed. A. C. Keller. Seattle: U. of Washington Pr., 1966.

1061 Bénichou, Paul. *Le Sacre de l'écrivain, 1750-1830, essai sur l'avènement d'un pouvoir spirituel laïque dans la France moderne.* P.: J. Corti, 1973.

1062 Bollème, Geneviève; Ehrard, Jean; Furet, François; Roche, Daniel; et collaborateurs. *Livre et société dans la France du XVIIIe siècle.* P.-La Haye: Mouton, 1965.

1063 Dédéyan, Charles. *Jean-Jacques Rousseau et la sensibilité littéraire à la fin du dix-huitième siècle.* P.: CDU-SEDES, 1966.

1064 Dufrenoy, Marie-Louise. *L'Orient romanesque en France 1709-1789.* Etude d'histoire et de critique littéraires. 2 vols. Montréal: Beauchemin, 1946; rpt., 2 vols. Montréal: Fides, 1958.

1065 Gossman, Lionel. *French Society and Culture: Background for 18th Century Literature.* Englewood Cliffs, N.J.: Prentice-Hall, 1972.

066 Grenet, André, et Jodry, Claude. *La Littérature de senti-
      ment au XVIIIe siècle*. 2 vols. P.: Masson, 1971.

067 Grimsley, Ronald. *From Montesquieu to Laclos. Studies on
      the French Enlightenment*. Geneva: Droz, 1974.

068 Hepp, Noémi. *Homère en France au XVIIIe siècle*. P.:
      Klincksieck, 1968.

069 Laufer, Roger. *Style rococo, style des Lumières*. P.:
      J. Corti, 1963.

070 Launay, Michel, et Mailhos, Georges. *Introduction à la
      vie littéraire du XVIIIe siècle*. P.: Bordas, 1969;
      rpt., 1973.

071 Mackrell, J. Q. C. *The Attack on "feudalism" in Eighteenth
      Century France*. London: Routledge and Kegan Paul,
      1973.

072 May, Gita. *De Jean-Jacques Rousseau à Madame Roland.
      Essai sur la sensibilité préromantique et révolu-
      tionnaire*. Genève: Droz, 1964.

073 Minguet, J.-Philippe. *Esthétique du rococo*. P.: Vrin,
      1966.

074 Monglond, André. *Le Pré-romantisme français*. 2 vols.
      P.: J. Corti, 1966; nouv. éd. 1969.

075 Mortier, Roland. *Clartés et ombres du Siècle des Lumières.
      Etudes sur le XVIIIe siècle littéraire*. Genève:
      Droz, 1969.

076 Trousson, Raymond. *Socrate devant Voltaire, Diderot,
      Rousseau. La Conscience en face du mythe*. P.:
      Lettres Modernes   Minard, 1967.

077 Van Tieghem, Paul. *Le Sentiment de la nature dans le
      préromantisme européen*. P.: Nizet, 1960.

III.   ANTHOLOGIES AND STUDIES BY GENRES

a.   POETRY

Anthologies
078 Finch, Robert, and Joliat, Eugène. *French Individualist
      Poetry 1686-1760: An Anthology*. Toronto: U. of
      Toronto Pr., 1971.

079 Roudaut, Jean, éd. *Poètes et grammairiens au XVIIIe
      siècle: Anthologie*. P.: Gallimard, 1971.

Studies

1080 Finch, Robert. *The Sixth Sense: Individualism in French Poetry, 1686-1760.* Toronto: U. of Toronto Pr., 1969.

1081 Muller, Henry. *Petit Enfer poétique du XVIIIe siècle.* P.: Cercle du livre précieux, 1959.

b. PROSE

Anthologies

1082 Etiemble, René, éd. *Romanciers du XVIIIe siècle.* 2 vols. P.: Gallimard, "Bibliothèque de la Pléiade," 1960-6

1083 Marchand, Jacqueline, éd. *Les Romanciers libertins du XVIIIe siècle.* Textes choisis. P.: Eds. Rationa-listes, 1972.

Studies

1084 Barchilon, Jacques. *Le Conte merveilleux français de 1690 à 1790: cent ans de féerie et de poésie ignorées de l'histoire littéraire.* P.: Champion, 1975.

1085 Brooks, Peter. *The Novel of Worldliness: Crébillon, Marivaux, Laclos, Stendhal.* Princeton: Princeton U Pr., 1969.

1086 Fauchery, Pierre. *La Destinée féminine dans le roman européen du dix-huitième siècle, 1713-1807: essai de gynécomythie romanesque.* P.: Colin, 1972.

1087 May, Georges. *Le Dilemme du roman au XVIIIe siècle: Etude sur les rapports du roman et de la critique (1715-1761).* P.: PUF, 1963.

1088 Mylne, Vivienne. *The Eighteenth Century French Novel: Techniques of Illusion.* Manchester: U. Pr., 1965.

1089 *Roman et Lumières au XVIIIe siècle. Colloque sous la présidence de Werner Krauss.* P.: Eds. Sociales, 1970.

1090 Stewart, Philip. *Imitation and Illusion in the French Memoir-Novel, 1700-1750. The Art of Make-Believe.* New Haven: Yale U. Pr., 1969.

c. THEATRE

Anthologies

1091 Brenner, Clarence Dietz, and Goodyear, Nolan A. *Eighteent. Century French Plays.* N.Y.: Appleton-Century-Croft. 1927.

1092 Truchet, Jacques, éd. *Théâtre du dix-huitième siècle.* Textes choisis, établis, présentés et annotés par

Jacques Truchet. 2 vols. P.: Gallimard, "Bibliothèque de la Pléiade," 1972-74.

Studies

093 Alasseur, Claude. *La Comédie Française au 18e siècle: étude économique.* P.-La Haye: Mouton, 1967.

094 Brenner, Clarence Dietz. *The Théâtre Italien, Its repertory, 1716-93.* Berkeley: U. of California Pr., 1961.

095 Carlson, Marvin. *The Theatre of the French Revolution.* Ithaca, N.Y.: Cornell U. Pr., 1966.

096 Courville, Xavier de. *Un apôtre de l'art du théâtre au XVIIIe siècle, Luigi Riccoboni dit Lélio.* 3 vols. P.: Droz, 1943-58. (Vol. 3 pub. by Lib. théâtrale.)
Vol. I: *Introduction et bibliographie. L'Expérience italienne (1676-1715).* 1943.
Vol. II: *L'Expérience française (1716-1731).* 1945.
Vol. III: *Lélio, premier historien de la Comédie Italienne et premier animateur du théâtre de Marivaux.* 1958.

097 Davis, James Herbert. *Tragic Theory and the Eighteenth Century French Critics.* Chapel Hill, North Carolina: U. of North Carolina Pr., 1967.

098 Gaiffe, Félix. *Le Drame en France au XVIIIe siècle.* P.: Colin, 1910; rpt., 1970.

099 Hamiche, Daniel. *Le Théâtre et la Révolution. La lutte de classes au théâtre en 1789 et en 1793.* P.: Union générale d'éditions, 1973.

100 Hawkins, Frederick William. *The French Stage in the Eighteenth Century.* 2 vols. Grosse Pointe, Michigan: Scholarly Pr., 1968.

101 Jourdain, Eleanor Frances. *Dramatic Theory and Practice in France, 1690-1808.* London: Longmans, Green, 1921; N.Y.: Blom, 1968.

102 Lagrave, Henri. *Le Théâtre et le public à Paris de 1715 à 1750.* P.: Klincksieck, 1972.

103 Lanson, Gustave. *Nivelle de La Chaussée et la Comédie larmoyante.* P.: Hachette, 1887.

104 Mamczarz, Irène. *Les Intermèdes comiques italiens au XVIIIe siècle en France et en Italie.* P.: CNRS, 1972.

CHAPTER 18

NINETEENTH CENTURY

A. GENERAL WORKS

See Ch. 13.

I. BIBLIOGRAPHIES

See Chs. 2 and 3, especially in Ch. 2 the retrospective
bibliographies of Lanson, 1931(no. 18), Talvart et Place,
1928-(no. 30), Thieme, 1933(no. 31), continued by
Dreher et Rolli, 1948(no. 32), and Drevet, 1954(no. 33);
the current bibliographies of Klapp, 1960-(no. 17), *MLA
Bibliography*, 1921-(no. 22), *MLA French VI Bibliography*,
1952-(no. 24), and *French VII-XX Bibliography*, 1949-
(no. 25), Rancoeur, 1953-(no. 26), and *The Year's Work in
Modern Language Studies*, 1931-(no. 34).

1105 Carteret, Léopold. *Le Trésor du bibliophile romantique et
        moderne, 1801-1875.* 4 vols. P.: Carteret, 1924-
        28. 1e réimpression rev., corr., et augm. P.: Eds
        Vexin français et Laurent Carteret, 1976; distribute
        P.: C. Coulet et A. Faure.

        Bibliography of choice first editions and illus-
    trated books.

1106 Peyre, Henri. *Bibliographie critique de l'hellénisme en Fr
        de 1843 à 1870.* New Haven: Yale U. Pr., 1932.

1107 Vicaire, Georges. *Manuel de l'amateur de livres du 19e si
        1801-1893.* 8 vols. P.: Rouquette, 1894-1920; rpt.
        Burt Franklin, 1973; P.: C. Coulet et A. Faure, 197

        Annotated bibliography of French nineteenth centu
    literature similar in presentation to Brunet's *Manuel*. . .

II. JOURNALS
    See Ch. 6.
Amis de Flaubert (Les). Rouen.
Amitié Guérinienne (L'). Carmaux.
Annales Romantiques. 12 vols. P., 1823-36; rpt., Genève:
        Slatkine, 1971.
Annales Romantiques. 2 vols. P., 1836-37; rpt., Genève:
        Slatkine, 1971.
Annales Romantiques. Revue d'Histoire du Romantisme. Vols.
        11. P., 1904-14; rpt., Genève: Slatkine, 1967.
Année Balzacienne (L'). P.
Association des Amis d'Alfred de Vigny. Bulletin. P.
Balzac à Saché. Bulletin de la Société Honoré de Balzac d
        Touraine. Saché.

Bulletin Baudelairien.   Nashville, Tennessee.
Bulletin de la Société Chateaubriand.   P.
Bulletin de la Société J.-K. Huysmans.   P.
Bulletin de la Société J. Verne.   P.
Bulletin de la Société "Les Amis de M. Rollinat."   Boulogne-
        sur-Seine.
Bulletin de l'Association des Amis d'Alexandre Dumas.
        Marly-le-Roi.
Cahiers Internationaux de Symbolisme.   Mons, Belgique.
Cahiers Naturalistes.   P.
Cahiers Paul-Louis Courier.   Véretz.
Cahiers Pierre Loti.   P.
Cahiers Staëliens.   P.
Etudes Baudelairiennes.   Neuchâtel.
Etudes Gobiniennes.   P.
Etudes Renaniennes.   P.
Nineteenth-Century French Studies.   Fredonia, N.Y.
Romantisme.   P.
Stendhal-Club.   Grenoble.*

III.   DICTIONARIES

See Ch. 8.

IV.   STUDIES ON THE LANGUAGE OF THE NINETEENTH CENTURY

See Chs. 11 and 12.

1108 Matoré, Georges. *Le Vocabulaire et la société sous Louis-
        Philippe.* Genève, 1951; rpt., Genève: Slatkine, 1967.

1109 Robert, Guy. *Mots et dictionnaires (1798-1878).* P.: Les
        Belles Lettres, 1966-. (With René Journet for the
        first 5 vols.) (In progress.)

        By the end of 1974, 9 vols. have been pub., up
to word "tâte."
        Reports and compares definitions in the *Diction-
naire de l'Académie.* . ., *Le Dictionnaire portatif.* . .
de Pierre Richelet, 1780, *Le Dictionnaire critique de la
langue française,* par l'Abbé Féraud, 1787, and *Le Nouveau
Dictionnaire portatif de la langue française,* refondu par
C. M. Gattel, 1797. In addition, more than twenty French
dictionaries are used to clarify definitions and record
various usages.

1110 Sainéan, Lazar. *Le Langage parisien au XIXe siècle.
        Facteurs sociaux, contingents linguistiques, faits
        sémantiques, influences littéraires.* P.: Boccard,
        1920.

V.   HISTORY, CIVILIZATION
See Ch. 13.

* Also rpt. *Cinquante Petites Revues françaises.* *Romantisme.
        Symbolisme.* . . . Genève: Slatkine, 1970.

1111 Bertier de Sauvigny, Guillaume de. *Les Débuts de l'époque
    contemporaine. 1789-1848.* 7e éd. P.: de Gigord,
    1969.

1112 _____. *La Restauration.* P.: Flammarion, 1955; nouv.
    éd. 1963.

1113 Gérard, Alice, éd. *Le Second Empire, innovation et créa-
    tion,* documents choisis et présentés par Alice
    Gérard. P.: PUF, 1973.

1114 Guiral, Pierre, et al. *La Société française (1815-1914)
    vue par les romanciers.* P.: Colin, 1969.

1115 Hemmings, Frederick William John. *Culture and Society in
    France, 1848-1898. Dissidents and Philistines.*
    N.Y.: Scribner, 1971.

1116 Labrousse, Camille-Ernest. *Aspects de l'évolution écono-
    mique et sociale de la France et du Royaume-Uni de
    1815 à 1880.* P.: CDU, 1949, 1954.

1117 Leroy, Alfred. *La Civilisation française du XIXe siècle.*
    Tournai: Casterman, 1963.

1118 Mayeur, Jean. *Les Débuts de la Troisième République.
    1871-1898.* P.: Eds. du Seuil, 1973.

1119 Rémond, René. *La Vie politique en France depuis 1789.*
    2 vols. P.: Colin, 1965-69.
    I: *1789-1848.*
    II: *1848-1879.*

1120 Tulard, Jean. *Nouvelle Histoire de Paris. Le Consulat et
    l'Empire.* P.: Hachette, 1970.

1121 Vigier, Philippe. *La Seconde République.* 3e éd. mise à
    jour. P.: PUF, "Que sais-je?" 1975.

VI.   RELIGION AND PHILOSOPHY

1122 Bérence, F. *Grandeur spirituelle du XIXe siècle français.*
    2 vols. P.: La Colombe, 1958-59.

1123 Bessède, Robert. *La Crise de la conscience catholique dans
    la littérature et la pensée française à la fin du
    XIXe siècle.* P.: Klincksieck, 1975.

1124 Charléty, Sébastien. *Histoire du saint-simonisme.* P.:
    Hachette, 1896; rpt., Genève: Gonthier, 1965.

1125 Charlton, Donald Geoffrey. *Positivist Thought in France
    during the Second Empire, 1852-1870.* Oxford:
    Clarendon Pr., 1959.

126 _____. *Secular Religions in France, 1815-1870*. London: Oxford U. Pr., 1963.

127 Derré, Jean-René. *Lamennais, ses amis et le mouvement des idées à l'époque romantique (1824-1834)*. P.: Klincksieck, 1962.

128 Guillemin, Henri. *Histoire des catholiques français au XIXe siècle*. P.: Milieu du monde, 1947.

B. LITERATURE

I. LITERARY HISTORIES AND GENERAL STUDIES

See Ch. 13.

129 Borie, Jean. *Le Tyran timide, le naturalisme de la femme au XIXe siècle*. P.: Klincksieck, 1973.

130 Charvet, Patrick Edward. *The Nineteenth Century, 1789-1870*. (*A Literary History of France*, ed. P. E. Charvet, Vol. IV.) London: Benn; N.Y.: Barnes and Noble, 1967.

131 _____. *The Nineteenth and Twentieth Centuries, 1870-1940*. (*A Literary History of France*, ed. P. E. Charvet, Vol. V.) London: Benn; N.Y.: Barnes and Noble, 1967.

132 Dakyns, Janine Rosalind. *The Middle Ages in French Literature 1851-1900*. London: Oxford U. Pr., 1973.

133 Descotes, Maurice. *La Légende de Napoléon et les écrivains français au XIXe siècle*. P.: Lettres Modernes Minard, 1967.

134 *Dictionnaire des lettres françaises*. (V) *Le Dix-neuvième siècle*. 2 vols. P.: Fayard, 1971-72.

135 Pia, Pascal. *Romanciers, poètes, essayistes du XIXe siècle*. P.: Denoël, 1971.

136 Prévost, John C. *Le Dandysme en France (1817-1839)*. Genève: Droz, 1957.

137 *Romantisme (Le)*. (*Littérature française*, éd. par Claude Pichois, vols. 12, 13, 14.) P.: Arthaud, 1968-.
  Vol. I: *1820-1843*, par Max Milner, 1973.
  Vol. II: *1843-1869*, par Claude Pichois (en préparation).
  Vol. III: *1869-1896*, par Raymond Pouilliart, 1968.

138 Sagnes, Guy. *L'Ennui dans la littérature française de Flaubert à Laforgue (1848-1884)*. P.: Colin, 1969.

1139 Saulnier, Verdun-Louis. *La Littérature française du siècle romantique*. P.: PUF, "Que sais-je?" 1945; 9e éd. 1969.

1140 Schwab, Raymond. *La Renaissance orientale*. P.: Payot, 1950.

1141 Swart, Koenraad Wolter. *The Sense of Decadence in Nineteenth-Century France*. The Hague: M. Nijhoff, 1964.

II. ANTHOLOGIES AND STUDIES BY GENRES

a. POETRY

Anthologies
1142 Maynial, Edouard, éd. *Anthologie des poètes du XIXe siècle*. P.: Hachette, 1929. (Frequently reprinted.)

1143 Parmée, Douglas, ed. *Twelve French Poets. 1820-1900. An Anthology of 19th Century French Poetry*, with an intro. and notes by Douglas Parmée. London: Longmans; N.Y.: David McKay Co., 1957, 1962.

Studies
1144 Cutler, Maxine G. *Evocation of the Eighteenth Century in French Poetry, 1800-1869*. Geneva: Droz, 1970.

b. PROSE

1. Historical Writings
1145 Moreau, Pierre. *L'Histoire en France au XIXe siècle. Etat présent des travaux et esquisse d'un plan d'études*. P.: Les Belles Lettres, 1935.

2. Literary Criticism
1146 Molho, Raphaël. *La Critique littéraire en France au XIXe siècle*. P.: Buchet-Chastel, 1963.

3. Novel and Short Story
Anthologies
1147 *Anthologie des préfaces de romans français du XIXe siècle*. Présentation de Herbert S. Gershman et Kersman B. Whitworth Jr. P.: Union générale d'éditions, 1972.

1148 Carlut, Charles E., ed. *19th Century French Short Stories* in the original French. N.Y.: Dell Publishing Co., 1966.

1149 Maynial, Edouard, éd. *Anthologie des romanciers du XIXe siècle*. P.: Hachette, 1931; rpt., 1966.

1150 _____. *Contes et récits du XIXe siècle*. P.: Hachette 1932; rpt., 1966.

1151 Sachs, Murray, ed. *The French Short Story in the Nine-teenth Century: A Critical Anthology.* N.Y.: Oxford U. Pr., 1969.

Studies
1152 Castex, Pierre-Georges. *Le Conte fantastique en France de Nodier à Maupassant.* P.: J. Corti, 1951; rpt., 1971.

1153 Clark, Priscilla P. *The Battle of the Bourgeois. The Novel in France, 1789-1848.* P.: Didier, 1973.

1154 Evans, David Owen. *Le Roman social sous la Monarchie de Juillet.* P.: Picart, 1930.

1155 George, Albert Joseph. *Short Fiction in France, 1800-1850.* Syracuse: Syracuse U. Pr., 1964.

1156 Giraud, Raymond Dorner. *The Unheroic Hero in the Novels of Stendhal, Balzac, and Flaubert.* New Brunswick, N.J.: Rutgers U. Pr., 1957.

1157 Lowrie, Joyce O. *The Violent Mystique: Thematics of Retribution and Expiation in Balzac, Barbey d'Aure-villy, Bloy, and Huysmans.* Geneva: Droz, 1974.

1158 Vernois, Paul. *Le Roman rustique de George Sand à Ramuz. Ses tendances et son évolution (1860-1925).* P.: Nizet, 1962.

c. THEATRE

Anthologies
1159 Borgerhoff, Joseph Leopold, ed. *Nineteenth Century French Plays.* N.Y.: Appleton-Century-Crofts, 1959.

1160 Bourgeois, René, et Mallion, Jean, éds. *Le Théâtre au XIXe siècle.* P.: Masson, 1971.

Studies
1161 Carlson, Marvin. *The French Stage in the Nineteenth Century.* Metuchen, N.J.: Scarecrow Pr., 1972.

1162 Des Granges, Charles-Marc. *La Comédie et les moeurs sous la Restauration et la Monarchie de Juillet (1815-1848).* P.: Fontemoing, 1904.

1163 Doumic, René. *De Scribe à Ibsen: causeries sur le théâtre contemporain.* P.: Perrin, 1896.

1164 Ginisty, Paul. *Le Mélodrame.* P.: Louis Michaud, 1910.

1165 Henderson, John A. *The First Avant-Garde (1887-1894). Sources of the Modern French Theatre.* London: Harrap, 1971.

1166 Jones, Michèle H. *Le Théâtre national en France de 1800 à 1830*. P.: Klincksieck, 1975.

1167 Lenient, Charles. *La Comédie en France au XIXe siècle*. 2 vols. P.: Hachette, 1898.

1168 Nostrand, Howard Lee. *Le Théâtre antique et à l'antique en France de 1840 à 1900*. P.: Droz, 1934.

1169 Wicks, Charles Beaumont. *The Parisian Stage. Alphabetical Indexes of Plays and Authors (1800-75)*. 4 vols. University, Alabama: U. of Alabama Pr., 1950-67.

     Vol. IV contains a "Cumulative Index of Authors, 1800-1875."

C. ANTHOLOGIES AND STUDIES ON LITERARY MOVEMENTS

    See Ch. 13, and Ch. 18, Pts. A and B.

I. ROMANTICISM

a. BIBLIOGRAPHY

1170 "The Romantic Movement: A Bibliography" (Annual), in *English Literary History*, 1937-49, then in *Philological Quarterly*, 1950-64. Thereafter: "The Romantic Movement: A Selective and Critical Bibliography," Sept. Supp. of *English Language Notes*. 1965-.

    French section pub. now under the dir. of James S. Patty.

b. LITERARY HISTORY AND CRITICISM

1171 Canat, R. *L'Hellénisme des romantiques* (jusqu'à 1852). 3 vols. P.: Didier, 1951-55.

1172 Cellier, Léon. *L'Epopée romantique*. P.: PUF, 1954; rpt., under the title: *L'Epopée humanitaire et les grands mythes romantiques*. P.: CDU-SEDES, 1971.

1173 Furst, Lilian R. *Romanticism in Perspective: A Comparative Study of Aspects of the Romantic Movements in England, France, and Germany*. London: Macmillan; N.Y.: St. Martin's Pr., 1969.

1174 Hoffmann, Léon-François. *Le Nègre romantique; personnage littéraire et obsession collective*. P.: Payot, 1973.

1175   . *Romantique Espagne: l'Image de l'Espagne en France entre 1800 et 1850*. Princeton: Princeton U. Pr., P.: PUF, 1961.

1176 Juden, Brian. *Traditions orphiques et tendances mystiques dans le romantisme français (1800-1855).* P.: Klinck-sieck, 1971.

1177 Marmier, Jean. *La Survie d'Horace à l'époque romantique.* P.: Didier, 1965.

1178 Moreau, Pierre. *Le Romantisme. (Histoire littéraire française,* éd. J. Calvet, vol. VIII.) P.: de Gigord, 1932; 2e éd., del Duca, 1957.

1179 Peyre, Henri. *Qu'est-ce que le romantisme?* P.: PUF, 1971.

1180 Richard, Jean-Pierre. *Etudes sur le romantisme.* P.: Eds. du Seuil, 1971.

On Balzac, Lamartine, Vigny, Hugo, Musset, Sainte-Beuve, Guérin.

c. ROMANTIC POETRY

Anthologies
1181 Decaunes, Luc. *La Poésie romantique française.* P.: Seghers, 1973.

Studies
1182 Avni, Abraham Albert. *The Bible and Romanticism: The Old Testament in German and French Romantic Poetry.* P.-The Hague: Mouton, 1969.

1183 Houston, John Porter. *The Demonic Imagination: Style and Theme in French Romantic Poetry.* Baton Rouge: Louisiana State U. Pr., 1969.

On Hugo, Musset, Vigny, Baudelaire, Nerval, Sainte-Beuve, Gautier, Ph. O'Neddy, P. Borel.

1184 Riffaterre, Hermine B. *L'Orphisme dans la poésie romantique: thèmes et style surnaturalistes.* P.: Nizet, 1970.

d. ROMANTIC PROSE

1185 Evans, David Owen. *Le Socialisme romantique: Pierre Leroux et ses contemporains.* P.: M. Rivière, 1948.

1186 _____. *Social Romanticism in France, 1830-1848, with a Selective Bibliography.* Oxford: Clarendon Pr., 1951.

Novel and Short Story
1187 Salomon, Pierre, éd. *Le Roman et la nouvelle romantiques.* Textes choisis et présentés par Pierre Salomon. P.: Masson, 1970.

e. ROMANTIC THEATRE

Anthologies

1188 Touchard, Pierre-Aimé, et Richer, Jean, éds. *Le Drame romantique*. P.: Club des libraires de France, 1957.

Studies

1189 Affron, Charles. *A Stage for Poets: Studies in the Theatre of Hugo and Musset*. Princeton: Princeton U. Pr., 1971.

1190 Ascoli, Georges. *Le Théâtre romantique*. P.: CDU, 1936, 1953.

1191 Brun, Auguste. *Deux Proses de théâtre: drame romantique, Comédies et proverbes*. Gap: Ophrys, 1954.

1192 Descotes, Maurice. *Le Drame romantique et ses grands créateurs, 1827-1839*. P.: PUF, 1955.

1193 Evans, David Owen. *Le Drame moderne à l'époque romantique (1827-1850)*. P.: PUF, 1937.

1194 _____. *Le Théâtre pendant la période romantique (1827-1848)*. P.: PUF, 1925.

1195 Ihrig, Grace Pauline. *Heroines in French Drama of the Romantic Period, 1829-1848*. N.Y.: King's Crown Pr., Columbia U., 1950. (Thesis.)

II. REALISM AND NATURALISM

1196 Becker, George Joseph, ed. *Documents of Modern Literary Realism*. Princeton: Princeton U. Pr., 1963.

1197 Beuchat, Charles. *Histoire du naturalisme français*. 2 vols. P.: Corrêa, 1949.

1198 Bornecque, Jacques-Henry, et Cogny, Pierre. *Réalisme et Naturalisme: l'histoire, la doctrine, les oeuvres*. Présenté par J.-H. Bornecque et P. Cogny. P.: Hachette, 1959.

1199 Cogny, Pierre. *Le Naturalisme*. P.: PUF, "Que sais-je?" 1953; 7e éd. 1976.

1200 Dumesnil, René. *Le Réalisme et le Naturalisme*. (*Histoire de la littérature française*, éd. J. Calvet, vol. IX.) P.: de Gigord, 1936; P.: del Duca, 1955.

1201 Lapp, John C. *Les Racines du naturalisme*. P.: Bordas, 1972.

1202 Martino, Pierre. *Le Naturalisme français (1870-1895)*.
P.: Colin, 1923; 7e éd. compl. par Rigatte, 1965;
8e éd. 1969.

III. *L'ART POUR L'ART*
PARNASSE, SYMBOLISM, *MOUVEMENT DECADENT*

See also Pt. IV hereafter.

Anthologies
1203 Léoutre, Gilbert, et Salomon, Pierre, éds. *Baudelaire et
le Symbolisme*. P.: Masson, 1970.

1204 MacIntyre, Carlyle Ferren. *French Symbolist Poetry* (A
Bilingual Edition). Tr. by C. F. MacIntyre.
Berkeley: U. of California Pr., 1958.

Studies
1205 Balakian, Anna. *The Symbolist Movement in Literature:
A Critical Appraisal*. N.Y.: Random House, 1967.

1206 Cassagne, Albert. *La Théorie de l'art pour l'art en France
chez les derniers romantiques et les premiers
réalistes*. P.: Hachette, 1906; Dorbon, 1959.

1207 Chadwick, Charles. *Symbolism*. London: Methuen, 1971.

On Baudelaire, Verlaine, Rimbaud, Mallarmé,
Valéry.

1208 Denommé, Robert Thomas. *The French Parnassian Poets*.
Pref. by Harry T. Moore. Carbondale: Southern
Illinois U. Pr.; London and Amsterdam: Feffer and
Simons, 1972.

On T. Gautier, T. de Banville, Leconte de Lisle,
J.-M. de Heredia.

1209 Estève, Edmond. *Le Parnasse*. P.: Guillon, 1931.

1210 Guiraud, Pierre. *Index du vocabulaire du symbolisme*.
6 vols. P.: Klincksieck, 1953-54.

1211 Lawler, James. *The Language of French Symbolism*. Princeton: Princeton U. Pr., 1969.

1212 Martino, Pierre. *Parnasse et Symbolisme*. P.: Colin,
1925, 1967.

1213 Michaud, Guy. *La Doctrine symboliste*. P.: Nizet, 1947.

1214 _____. *Message poétique du symbolisme (Le)*. 3 vols.
P.: Nizet, 1947, 1961.

I: *L'Aventure poétique.*
II: *La Révolution poétique.*
III: *L'Univers poétique.*

1215 Peyre, Henri. *Qu'est-ce que le symbolisme?* P.: PUF, 197▮

1216 Richard, Noël. *Le Mouvement Décadent: dandys, esthètes et quintessents.* P.: Nizet, 1968.

1217 Schmidt, Albert-Marie. *La Littérature symboliste (1870-1900).* P.: PUF, "Que sais-je?" 1942, 1950, 1967.

1218 Walzer, Pierre-Olivier. *La Révolution des Sept.* Neuchâte_
La Baconnière, 1970.

On Lautréamont, Mallarmé, Rimbaud, Corbière, Cros, Nouveau, and Laforgue.

IV. THEATRE IN THE SECOND HALF OF THE NINETEENTH CENTURY

Bibliography
1219 SantaVicca, Edmund F., comp. *Four French Dramatists: A Bibliography of Criticism of the Works of Eugène Brieux, François de Curel, Emile Fabre, Paul Hervieu.* Metuchen, N.J.: Scarecrow Pr., 1974.

Anthology
1220 Pellissier, Georges. *Anthologie du théâtre français contemporain (prose et vers) (1850 à nos jours).* 5e éd. P.: Delagrave, 1930.

Studies
1221 Allard, Louis. *La Comédie de moeurs en France au dix-neuvième siècle.* . . . 2 vols. P.: Hachette, 1924-33.

1222 Benoist, Antoine. *Le Théâtre d'aujourd'hui.* 2 vols.
P.: Soc. française d'imprimerie et de librairie, 1911-12.

1223 Chandler, Frank Wadleigh. *The Contemporary Drama of France.* Boston: Little, Brown and Co., 1920.

1224 Clark, Barrett Harper. *Contemporary French Dramatists: Studies on the Théâtre libre, Curel, Brieux, Porto-Riche, Hervieu, Lavedan,* . . . . Cincinnati: Stewart and Kidd Co., 1915.

1225 Doumic, René. *Le Théâtre nouveau.* P.: Perrin, 1908.

1226 Ernest-Charles, J. *Le Théâtre des poètes. Histoire du théâtre poétique en France, 1850-1910.* P.: Ollendorff, 1910.

1227 Filon, Pierre-Marie-Augustin. *De Dumas à Rostand. Esquisse du mouvement dramatique contemporain.* P.: Colin, 1898.

1228 Got, Maurice. *Théâtre et Symbolisme: recherches sur l'essence et la signification spirituelle de l'art symboliste.* P.: Cercle du Livre, 1955. (Thèse.)

1229 Kahn, Armand. *Le Théâtre social en France de 1870 à nos jours.* Lausanne: Ami Fatio, 1907.

1230 Marie, Gisèle. *Le Théâtre symboliste: ses origines, ses sources, pionniers et réalisateurs.* P.: Nizet, 1973.

1231 Marsan, Jules. *Théâtre d'hier et d'aujourd'hui.* P. Cahiers Libres, 1926.

1232 Pruner, Francis. *Les Luttes d'Antoine au Théâtre libre.* P.: Lettres Modernes Minard, 1964.

1233 Robichez, Jacques. *Le Symbolisme au théâtre: Lugné-Poe et les débuts de l'Oeuvre.* P.: L'Arche, 1957.

1234 Smith, Hugh Allison. *Main Currents of Modern French Drama.* N.Y.: Holt, 1925.

1235 Sorel, Albert-Emile. *Essais de psychologie dramatique.* P.: Sansot, 1910.

1236 Zola, Emile. *Le Naturalisme au théâtre.* P.: Charpentier, 1881.

1237 _____. *Nos Auteurs dramatiques.* P.: Charpentier, 1881.

    This work and the preceding one are reproduced in Zola's *Oeuvres complètes*, éd. Henri Mitterand. P.: Cercle du livre précieux, 1966, vol. XI.

CHAPTER 19

TWENTIETH CENTURY

A.   GENERAL WORKS

See Ch. 13.

I.   BIBLIOGRAPHIES

See Chs. 2 and 3; especially in Ch. 2 the retrospective bibliographies of Talvart, 1928-(no. 30), Thieme,
1933(no. 31); continued by Dreher et Rolli, 1948(no. 32),
and Drevet, 1954(no. 33); the current bibliographies of
Klapp, 1960-(no. 17), *MLA Bibliography*, 1921-(no. 22),
MLA French VII-XX Bibliography, 1949-(no. 25), Rancoeur,
1953-(no. 26), and *The Year's Work in Modern Language
Studies*, 1931-(no. 34).

1238   Nigay, Gilbert. "Les Recherches bibliographiques dans le
domaine de la littérature française contemporaine."
L'Information Littérature, t. 19, No. 2 (1967),
57-61.

II.   JOURNALS

See Ch. 6.

1239   Admussen, Richard L. *Les Petites Revues littéraires
(1914-1939). Répertoire descriptif.* St. Louis,
Missouri: Washington U. Pr.; P.: Nizet, 1970.

1240   Arbour, Romeo. *Les Revues littéraires éphémères paraissant
à Paris entre 1900 et 1914. Répertoire descriptif.*
P.: J. Corti, 1956.

A list of 154 little Parisian magazines, published
less than four years. It gives editors, publishing details,
names of principal contributors, location in Paris librarie
and index of names of persons. Appendix lists thirty-one
titles not located in Parisian libraries.

Amis de La Varende (Les). P.
Amis de Louis Pergaud (Les). Valentigney.
Amitié Charles Péguy (L'). P.
Annales de la Fondation M. Maeterlinck. Bruxelles.
Association des amis d'Alain. Bulletin d'informations. P
Bulletin de la Société des Amis de Colette. St.-Sauveur-
en-Puisaye.
*Bulletin de la Société des Amis de M. Proust et des Amis
de Combray.* P.

Bulletin de la Société Paul Claudel. P.
Bulletin des Amis d'André Gide, publié. . .par l'Unité
    d'études françaises de l'Université de Lyon II. Bron.
Cahiers Charles Du Bos. Neuilly-sur-Seine.
Cahiers Charles Maurras. P.
Cahiers Dada-Surréalisme. Cahiers de l'Association
    Internationale pour l'Etude de Dada et du Surréalisme.
    P. Nos. 1-4, 1966, 1968, 1969, 1970. Continuation of
    Revue de l'Association pour l'étude du mouvement Dada,
    No. 1, oct. 1965. Continued by *Le Siècle éclaté,*
    No. 1-, 1974-.
Cahiers des Amis de Valéry Larbaud. Vichy.
Cahiers Jean Cocteau. P.
Cahiers Jean Giraudoux. P.
Cahiers Marie Noël. P.
Cahiers Paul Eluard. Nice.
Claudel Studies. Irving, Texas.
Création (Association de recherches sur la poésie moderne et
    contemporaine). P.
Etudes Maurrassiennes. Centre Charles Maurras. Aix-en-
    Provence.
Lys Rouge (Le). Société Anatole France. P.
Proust Research Association Newsletter. Lawrence, Kansas.
Révolution Surréaliste (La). P. 1er déc. 1924-15 déc.
    1929; rpt., P.: Eds. J.-M. Place, 1975. Continued as *Le
    Surréalisme au Service de la Révolution.* P.Juil. 1930-mai 1933, 1976.
Société Claudel en Belgique, Bulletin Régional. Hannut,
    Belgique.
Société des Amis de Jules Romains. Bulletin. P.
Société d'Etude du XXe Siècle. Bulletin. P.

III. DICTIONARIES

See Ch. 8.

IV. CONTEMPORARY FRENCH LANGUAGE

See Chs. 11 and 12.

1 Galichet, Georges. *Le Français moderne. Structures et fonction-
    nement.* P.: PUF, "Que sais-je?" 1949; 6e éd. rev., 1975.

V. HISTORY, CIVILIZATION

See Ch. 13.

2 Ambrosi, Charles, et Ambrosi, Arlette. *La France, 1870-1975.*
    2e éd. rev. et compl. P.:Masson, 1976.

3 Beaujour, Michel, et Ehrmann, Jacques. *La France contempo-
    raine.* 3e éd. P.: Colin, 1969.

1244 Bouju, Paul M., et Dubois, H. *La Troisième République*.
6e éd. P.: PUF, "Que sais-je?" 1967.

1245 Calvet, Henri. *La Société française contemporaine*.
P.: Nathan, 1956.

1246 Dupeux, Georges. *La France de 1945 à 1965*. P.: Colin,
1969.

1247 Duroselle, Jean-Baptiste. *La France de la Belle Epoque*.
La France et les Français 1900-1914. P.: Eds.
Richelieu, 1973.

1248 Duverger, Maurice. *La Cinquième République*. 4e éd. P.:
PUF, 1968.

1249 Fauvet, Jacques. *La IVe République*. P.: Fayard, 1959, 1

1250 *Troisième République (La)*. 2 vols. P.: Colin, 1969-70.
I: *1870-1914* par Georges Bourgin, 1969.
II: *1914-1940* par Jacques Néré, 3e éd. 1970.

1251 Trotignon, Yves. *La France au XXe siècle*. 2e éd. P.:
Bordas, 1969.

VI. RELIGION AND PHILOSOPHY

See Ch. 13.

1252 Chalumeau, Jean-Luc. *La Pensée en France de Sartre à
Foucault*. P.: F. Nathan, Alliance Française,
1974. Ills.

1253 Duméry, Henry. *Regards sur la philosophie contemporaine*.
P.: Casterman, 1956.

1254 Foulquié, Paul. *L'Existentialisme*. P.: PUF, "Que sais-je
1947; 16e éd. 1971.

1255 Gardner, Howard. *The Quest for Mind: Piaget, Lévi-Strauss
and the Structuralist Movement*. N.Y.: Knopf, 1973.

1256 Harari, Josué V. *Structuralists and Structuralisms: A
Selected Bibliography of French Contemporary Thought
(1960-1970)*. Ithaca, N.Y.: Diacritics, 1971.

1257 Morot-Sir, Edouard. *La Pensée française d'aujourd'hui*.
P.: PUF, 1971.

1258 Mourre, Michel, éd. *Dictionnaire des idées contemporaines*.
P.: Eds. universitaires, 1975.

1259 Picon, Gaëtan, éd. *Panorama des idées contemporaines*.
P.: Gallimard, 1957.

B. THE LITERATURE

I. LITERARY HISTORIES, ANTHOLOGIES, AND GENERAL STUDIES

See Chs. 13 and 18.

a. LITERARY HISTORIES

1260 Marill, René (Albérès). *L'Aventure intellectuelle du XXe siècle. Panorama des littératures européennes. (1900-1963).* P.: A. Michel, 1963; 4e éd. rev. et corr. 1969.

1261 Astorg, Bertrand d'. *Aspects de la littérature européenne depuis 1945.* P.: Eds. du Seuil, 1952.

1262 Baldensperger, Fernand. *L'Avant-guerre dans la littérature française (1900-1914).* P.: Payot, 1919.

1263 _____ . *La Littérature française entre les deux guerres (1919-1939).* Los Angeles: Lymanhouse, 1941.

1264 Bersani, Jacques; Autrand, Michel; Lecarme, Jacques; et Vercier, Bruno. *La Littérature en France depuis 1945.* P., Montréal: Bordas, 1970, 1974. Ills.

1265 Boisdeffre, Pierre de , sous la dir. de. *Dictionnaire de littérature contemporaine.* 3e éd. rev. et mise à jour. P.: Eds. universitaires, 1966.

1266 _____ . *Les Ecrivains français d'aujourd'hui.* 5e éd. rev. et mise à jour. P.: PUF, "Que sais-je?" 1963, 1973.

1267 _____ . *Une histoire vivante de la littérature d'aujourd'hui, 1939-1968.* 7e éd. entièrement remise à jour. P.: Perrin, 1968. Abridged under the title: *Abrégé d'Une histoire de la littérature d'aujourd'hui.* Texte revu et abrégé par l'auteur d'après la 7e éd. (1968). 2 vols. P.: Union générale d'éditions, 1969.

1268 Bourin, André, et Rousselot, Jean. *Dictionnaire de la littérature française contemporaine.* P.: Larousse, 1966.

1269 Bouvier, Emile. *Les Lettres françaises au XXe siècle.* P.: PUF, 1962.

1270 Bruézière, Maurice. *Histoire descriptive de la littérature contemporaine.* 2 vols. P.: Berger-Levrault, 1975-76.

1271 Chaigne, Louis. *Les Lettres contemporaines. (Histoire de*

213

la littérature française, éd. J. Calvet, vol. X.)
P.: del Duca, 1964.

1272 Clouard, Henri. *Histoire de la littérature française du symbolisme à nos jours.* 2 vols. P.: A. Michel, nouv. éd. 1962. I: *1885-1914.* II: *1915-1960.*

1273 Girard, Marcel. *Guide illustré de la littérature française moderne de 1918 à nos jours.* Nouv. éd. P.: Seghers 1971.

1274 Jeanneau, Augustin, et Chaigne, Louis. *Petit Guide de la littérature d'aujourd'hui.* P.: Lanore, 1966.

1275 Junod, Roger-Louis. *Ecrivains français du XXe siècle.* 2e éd. rev. et augm. Lausanne: Payot, 1973.

1276 Kanters, Robert. *L'Air des lettres, ou tableau raisonnable des lettres françaises d'aujourd'hui.* P.: Grasset, 1973.

1277 Moore, Harry T. *Twentieth-Century French Literature.* 2 vols. in 1. Carbondale: South Illinois U. Pr., 1966; N.Y.: Dell Pub. Co., 1967.

1278 Nathan, Jacques. *Histoire de la littérature française contemporaine, 1919-1960.* P.: F. Nathan, 1954.

1279 Picon, Gaëtan. *Panorama de la nouvelle littérature française.* Ed. rev. et corr. P.: Gallimard, 1976.

1280 Simon, Pierre-Henri. *Histoire de la littérature française au XXe siècle. 1900-1950.* 2 vols. P.: Colin, 1956, 5e éd. 1959; rpt., 1967.

1281 *Vingtième Siècle (Le). (Littérature française,* éd. Claude Pichois, vols. 15 et 16.) P.: Arthaud, 1975-.
I: *1896-1920,* par Pierre-Olivier Walzer. 1975.
II: *1920-1960,* par Germaine Brée (en préparation).

b. GENERAL ANTHOLOGIES

1282 Boisdeffre, Pierre de. *Une anthologie vivante de la littérature d'aujourd'hui.* 2 vols. P.: Perrin, 1965-66
I: *Roman, Théâtre, Idées, 1945-1965.* II: *La Poésie française de Baudelaire à nos jours.*

1283 Brée, Germaine, and Bernauer, George, eds. *Defeat and Beyond: An Anthology of French Wartime Writing, 1940-1945.* N.Y.: Panthéon, 1970.

1284 Brée, Germaine, ed. *Twentieth Century French Literature. An Anthology of Prose and Poetry.* Ed. with a Preface,

Introductions, and Notes by Germaine Brée. N.Y.:
Macmillan, 1962.

1285 Cohn, Ruby, and Parker, Lily, éds. *Monologues de Minuit*.
N.Y.: Macmillan, 1965.

1286 Curnier, Pierre, éd. *Pages commentées d'auteurs contemporains*. 3 vols. P.: Larousse, 1962-67.

1287 Guthrie, Ramon, and Diller, George E., eds. *Prose and
Poetry of Modern France*. N.Y.: Scribner, 1964.

1288 Peyre, Henri, ed. *Contemporary French Literature. A
Critical Anthology*. N.Y.: Harper and Row, 1964.

1289 Pingaud, Bernard, éd. *Ecrivains d'aujourd'hui. Dictionnaire anthologique et critique*. P.: Grasset, 1960.

c. GENERAL STUDIES

1290 Marill, René (Albérès). *Bilan littéraire du XXe siècle*.
Nouv. éd. P.: Aubier, 1962; 3e éd. rev. et augm.
P.: Nizet, 1971.

1291 Bernard, Jean-Pierre. *Le Parti communiste français et la
question littéraire, 1921-1939*. Grenoble: Pr.
universitaires de Grenoble, 1972.

1292 Boisdeffre, Pierre de. *Métamorphoses de la littérature.
Essais de psychologie littéraire*. 5e éd. entièrement
refondue. 2 vols. P.: Alsatia, 1963. I: *De
Barrès à Malraux* (Barrès, Gide, Bernanos, Mauriac,
Montherlant, Malraux). II: *De Proust à Sartre*
(Proust, Valéry, Cocteau, Anouilh, Camus, Sartre).
(Also sold bound in one vol. Bruxelles: Gérard,
1973.)

1293 Derrida, Jacques. *L'Ecriture et la différence*. P.: Eds.
du Seuil, 1967. (On A. Artaud, G. Bataille, M. Blan-
chot, et al.)

1294 Faÿ, Bernard. *Les Précieux*. P.: Perrin, 1966. (Claudel,
Cocteau, Gide, Giraudoux, Morand, Proust, Radiguet,
G. Stein, Valéry.)

1295 Griffiths, Richard M. *Reactionary Revolution: The Catholic
Revival in French Literature, 1870 through 1914*.
N.Y.: Ungar, 1965.

_____. *Révolution à rebours. Le renouveau catholique
dans la littérature en France de 1870 à 1914*, tr. de
l'anglais. P.: Desclée, 1971.

1296   Guiral, Pierre, et Temime, Emile. *La Société française*
       1914-1970, à travers la littérature. P.: Colin, 197'

1297   Hatzfeld, Helmut Anthony. *Trends and Styles in Twentieth*
       Century French Literature. Rev. enl. ed. Washington
       D.C.: Catholic U. of America Pr., 1966.

1298   Hugues, Henry Stuart. *The Obstructed Path: French Social*
       Thought in the Years of Desperation 1930-1960. N.Y.:
       Harper and Row, 1968. (On J. Maritain, R. Martin du
       Gard, G. Bernanos, A. de Saint-Exupéry, A. Malraux,
       J.-P. Sartre, A. Camus, et al.)

1299   Jacob, Jean-Marie, et Weiler, Maurice, éds. *Ecrivains*
       français du vingtième siècle. P.: Belin, 1966.

1300   Mansuy, Michel. *Etudes sur l'imagination de la vie: Jules*
       Supervielle, Henri Bosco, Alain Robbe-Grillet, Henri
       Michaux, Jean Rostand, Pierre Teilhard de Chardin.
       P.: J. Corti, 1970.

1301   Maurois, André. *Nouvelles Directions de la littérature*
       française. Oxford: Clarendon Pr., 1967.

1302   Moreau, Pierre. *Le Moi et le sentiment de l'existence*
       dans la littérature française contemporaine.
       (1966-70.) P.: Lettres Modernes Minard, 1973.

1303   Mounier, Emmanuel. *Malraux, Camus, Sartre, Bernanos.*
       L'Espoir des désespérés. P.: Eds. du Seuil, 1970.

1304   Psichari, Henriette. *Les Convertis de la Belle Epoque.*
       Préf. de Jean Pommier. P.: Les Eds. rationalistes,
       1971. (On E. Psichari, L. Bloy, Ch. Péguy, et al.)

1305   Sénart, Philippe. *Chemins critiques. D'Abellio à Sartre.*
       P.: Plon, 1966.

1306   Simon, Pierre-Henri. *Diagnostic des lettres françaises*
       contemporaines: de François Mauriac à Jean-René
       Huguenin, de Julien Green à Philippe Sollers, de Sar-
       tre à Robbe-Grillet. Bruxelles: La Renaissance du
       Livre; P.: Nizet, 1966.

1307   _____. *Témoins de l'homme. La condition humaine dans*
       la littérature du XXe siècle, Proust, Gide, Valéry,
       Claudel, Montherlant, Bernanos, Malraux, Sartre,
       Camus. P.: Payot, 1967.

1308   Sturrock, John. *The French New Novel: Claude Simon,*
        Michel Butor, Alain Robbe-Grillet. London: Oxford
        U. Pr., 1969.

1309   Tison-Braun, Micheline. *La Crise de l'humanisme. Le Con-*
        flit de l'individu et de la société dans la litté-
        rature française moderne. 2 vols. P.: Nizet,
        1958-67. Tome I: *1890-1914.* Tome II: *1914-1939.*

        d. ANTHOLOGIES AND STUDIES BY GENRES

        1. Poetry

        Anthologies
1310   *L'Année poétique 1974-* *(L').* Seghers, 1975-.

                First of a New series, whose annual volume is pub.
        in Feb. It is an anthology of poems in French, by well-known
        or unknown poets published during the preceding year in
        anthologies or in periodicals. Completed by a list of the
        most important journals where poets might submit their poems.

1311   Brindeau, Serge, et al., éds. *La Poésie contemporaine de*
        langue française depuis 1945. P.: Eds. Saint-
        Germain-des-Prés, 1973.

                This is a monumental undertaking gathering all the
        poets of French expression having published after 1945,
        whether or not they are of French nationality. The poetry
        is classified according to main themes of each work con-
        sidered. It is a successful attempt to cover in depth the
        poetic currents of the very diverse and complex contemporary
        poetry in French.

1312   Delvaille, Bernard. *La Nouvelle Poésie française.*
        Anthologie. Nouv. éd. P.: Seghers, 1974.

1313   Gavronsky, Serge, comp. and tr. *Poems and Texts: An*
        Anthology of French Poems, Translations and Inter-
        views with Ponge, Follain, Guillerie, Frénaud,
        Bonnefoy, Du Bouchet, Roche, and Pleynet. Selected
        and trans., with interviews and an introduction, by
        S. Gavronsky. N.Y.: October House, 1969.

1314   Hackett, Cecil Arthur, ed. *New French Poetry. An*
        Anthology. Oxford: Blackwell, 1973.

1315   Hubert, Renée Riese, et Judd D., éds. *Anthologie de la*
        poésie française du vingtième siècle. N.Y.: Appleton-
        Century-Crofts, 1971.

1316   Loisy, Jean, éd. *Un certain choix de poèmes (1935-1965),*
        précédé d'une introduction. P.: Points et contre-
        points, 1968.

1317 *Les Poèmes de l'année 1955(-70)*. Présentés par Alain
       Bosquet et Pierre Seghers. P.: Seghers, 1955-71.

       Anthology of poems published the preceding year in
French around the world. Similar anthologies have been
published irregularly in the following years.

1318 Rousselot, Jean, éd. *Panorama critique des nouveaux
       poètes français*. Nouv. éd. P.: Seghers, 1952.
       Reworked and enl. under the title:

       _____. *Les Nouveaux Poètes français, panorama critique*.
       P.: Seghers, 1959.

1319 Roy, Claude, éd. *Trésor de la poésie populaire*. Textes
       choisis avec la collaboration de Claire Vervin. P.:
       Seghers, 1967.

1320 Seghers, Pierre. *Poètes maudits d'aujourd'hui*. P.:
       Seghers, 1972. Ills.

1321 _____. *La Résistance et ses poètes, (France 1940-1945)*.
       P.: Seghers, 1974; 3e éd. complétée et corrigée,
       1975.

       On Aragon, Jean Paulhan, Eluard, Desnos, Loys
Masson, Max Jacob, Pierre Seghers.

1322 Taylor, Simon Watson, and Lucie-Smith, Edward, eds.
       French Poetry Today: A Bilingual Anthology.
       N.Y.: Schocken Books, 1971.

       Studies
1323 Boisdeffre, Pierre de. *Les Poètes français d'aujourd'hui*.
       P.: PUF, "Que sais-je?" 1973.

1324 Caws, Mary Ann, ed. *About French Poetry from Dada to
       "Tel Quel." Text and Theory*. Ed. by Mary Ann Caws,
       with a Foreword by Henri Peyre. Detroit: Wayne
       State U. Pr., 1974.

       Sixteen essays, by the most outstanding special-
ists in the field of contemporary French poetry, on text
or theory.

1325 _____. *The Inner Theatre of Recent French Poetry:
       Cendrars, Tzara, Péret, Artaud, Bonnefoy*. Princeton:
       Princeton U. Pr., 1972.

1326 Cornell, Kenneth. *The Post-Symbolist Period. French
       Poetic Currents, 1900-1920*. New Haven: Yale U. Pr.,
       1958; new ed. without change, New Haven: Archon
       Books, 1970.

1327   Décaudin, Michel. *La Crise des valeurs symbolistes,*
        vingt ans de poésie française, 1895-1914. Toulouse:
        Privat, 1960.

1328   Onimus, Jean. *Expérience de la poésie. Saint-John Perse,*
        Henri Michaux, René Char, Guillevic, Jean Tardieu,
        Jean Follain, Pierre Emmanuel. P.: Desclée de
        Brouwer, 1973.

1329   Raymond, Marcel. *De Baudelaire au surréalisme.* Ed. nouv.
        rev. et remaniée. P.: J; Corti, 1952.

1330   Richard, Jean-Pierre. *Onze Etudes sur la poésie moderne.*
        P.: Eds. du Seuil, 1964.

1331   Rousselot, Jean. *Dictionnaire de la poésie française*
        contemporaine. P.: Larousse, 1968.

            Mainly a biographical dictionary with brief
        notices on the lives and works of twentieth century poets
        in France, and poets of French expression outside of
        France. Includes also short articles on the principal
        movements, schools, important collections of poetry,
        periodicals, doctrines, and theories.

        2. Prose

                            Diaries

1332   "Journaux intimes et carnets," *La Nouvelle Revue Française,*
        Sept. 1975. (Special issue.)

                            Essays

1333   Brée, Germaine, et Solomon, Philip, éds. *Choix d'essais*
        du vingtiéme siècle. Waltham, Mass.: Blaisdell,
        1969.

                      Literary Criticism

1334   Simon, John K., ed. *Modern French Criticism: from Proust*
        and Valéry to Structuralism. Chicago: U. of Chicago
        Pr., 1971.

                            Novels

        Anthologies
1335   Baudin, Henri, et Bourgeois, René. *De Proust au nouveau*
        roman. P.: Masson, 1971.

1336   Petit, Jacques, éd. *Roman 61(-66). Anthologie des*
        principaux romans français publiés en 1961(-1966).
        P.: Didier, 1962(-1967).

1337 Marill, René (Albérès). *Le Roman d'aujourd'hui, 1960-1970.*
     P.: A. Michel, 1970.

1338 Astier, Pierre. *La Crise du roman français et le nouveau
     réalisme. Essai de synthèse sur les nouveaux romans.*
     P.: Debresse, 1969.

1339 _____. *Encyclopédie du nouveau roman et le nouveau
     réalisme.* . . . P.: Debresse, 1969.

1340 Baqué, Françoise. *Le Nouveau Roman.* P.: Bordas, 1972.

1341 Barrère, Jean-Bertrand. *La Cure d'amaigrissement du roman.*
     P.: A. Michel, 1964.

1342 Bloch-Michel, Jean. *Le Présent de l'indicatif. Essai sur
     le nouveau roman.* P.: La Table Ronde, 1967.

1343 Boisdeffre, Pierre de. *La Cafetière est sur la table, ou
     Contre le nouveau roman.* P.: La Table Ronde, 1967.

1344 _____. *Où va le roman? Essai.* P.: del Duca, 1962;
     nouv. éd. remaniée, augm. et mise à jour, 1972.

1345 Frohock, Wilbur Merrill, ed. *Image and Theme: Studies in
     Modern French Fiction (Bernanos, Malraux, Sarraute,
     Gide, Martin du Gard),* by Susan M. Keane and others.
     Ed. with an introduction by W. M. Frohock. Cam-
     bridge, Mass.: Harvard U. Pr., 1969.

1346 Huvos, Kornel. *Cinq Mirages américains: Les Etats-Unis
     dans l'oeuvre de Georges Duhamel, Jules Romains,
     André Maurois, Jacques Maritain et Simone de Beauvoir*
     P.: Didier, 1972.

1347 Kern, Edith. *Existential Thought and Fictional Technique:
     Kierkegaard, Sartre, Beckett.* New Haven: Yale U.
     Pr., 1970.

1348 Lalou, René. *Le Roman français depuis 1900.* P.: PUF,
     "Que sais-je?" 1941; nouv. éd. 1963; 11e éd. mise à
     jour par Georges Versini, 1969.

1349 Magny, Claude-Edmonde. *Histoire du roman français depuis
     1918.* P.: Eds. du Seuil, 1950, 1971.

1350 Mercier, Vivian. *The New Novel: from Queneau to Pinget.*
     N.Y.: Farrar, Straus and Giroux, 1971.

1351 Monnier, Jean-Pierre. *L'Age ingrat du roman.* Neuchâtel:
     La Baconnière, 1967.

352 Müller, A. *Les Passions humaines dans le roman contempo-rain.* P., 1968. Dépôt: Procure de l'Assomption, 6 rue de Lübeck, P.

353 Nadeau, Maurice. *Le Roman français depuis la guerre.* P.: Gallimard, 1963; nouv. éd. rev. et augm. 1970.

354 O'Flaherty, Kathleen. *The Novel in France, 1945-1965. A General Survey.* Cork, Ireland: Cork U. Pr., 1973.

355 Ouellet, Réal, éd. *Les Critiques de notre temps et le Nouveau roman.* Présentation par Réal Ouellet. P.: Garnier, 1972.

356 Peyre, Henri. *French Novelists of Today.* 2nd ed. N.Y.: Oxford U. Pr., 1967. (1st ed., 1955 under title: *The Contemporary French Novel.*)

357 Prévost, Claude. *Littérature, politique, idéologie. Aragon, Malraux, Kafka, Lénine, la politique et la littérature. Le roman socialiste.* P.: Eds. Sociales, 1973.

358 Rahv, Betty T. *From Sartre to the New Novel.* Port Washington, N.Y.: Kennikat Pr., 1974.

   About the novels of Sartre, Camus, Sarraute, Robbe-Grillet, Butor.

359 Reck, Rima Drell. *Literature and Responsibility. The French Novelist in the Twentieth Century.* Baton Rouge: Louisiana State U. Pr., 1969.

360 Ricardou, Jean. *Le Nouveau Roman.* P.: Eds du Seuil, 1974.

361 Robbe-Grillet, Alain. *Pour un nouveau roman.* P.: Eds. de Minuit, 1963.

362 Roger, Alain, et Maraud, André. *Le Roman contemporain.* P.: PUF, 1973.

363 Roger, Georges. *Maîtres du roman de terroir.* P.: A. Silvaire, 1959.

   On E. Leroy, H. Pourrat, L. Hémon, M. Genevoix, A. de Chateaubriant.

364 Roudiez, Léon Samuel. *French Fiction Today: A New Direction.* New Brunswick, N.J.: Rutgers U. Pr., 1972.

3. Theatre
Anthologies

1365 Benay, Jacques G., et Kuhn, Reinhard, éds. *Panorama du théâtre nouveau.* 4 vols. N.Y.: Appleton-Century-Crofts, 1967-68.

1366 Bishop, Thomas, éd. *L'Avant-garde théâtrale: French Theatre since 1950.* Lexington, Mass.: Heath, 1970; N.Y.: N.Y.U. Pr., 1975.

1367 Brée, Germaine, and Kroff, Alexander Y., eds. *Twentieth Century French Drama.* N.Y.: Macmillan, 1969.

Studies

1368 Bonnerot, Sylviane. *Le Théâtre de 1920 à 1950.* P.: Masson, 1972.

1369 _____. *Visages du théâtre contemporain.* P.: Masson, 1971.

1370 Cohn, Ruby. *Currents in Contemporary Drama.* Bloomington: Indiana U. Pr., 1969.

1371 Corvin, Michel. *Le Théâtre nouveau en France.* 3e éd. mise à jour. P.: PUF, "Que sais-je?" 1969.

1372 *Dictionnaire des hommes de théâtre français contemporains, auteurs, compositeurs, choréauteurs,* éd. par André Boll et Serge Zaneth. Préf. de A. Salacrou, H. Sauguet, et S. Lifar. 2 vols. P.: Perrin, 1957-67.

1373 Guicharnaud, Jacques, and Guicharnaud, June. *Modern French Theater from Giraudoux to Genet.* Rev. ed. New Haven: Yale U. Pr., 1967.

1374 Jacquart, Emmanuel. *Le Théâtre de dérision: Beckett, Ionesco, Adamov.* P.: Gallimard, 1974.

1375 Knowles, Dorothy. *French Drama of the Inter-War Years, 1918-1939.* London: Harrap, 1967.

1376 Mignon, Paul-Louis. *Le Théâtre contemporain.* P.: Hachette, 1969.

1377 Pillement, Georges. *Le Théâtre d'aujourd'hui: de Jean-Paul Sartre à Arrabal.* P.: Le Bélier, 1970.

1378 Simon, Alfred. *Dictionnaire du théâtre français contemporain.* P.: Larousse, 1970.

1379 Surer, Paul. *Cinquante Ans de théâtre* (1919-1969). P.: CDU-SEDES, 1969.

1380 Versini, Georges. *Le Théâtre français depuis 1900.*
P.: PUF, "Que sais-je?" 1970.

II. ANTHOLOGIES AND STUDIES ON

DADA AND SURREALISM

Bibliographies
1381 "Bibliographie" (on Dada and surrealism), in *Revue de
l'Association pour l'étude du mouvement Dada*, No. 1,
1965; thereafter in *Cahiers Dada Surréalisme.* P.:
Lettres Modernes Minard, Nos. 1-4, 1966, 1968,
1969, 1970 (this journal is no longer published).

1382 Gershman, Herbert S. *A Bibliography of the Surrealist
Revolution in France.* Ann Arbor: U. of Michigan
Pr., 1969.

Anthologies
1383 Bédouin, Jean-Louis, éd. *La Poésie surréaliste.* P.:
Seghers, 1964; éd. rev. et augm. 1970.

1384 Benedikt, Michael, and Wellwarth, George E., eds. and trs.
*Modern French Theatre. The Avant-Garde, Dada and
Surrealism.* An Anthology of plays ed. and tr. by
Michael Benedikt and George E. Wellwarth. N.Y.:
Dutton, 1964.

1385 Huguet, Georges. *L'Aventure Dada (1916-1922).* P.:
Seghers, 1971.

1386 Légoutière, Edmond. *Le Surréalisme.* P.: Masson, 1972.

1387 Marshall, Robert G., et St. Aubyn, Frederic C., eds.
Trois Pièces surréalistes. N.Y.: Appleton-Century-
Crofts, 1969.

1388 Matthews, J. H., ed. *An Anthology of French Surrealist
Poetry.* London: U. of London Pr., 1966.

1389 Poupard-Lieussou, Yves, éd. *Dada en verve.* Choix de
Yves Poupard-Lieussou. Présentation d'Henri Béhar.
P.: P. Horay, 1972.

1390 Tison-Braun, Micheline, éd. *Dada et le surréalisme.
Textes théoriques sur la poésie*, avec des notices
historiques et bibliographiques. P.: Bordas, 1973.

Studies
1391 Abastado, Claude. *Introduction au surréalisme.* P.:
Bordas, 1971.

1392 Alexandrian, Sarane. *Le Surréalisme et le rêve.* P.:
Gallimard, 1974.

1393 Audoin, Philippe. *Les Surréalistes*. P.: Eds. du Seuil, 1973.

1394 Balakian, Anna. *Surrealism: the road to the absolute*. Rev. and enl. London: Dutton, 1970. (1st ed. 1959.)

1395 Bancquart, Marie-Claire. *Paris des surréalistes*. P.: Seghers, 1972.

1396 Baron, Jacques. *L'An I du surréalisme, suivi de l'An dernier*. P.: Denoël, 1969.

1397 Béhar, Henri. *Etude sur le théâtre dada et surréaliste*. P.: Gallimard, 1967.

1398 Bigsby, C. W. E. *Dada and Surrealism*. London: Methuen, 1972.

1399 Bonnet, Marguerite. *André Breton et les débuts de l'aventure surréaliste*. P.: J. Corti, 1975.

1400 Bréchon, Robert. *Le Surréalisme*. 2e éd. P.: Colin, 1971.

1401 Caws, Mary Ann. *The Poetry of Dada and Surrealism: Aragon, Breton, Tzara, Eluard and Desnos*. Princeton: Princeton U. Pr., 1970.

1402 _____. *Surrealism and the Literary Imagination, a Study of Breton and Bachelard*. La Haye: Mouton, 1966.

1403 *Dictionnaire abrégé du surréalisme*. Nouv. éd. P.: J. Corti, 1969.

1404 Duplessis, Y. *Le Surréalisme*. 10e éd. mise à jour. P.: PUF, "Que sais-je?" 1974.

1405 Durozoi, Gérard, et Lecherbonnier, Bernard. *Le Surréalisme: théories, thèmes, techniques*. P.: Larousse, 1972.

1406 *Entretiens sur le surréalisme*, Cerisy-la-Salle, 1966. Sous la dir. de Ferdinand Alquié (Décades du Centre culturel international de Cerisy-la-Salle, nouv. sér. 8.) P.-La Haye: Mouton, 1968.

1407 Gauthier, Xavière. *Surréalisme et sexualité*. Préf. de J.-B. Pontalis. P.: Gallimard, 1972.

1408 Gershman, Herbert S. *The Surrealist Revolution in France*. Ann Arbor: U. of Michigan Pr., 1969.

1409 Jannini, Pasquale Anil, et Zoppi, S. *Surréalisme/Surrealism* Avec la collaboration de la Société d'étude du XXe

siècle. Articles de M. Décaudin, et al. P.:
Nizet, 1974.

1410 Lemaître, Maurice. *Le Lettrisme devant Dada et les nécro-
phages de Dada!* P.: Centre de Créativité, 1967.

1411 Matthews, J. H. *Surrealist Poetry in France.* Syracuse,
N.Y.: Syracuse U. Pr., 1969. (On Ph. Soupault,
L. Aragon, B. Péret, R. Desnos, R. Vitrac, M.
Leiris, J. Arp, P. Eluard, R. Char, et al.)

1412 Nadeau, Maurice. *Histoire du Surréalisme, suivie de Documents surréalistes.* P.: Eds. du Seuil, 1964.

1413 Sanouillet, Michel. *Dada à Paris.* P.: Pauvert, 1965.

1414 _____. *Dada 1915-1923.* P.: F. Hazan, 1969.

1415 Somville, Léon. *Devanciers du surréalisme. Les groupes
d'avant-garde et le mouvement poétique 1912-1925.*
Genève: Droz, 1971.

CHAPTER 20

LITERATURES OF FRENCH EXPRESSION OUTSIDE OF FRANCE

A. GENERAL WORKS

Most of the books we have mentioned in the preceding
chapters cover also literatures of French expression outsid
of France proper. In this chapter we shall indicate works
entirely devoted to them.

I. GENERAL BIBLIOGRAPHIES

See in particular:
Pt. 1, Ch. 2: *Bulletin Signalétique 523* (no. 12),
Klapp, 1960-(no. 17), *MLA Bibliography*, 1921-(no. 22),
Rancoeur, 1953-(no. 26), *Zeitschrift für Romanische
Philologie*, 1877-1964, later *Romanische Bibliographie*,
1965-(no. 27).
Ch. 3: *Répertoire des livres de langue française
disponibles*, 1972-(no. 71); *Douze Mois d'édition franco-
phone*, 1973-(no. 87), *L'Année francophone 1974*, 1975
(no. 88).

II. JOURNALS

See in particular in Ch. 2: *Bulletin Signalétique 523*,
1940-(no. 12), *Francophonie-Edition*, 1972-(no. 87); and
in Ch. 6: Duprat, G.; Lutova, K.; et Bossuat, M.-L.,
*Bibliographie des répertoires nationaux de périodiques en
cours* (no. 137), and international periodical directories
(nos. 157-161).

III. GENERAL REFERENCES

Ch. 5: *International Library Directory*. . .(no. 107).
Ch. 7: Catalogs of Dissertations and Theses.
Ch. 9: Biographical Dictionaries.
Ch. 10: Main Publishers and Collections.
Pt. 2: Chs. 11-12, on French Language.
Pt. 3: Chs. 13-19, on French Literature.

IV. GENERAL STUDIES

1416 Boly, Joseph, éd. *La Voix au coeur multiple, petite
      anthologie mondiale de la littérature française
      contemporaine.* P.: Ed. de l'Ecole, 1966.

          Concerns authors from France, Africa, Madagascar,
the Middle East, etc. Gives for each author a brief biography, information on his work, and an excerpt. Bib-

liographies and photographs.

1417 Tougas, Gérard. *Les Ecrivains d'expression française et la France. Essai.* P.: Denoël, 1973.

   Literary history of French speaking regions: Switzerland, Belgium, Quebec, Haiti, Martinique, Africa, and the Maghreb.

1418 Viatte, Auguste, éd. *Anthologie littéraire de l'Amérique francophone; littératures canadienne, louisianaise, haïtienne, de la Martinique, de la Guadeloupe et de la Guyane.* Sherbrooke, Québec: CELEF (Centre d'étude des littératures d'expression française), 1971.

1419 _____. *Histoire littéraire de l'Amérique française, des origines à 1950.* Québec: Presses de l'U. Laval; P.: PUF, 1954.

   On French Canada and French-speaking West Indies.

B. BELGIUM

I. GENERAL BIBLIOGRAPHIES

   See in Ch. 3, Belgian retrospective bibliographies: *Bibliographie Nationale. Dictionnaire des écrivains belges.* . .(no. 48), *Bibliographie des écrivains français de Belgique.* . .(no. 49), *Bibliotheca belgica.* . . (no. 50); and current bibliography: *Bibliographie de Belgique. Liste mensuelle des publications belges.* . . (no. 72).

1420 *Bibliographie de l'humanisme belge précédée d'une bibliographie générale concernant l'humanisme européen,* par A. Gerlo avec la collaboration d'E. Lauf. Bruxelles: Presses universitaires de Bruxelles, 1965.

1421 Delecourt, Jules Victor. *Dictionnaire des anonymes et pseudonymes, XVe siècle-1900.* Mis en ordre par G. Delecourt. Bruxelles: Académie royale de Belgique, 1960-. Vol. 1-.

II. JOURNALS

   See Ch. 6: repertories, nos. 138-143.

III. DISSERTATIONS AND THESES

   See in Ch. 7: *Liège. Université de. Répertoire des thèses de doctorat.* . .(no. 194); *Louvain. Université Catholique. Bibliographie académique* (no. 195) and *Résumé des dissertations.* . .(no. 196).

IV. BIOGRAPHICAL DICTIONARIES

See in Ch. 9: Académie Royale. . .*Biographie nationale* (no. 339) and its repertories (nos. 340-342), Hanlet, C., *Les Ecrivains belges*. . .(no. 343), *Who's Who in Belgium*. . (no. 344), Dhondt, J., et Vervaeck, S., *Instruments Biographiques*. . .(no. 345).

V. HISTORY

1422 Dhondt, Jean. *Histoire de la Belgique*. P.: PUF, "Que sais-je?" 1968.

VI. LITERARY HISTORIES

1423 Burniaux, Robert, et Frickx, Robert. *La Littérature belge d'expression française*. P.: PUF, "Que sais-je?" 1973.

1424 Charlier, Gustave, et Hanse, Joseph, éds. *Histoire illustrée des lettres françaises de Belgique*. Bruxelles: La Renaissance du Livre, 1958. (Bibliographies.)

1425 Galand, Guy. *Les Lettres françaises de Wallonie des origines au début du XXe siècle*. 2e éd. Charleroi: Inst. J. Destrée, 1962.

1426 Mor, Antonio, e Weisgerber, Jean. *Le Letterature del Belgio*. Nuova ed. Firenze e Milano: Sansoni, Accademia, 1968.

1427 Wilmotte, Maurice. *La Culture française en Belgique*. P.: Champion, 1912.

1428 _____. *Le Wallon. Histoire et littérature, des origines à la fin du XVIIIe siècle*. Bruxelles: Rozez, 1893.

VII. ANTHOLOGIES

1429 Bussy, Christian, éd. *Anthologie du surréalisme en Belgique*. P.: Gallimard, 1972.

VIII. GENERAL STUDIES

1430 Braet, Herman. *L'Accueil fait au symbolisme en Belgique (1885-1900)*. Bruxelles: Palais des Académies, 1967.

1431 Charlier, Gustave. *Le Mouvement romantique en Belgique (1815-1850)*. 2 vols. Bruxelles: Palais des Académies, 1948-59.

1432 *Lettres belges, lettres mortes?* Bruxelles: Le Groupe du roman, 1972.

1433 Vovelle, José. *Le Surréalisme en Belgique.* Bruxelles: André de Rache, 1972.

1434 Warmoes, Jean. *Un demi-siècle de lettres françaises en Belgique.* (Exposition organisée en collaboration par l'Académie royale de langue et de littérature françaises et la Bibliothèque royale de Belgique, Bruxelles, Bibliothèque royale Albert Ier, du 25 avril au 30 juin 1972.) Catalogue rédigé par Jean Warmoes. Bruxelles: Académie royale de langue et de littérature françaises, 1972.

IX. POETRY

1435 Guiette, R. *Poètes français de Belgique, de Verhaeren au surréalisme.* P.: Ed. Lumière, 1948.

C. SWITZERLAND

I. BIBLIOGRAPHIES

See in particular in Ch. 3, Swiss retrospective bibliographies: *Catalogue des éditions de la Suisse Romande* (no. 63), *Katalog. . .Systematisches Verzeichnis. . .* (no. 64), *Schweizer Bücherverzeichnis* (no. 65); and current bibliographies: *Bibliographie und literarische Chronik der Schweiz* (no. 91), *Bibliographisches Bulletin der Schweiz* (no. 92), *Das Schweizer Buch* (no. 93).

II. CATALOGS OF MANUSCRIPTS

See Ch. 5, nos. 128-129.

III. JOURNALS

See Ch. 6, repertories, nos. 156, 169-172.

IV. DISSERTATIONS AND THESES

See in Ch. 7, Soret, C., *Catalogue des. . .thèses. . .* (no. 230), *Jahresverzeichnis der schweizerischen Hochschulschriften. . .*(no. 231), *Les Thèses de doctorat à l'Université de Fribourg. . .*(no. 232).

V. BIOGRAPHICAL DICTIONARIES

See Ch. 9, *Dictionnaire historique et biographique de la Suisse. . .*(no. 356), *Who's Who in Switzerland. . .* (no. 357), *Schweizer Schriftsteller der Gegenwart*(no. 358).

VI. HISTORY

1436 Gilliard, Charles. *Histoire de la Suisse.* 5e éd. P.:
     PUF, "Que sais-je?" 1968.

VII. LITERATURE

a. LITERARY HISTORIES

1437 Berchtold, Alfred. *La Suisse romande au cap du XXe
     siècle, portrait littéraire et moral.* 2e éd.
     Lausanne: Payot, 1966.

1438 Godet, Philippe Ernest. *Histoire littéraire de la Suisse
     française.* 2e éd. P.: Fischbacher, 1895.

1439 Guyot, Charly. *Ecrivains de Suisse française.* Berne:
     Francke, 1961.

1440 Rossel, Virgile. *Histoire littéraire de la Suisse ro-
     mande, des origines à nos jours.* 2e éd. Neuchâtel:
     Kahn, 1904. (1e éd. 2 vols. Genève: Georg,
     1889-91.)

b. GENERAL ANTHOLOGIES

1441 *Anthologie romande de la littérature alpestre.* Ed. par
     Edmond Pidoux. Lausanne: Bibliothèque Romande,
     1972.

1442 *Chroniqueurs du seizième siècle. Bonivard, Pierrefleur,
     Jeanne de Jussy, Fromment.* Ed. par Maurice Bossard
     et Louis Junod. Lausanne: Bibliothèque Romande,
     1974.

c. GENERAL STUDIES

1443 Guyot, Charly. *La Vie intellectuelle et religieuse en
     Suisse française à la fin du XVIIIe siècle. Henri-
     David de Chaillet, 1751-1823.* Neuchâtel: La
     Baconnière, 1946.

1444 Kohler, Pierre. *La Littérature d'aujourd'hui dans la
     Suisse romande.* Lausanne: Payot, 1923.

1445 Reynold, Gonzague de. *Histoire littéraire de la Suisse au
     XVIIIe siècle. Le doyen Bridel et les origines de
     la littérature suisse romande.* Lausanne: Bridel,
     1909.

1446 Weck, René de. *La Vie littéraire dans la Suisse française.*
     P.: Fontemoing, 1912.

d. POETRY

Anthologies
447 Igly, France. *Un demi-siècle de poésie romande. Poètes d'hier et d'aujourd'hui.* Présentation et choix de poèmes par France Igly, avec la collaboration des auteurs. Remarque sur la poésie en Suisse romande, par M. Raymond. Présence du poète, par Maurice Zermatten. Travers: Nouvelle bibliothèque, 1969.

448 *Poètes de Suisse romande. Anthologie.* Genève: Rencontre, 1974.

Studies
449 Godel, Vahé. *Poètes à Genève et au-delà.* Genève: Georg, 1966.

D. CANADA AND LOUISIANA

See in this ch., Pt. A, nos. 1416-1419.

I. CANADA

a. GENERAL BIBLIOGRAPHIES

See in particular in Ch. 3: Canadian retrospective bibliographies: Lochhead, D., *Bibliography of Canadian Bibliographies*(no. 51), Dionne, N. E., *Inventaire chronologique des ouvrages publiés.* . .(no. 52), Tremaine, M., *A Bibliography of Canadian Imprints.* . .(no. 53), Haight, W. R., *Canadian Catalogue of Books.* . .(no. 54), Hare, J. E., et Wallot, J.-P., *Les Imprimés dans le Bas-Canada.* . . (no. 55), Martin, G., *Bibliographie sommaire du Canada français.* . .(no. 56), Tod, D., and Cordingley, A., *A Check List of Canadian Imprints.* . .(no. 57); catalogs of books in print: *Canadian Books in Print.* . .(no. 66), *Catalogue de l'édition au Canada français.* . .(no. 67), *Répertoire de l'édition au Québec.* . .(no. 68); and current bibliographies: *Canadian Catalogue of Books.* . .(no. 73), *Canadiana.* . .(no. 74), *Bibliographie du Québec.* . .(no. 75).

450 Bosa, Réal. *Les Ouvrages de référence du Québec; bibliographie analytique compilée sous la direction de Réal Bosa.* Montréal: Ministère des Affaires culturelles du Québec, 1969.

A general guide to reference books pub. in Quebec (mostly in French) with descriptive annotations. Broad subject coverage including generalities, philology, art, literature and history; nine chapters in all. The chapter on Canadian literature is classified into sections and includes bibliographies, societies, dictionaries, history, criticism, sociology of literature and anthologies.

1451 Chalifoux, Jean-Pierre. *Liste de sources bibliographiques relatives à la littérature canadienne-française.* 2e éd. rev. Montréal: La Bibliothèque, McGill U., Centre d'études canadiennes-françaises, 1967.

1452 Tougas, Gérard. *A Checklist of Printed Materials Relating to French-Canadian Literature, 1763-1968/Liste de référence d'imprimés relatifs à la littérature canadienne-française,* by/par Gérard Tougas. 2nd ed. Vancouver: University of British Columbia Pr., 1973.

b. CATALOGS OF MANUSCRIPTS

See Ch. 5, no. 135 and Supp.

c. JOURNALS

See Ch. 6, repertories, nos. 144-146, 162, 180-183.

Livres et auteurs québécois. Québec.

d. DISSERTATIONS AND THESES

See in Ch. 7, *Canadian Theses.* . .(nos. 197-199), Naaman, A. Y., *Guide bibliographique des thèses littéraires canadiennes.* . .(no. 200), Brodeur, L. A., *Répertoire des thèses littéraires canadiennes.* . .(no. 201).

e. BIOGRAPHICAL DICTIONARIES

See in Ch. 9: *Canadian Who's Who.* . .(no. 346), *Who's Who in Canada.* . .(no. 347), *The Macmillan Dictionary of Canadian Biography* (no. 348), *Standard Dictionary of Canadian Biography.* . .(no. 349), Sylvestre, Guy. *Ecrivains canadiens.* . .(no. 350), *Dictionnaire biographique du Canada.* . .(no. 351).

f. HISTORY AND CIVILIZATION

1453 Blanchard, Raoul. *Le Canada français.* P.: PUF, "Que sais-je?" 1964.

1454 Giraud, Marcel. *Histoire du Canada.* P.: PUF, "Que sais-je?" 1946; 2e éd., 1950.

g. FRENCH-CANADIAN LANGUAGE

1455 Bélisle, Louis Alexandre. *Dictionnaire général de la langue française au Canada.* Québec: Bélisle, 1957.

1456 Clapin, Sylva. *Dictionnaire canadien-français; ou Lexique-glossaire des mots, expressions et locutions ne se trouvant pas dans les dictionnaires courants et dont l'usage appartient surtout aux Canadiens-Français avec de nombreuses citations ayant pour but*

d'établir les rapports existant avec le vieux
français, l'ancien et le nouveau patois normand et
saintongeais, l'anglais, et les dialectes des premiers aborigènes, par Sylva Clapin. Montréal:
Beauchemin, 1891; rpt., Québec: Presses de l'U.
Laval, 1975.

457 Dulong, Gaston. Bibliographie linguistique du Canada
français. Québec: Presses de l'U. Laval, 1966.

h. LITERARY HISTORIES

458 Duhamel, Roger. Manuel de littérature canadienne-
française. Montréal: Ed. du Renouveau pédagogique,
1967.

459 Grandpré, Pierre de. Histoire de la littérature française
du Québec. 4 vols. Montréal: Beauchemin, 1967-69.

460 Mailhot, Laurent. La Littérature québécoise. P.: PUF,
"Que sais-je?" 1974.

461 Tougas, Gérard. Histoire de la littérature canadienne-
française. 2e éd. rev. et augm. P.: PUF, 1964
(1e éd. 1960).
_____. History of French-Canadian Literature. Tr. by
Alta Lind Cook. Toronto: Ryerson Pr., 1966.

i. GENERAL STUDIES

462 Grandpré, Pierre de. Dix Ans de vie littéraire au Canada
français. Montréal: Beauchemin, 1966.

463 Marcotte, Gilles. Présence de la critique. Critique et
littérature contemporaines au Canada français.
Textes choisis. Montréal: Eds. HMH, 1966.

464 Warwick, Jack. Long Journey: Literary Themes of French
Canada. Toronto: U. of Toronto Pr., 1968.
_____. L'Appel du Nord dans la littérature canadienne-
française, tr. par Jean Simard. Montréal: Eds.
Hurtubise, 1972. (Tr. into French of above.)

465 Wyczynski, Paul. Poésie et symbole, perspectives du
symbolisme: Emile Nelligan, Saint-Denys Garneau,
Anne Hébert et le langage des arbres. Montréal:
Déom, 1965.

j. LITERARY GENRES

1. Poetry
Bibliography and Anthologies
466 Bosquet, Alain, éd. Poésie du Québec. Anthologie composée
par Alain Bosquet: Alain Grandbois, Simone Routier,

François Hertel, Saint-Denys Garneau. . .et al. P.:
Seghers, 1968. (First pub. in 1962 under title:
La Poésie canadienne.)

1467 Cotnam, Jacques, éd. *Poètes du Québec, 1860-1968: anthologie. . .précédée d'une bibliographie.* Montréal:
Fides, 1969.

1468 Malouin, Reine, éd. *La Poésie il y a cent ans; essai et anthologie.* Québec: Garneau, 1968.

Studies

1469 Marcotte, Gilles. *Le Temps des poètes. Description critique de la poésie actuelle au Canada français.*
Montréal: Eds. HMH, 1969.

1470 Maugey, Axel. *Poésie et société au Québec (1937-1970).*
Québec: Presses de l'U. Laval, 1972.

   2. Prose

Essay

1471 Vigneault, Robert. "L'Essai québécois, 1968-1969."
Etudes françaises, fév. 1970, pp. 105-120.

Novel

Bibliography

1472 Hare, John Ellis. *Bibliographie du roman canadien-français. 1837-1962.* Montréal: Fides, 1965.

1473 Hayne, David M., et Tirol, Marcel. *Bibliographie critique du roman canadien-français, 1837-1900.* Toronto:
U. of Toronto Pr., 1968.

Anthology

1474 Rousseau, Guildo, éd. *Préfaces des romans québécois du XIXe siècle*, recueillies et présentées par G. Rousseau
Sherbrooke: Eds. Cosmos, 1970.

Studies

1475 Charbonneau, Robert. *Romanciers canadiens.* Québec:
Presses de l'U. Laval, 1972.

1476 Collet, Paulette. *L'Hiver dans le roman canadien-français.* Québec: Presses de l'U. Laval, 1965.

1477 Falardeau, Jean-Charles. *Notre Société et son roman.*
Montréal: Eds. HMH, 1967.

1478 Lemire, Maurice. *Les Grands Thèmes nationalistes du roman historique canadien-français.* Québec:
Presses de l'U. Laval, 1970.

1479 Racine, Claude. *L'Anticléricalisme dans le roman qué-
        bécois, 1940-1965.* Montréal: Hurtubise, 1972.

1480 Robidoux, Réjean, et Renaud, André. *Le Roman Canadien-
        français du vingtième siècle.* Ottawa: Eds. de
        l'U. d'Ottawa, 1966.

1481 Servais-Maquoi, Mireille. *Le Roman de la terre au Québec.*
        Québec: Presses de l'U. Laval, 1974.

1482 Sirois, Antoine. *Montréal dans le roman canadien.*
        Montréal: Didier, 1968.

II. LOUISIANA

LITERARY HISTORIES

1483 Caulfeild, Ruby Van Allen. *The French Literature of
        Louisiana.* N.Y.: Institute of French Studies,
        Columbia U., 1929.

1484 Giraud, Marcel. *Histoire de la Louisiane française.*
        4 vols. P.: PUF, 1953-74.
        _____. *A History of French Louisiana.* Tr. by Joseph
        C. Lambert. Rev. and corr. by the author. Baton
        Rouge: Louisiana State U. Pr., 1974-.

1485 Tinker, Edward Larocque. *Les Ecrits de langue française
        en Louisiane au XIXe siècle. Essais biographiques
        et bibliographiques.* P.: Champion, 1932; rpt., 1975.

E. FRENCH ANTILLES, GUIANA, HAITI, FRENCH-SPEAKING AFRICA, NEAR EAST

I. WORKS CONCERNING ALL THESE COUNTRIES

We group here works concerning all the above countries.
Even when titles refer only to "black" or "African" writers
of French expression, the above countries are often considered as well.

a. GENERAL BIBLIOGRAPHIES

See in Ch. 3: Baratte, *Bibliographie. Auteurs africains et malgaches de langue française* (no. 47).

1486 Agence de Coopération Culturelle et Technique, Paris.
        *Bibliographie sélective des pays d'expression
        française, d'Afrique, du Maghreb, d'Orient et des
        Antilles.* P.: IPEC, 1972.

This bibliography of twenty pages lists the books
in print in French (published or reprinted since 1960)
classified systematically. Useful but incomplete.

1487   Centre d'Analyse et de Recherche Documentaires pour
        l'Afrique Noire (CARDAN). Paris. *Bulletin d'Inform*
        tion et de Liaison. Etudes Africaines. P., 1971-.
        Quarterly.

        Continuation of *Recherche, enseignement, documen-*
tation africainistes francophones. This excellent publica
tion lists research in progress (including theses and
diplomas), teaching and documentation existing in the fiel
of African studies in French. CARDAN publishes also
Fiches analytiques since 1964, which analyzes eighty Frenc
and non-French journals on cards (geography, history,
ethnology, and linguistics).

1488   *Guide bibliographique du monde noir/Bibliographic Guide*
        to the Negro World, sous la dir. de J. R. Fontvielle
        et de R. P. Engelbert Mveng. 3 vols. Yaoundé:
        Ministère de l'Education, de la Culture et de la
        Formation professionnelle, 1971.

        Very useful research tool concerning all the Negro
world, in America and West Indies, Africa and islands of
the Indian Ocean. Bilingual catalog of the 1st International Exhibition of the African book in Yaoundé, 1968;
classified by alphabetical order of countries. The
second part is a bibliography.

                b. ENCYCLOPEDIAS, HANDBOOK

        See the passages concerning those countries in the
French encyclopedias listed in Ch. 8.

1489   *Africa, a handbook to the continent,* ed. by Colin L.
        Legum. Rev. and enl. ed. N.Y.: Praeger, 1966.

        Collection of good vulgarization studies written
by specialists.

        c. BIOGRAPHICAL DICTIONARIES AND REFERENCE BOOKS

1490   *(Bottin.) Afrique centrale. Algérie. Maroc. Tunisie.*
        Madagascar. Antilles. 2 vols. P.: Soc. Didot-
        Bottin, 1946-. Annual.

        Equivalent to a *Who's Who.*

1491   Anderson, Ian Gibson, ed. *Current African Directories,*
        Incorporating "African Companies, A Guide to Source
        of Information." Beckenham (Kent): CBD Research,
        1972.

        Useful repertory of the dictionaries of African
biography published in Africa or concerning it (alphabetical classification of titles).

1492 *Dictionary of African Biography.* 2nd ed. London: Melrose Pr., 1971.

　　　Biographies of the personalities of Africa (excluding South Africa, Rhodesia, and Portuguese territories).

1493 *The Middle-East and North-Africa. A Survey and Reference Book. 1972-1973.* . . . 21st ed. London: Europa Publications, 1974/75. (1st ed. 1948.)

　　　Completed since 1971 by another reference book, *Africa South of the Sahara.* Both study in detail these countries, and provide notably the list of their periodicals, the repertory of their main cultural institutions, and a *Who's Who* on c. 1,300 persons.

d. JOURNALS

　　　See Ch. 6.

e. HISTORY AND CIVILIZATION

1494 Balandier, Georges. *Afrique ambiguë.* P.: Union générale des éditeurs, 1962.

1495 Cornevin, Marianne. *Histoire de l'Afrique contemporaine de la Deuxième Guerre mondiale à nos jours.* P.: Payot, 1972.

1496 Cornevin, Robert et Marianne. *L'Afrique noire de 1919 à nos jours.* P.: PUF, 1973.

1497 Cornevin, Robert. *Histoire de l'Afrique.* Nouv. éd. mise à jour. 3 vols. P.: Payot, 1967-75. Cartes et croquis. 2e éd. compl. et mise à jour, 1976.
I: *Des origines au XVIe siècle.*
II: *Du tournant du XVIe siècle au tournant du XXe siècle. L'Afrique précoloniale (1500-1900).*
III: *Colonisation, décolonisation, indépendance.*

1498 Cornevin, Robert et Marianne. *Histoire de l'Afrique des origines à la Deuxième Guerre mondiale.* 3e éd. P.: Payot, 1970.

1499 Fage, J. D. *An Atlas of African History.* London: Arnold, 1958.

1500 France. Institut Géographique National. *Grand Atlas du continent africain.* Sous la dir. de Régine Van Chi-Bonnardel. P.: Editions Jeune Afrique, 1973.

1501 Frobenius, Léo. *Histoire de la civilisation africaine.* 3e éd. P.: Gallimard, 1936.

1502 Julien, Charles-André. *L'Histoire de l'Afrique blanche des origines à 1945*. P.: PUF, "Que sais-je?" 1966.

1503 Maquet, Jacques Jérôme. *Les Civilisations noires. Histoir€ techniques, arts, sociétés*. Verviers: Gérard, 1966.

1504 Merle, Marcel, sous la dir. de. *L'Afrique noire contemporaine*. P.: Colin, 1968.
_____. *Civilizations of Black Africa*. N.Y.: Oxford U. Pr., 1972. (Tr. of the above.)

1505 Paulme, Denise. *Les Civilisations africaines*. 5e éd. P.: PUF, "Que sais-je?" 1969.

1506 Senghor, Léopold Sédar. *Les Fondements de l'africanité, ou Négritude et arabité*. P.: Présence Africaine, 1967.

1507 Yacono, Xavier. *Les Etapes de la décolonisation française*. P.: PUF, "Que sais-je?" 1971; 2e éd. mise à jour, 19

1508 _____. *Histoire de la colonisation française*. P.: PUF, "Que sais-je?" 1969.

f. LITERATURE

1. Literary Histories

1509 Chevrier, Jacques. *Littérature nègre. Afrique, Antilles, Madagascar*. P.: Colin, 1974.

Fifty years of Negro-African literature in French in Africa, West Indies, and Madagascar.

1510 Colin, Roland. *Littérature africaine d'hier et de demain*. P.: ADEC, 1965.

1511 Eliet, Edouard, éd. *Panorama de la littérature négro-africaine (1921-1962)*. P.: Présence Africaine, 1965.

1512 Jahn, Janheinz. *Manuel de littérature néo-africaine du XVIe siècle à nos jours, de l'Afrique à l'Amérique*. Tr. de Gaston Bailly. P.: Resma, 1969.

1513 Kesteloot, Lilyan. *Les Ecrivains noirs de langue française: naissance d'une littérature*. Bruxelles: Presses de l'U. de Bruxelles, 1962; 3e éd. rev. 1967; 4e éd. 1971; 5e éd. 1976.

1514 Nantet, Jacques. *Panorama de la littérature noire d'expression française*. P.: Fayard, 1972.

The work and lives of one hundred French speaking writers of Black Africa and the Antilles.

2. General Studies

1515 Fanoudh-Siefer, Léon. *Le Mythe du nègre et de l'Afrique noire dans la littérature française (de 1800 à la 2e guerre mondiale)*. P.: Klincksieck, 1968.

1516 Melone, Thomas. *De la négritude dans la littérature négro-africaine*. P.: Présence Africaine, 1962.

3. General Anthologies

1517 Justin, Andrée, éd. *Anthologie africaine des écrivains noirs d'expression française*. P.: Institut Pédagogique africain, 1962.

1518 Kesteloot, Lilyan, éd. *Anthologie négro-africaine. Panorama critique des prosateurs, poètes et dramaturges noirs du XXe siècle*. Verviers: Gérard, "Marabout Un.," 1967.

1519 Mphahlele, Ezekiel, ed. *African Writing Today*. Harmondsworth: Penguin Books, 1967.

　　　　Anthology in English of African writers of French, English, and Portuguese languages. Biographical notes at the end of the volume.

4. Poetry
Anthologies

1520 Collins, Marie, ed. *Black Poets in French*. N.Y.: Scribner, 1972.

　　　　Poems in French by black poets of America and Africa. With the English tr. on the opposite page.

1521 Jones, Edward Allen, ed. *Voices of Negritude: the expression of Black experience in the poetry of Senghor, Césaire and Damas*. Valley Forge: Judson Press, 1971.

1522 Rombaud, Marc. *La Poésie négro-africaine de langue française*. P.: Seghers, 1976.

　　　　Anthology of fifty years of Negro-African poetry of Africa, Madagascar, West Indies.

* 1524 Senghor, Léopold Sédar. *Anthologie de la nouvelle poésie nègre et malgache de langue française*. P.: PUF, 1948; rpt. 1969.

　　　　Poets of Africa, West Indies, Madagascar.

5. Novel and Short Story
Anthologies

1525 Jadot, Joseph-Marie. *Contes d'ici et de là-bas*. Bruxelles: Marais, 1952.

* No. 1523 has been eliminated.

239

1526 Sainville, Léonard, éd. *Anthologie de la littérature négro-africaine; romanciers et conteurs.* 2 vols. P.: Présence Africaine, 1963-68.

Studies
1527 Anozie, Sunday Ogbonna. *Sociologie du roman africain. Réalisme, structure et détermination dans le roman moderne ouest-africain.* P.: Aubier, 1970.

1528 Leusse, Hubert de. *Afrique et Occident, heurs et malheurs d'une rencontre, les romanciers du pays noir.* P.: Eds. de l'Orante, 1971.

1529 Mouralis, Bernard. *Individu et collectivité dans le roman négro-africain d'expression française.* Abidjan: Annales de l'U. d'Abidjan, série D, Lettres, t. 2, 1969.

6. Theatre
1530 Béart, Charles. *Recherche des éléments d'une sociologie des peuples africains à partir de leurs jeux.* P.: Présence Africaine, 1960.

1531 Colloque sur le théâtre négro-africain, Abidjan, Côte d'Ivoire, 1970. *Actes du Colloque sur le théâtre négro-africain.* Abidjan, Ecole des lettres et sciences humaines, 15-29 avril 1970. P.: Présence Africaine, 1971.

1532 Cornevin, Robert. *Le Théâtre en Afrique noire et à Madagascar.* P.: Le Livre Africain, 1970.

1533 Scherer, Jacques. "Le Théâtre en Afrique noire francophone." In *Le Théâtre moderne. II.* Ed. par Jean Jacquot. P.: Eds. du CNRS, 1968, pp. 103-116.

1534 Traoré, Bakary. *Le Théâtre négro-africain et ses fonctions sociales.* P.: Présence Africaine, 1958. (English ed.: *The Black African Theatre and Its Social Functions.* Ibidan, Nigeria: Ibidan U. Pr., 1972.

II. FRENCH ANTILLES, GUIANA, AND HAITI

See in this chapter nos. 1416-1419, and the preceding section I.

a. FRENCH ANTILLES AND GUIANA

1. Journal
Cahiers Césairiens. University Park, Pennsylvania, 1975-.

2. Literary History and Criticism
1535 Bostick, Herman F. "Caribbean French Literature in Proper Perspective." *College Language Association Journal* (Morgan State Coll., Baltimore), 16 (1972), 1-6.

536 Chanover, Pierre. "Martinique and Guadeloupe: A Check List of Modern Literature." *Bulletin of the N.Y. Public Library*, 74 (1970), 514-31.

537 Conde, Maryse. "Autour d'une littérature antillaise." *Présence Africaine*, 81 (1972), 170-76.

538 *Littérature antillaise.* (*Encyclopédie antillaise*, 1-2). 2 vols. Fort-de-France: Gros Desormeaux, 1971-72. I: Poésie. II: Prose.

3. Poetry

1539 Shapiro, Norman R. "Negro Poets of French Caribbean: a Sampler." *The Antioch Review*, 27 (Summer 1967), 211-28.

1540 Wolitz, Seth L., ed. *Black Poetry of the French Antilles: Haiti, Martinique, Guadeloupe, Guiana.* Berkeley: Fybate Lecture Notes, 1968.

4. Novel

1541 Viatte, Auguste. "Le roman de la Louisiane, des Antilles françaises et de la Guyane française." In *Le Roman contemporain d'expression française*, éd. par Antoine Naaman et Louis Painchaud. Sherbrooke, Québec: Faculté des Arts, U. de Sherbrooke, 1971.

5. Theatre

542 Silenieks, Juris. "Deux Pièces antillaises: du témoignage local vers une tragédie moderne" (A. Césaire, *La Tragédie de Roi Christophe; Ed.* Glissant, *Monsieur Toussaint*). *Kentucky Romance Quarterly*, 15 (1968), No. 3, 245-54.

b. HAITI

1. Bibliography

543 Bissainthe, Max. *Dictionnaire de bibliographie haïtienne.* Washington: Scarecrow Pr., 1951. *Supplément*, 1973.

544 Primus, Wilma. "A Bibliography of Haitian Literature, 1900-1972." *Black Images: A Critical Quarterly on Black Culture*, 2, i (1973), 44-59.

2. Language

545 Ans, André-Marcel d'. *Le Créole français d'Haïti: Etude des unités d'articulation, d'expansion et de communication.* P.-La Haye: Mouton, 1968.

546 Faine, Jules. *Dictionnaire français-créole.* Montréal: Leméac, 1974.

3. Literary Histories

1547 Fouchard, Jean. *Langue et littérature des aborigènes d'Ayti*. P.: L'Ecole, 1973.

1548 Fouché, Franck. *Guide pour l'étude de la littérature haïtienne*. Port-au-Prince: Panorama, 1964.

1549 Gouraige, Ghislain. *Histoire de la littérature haïtienne*. Port-au-Prince: N. A. Théodore, 1960; rpt., Nendeln, Liechtenstein: Kraus Reprint, 1973.

1550 Lhérisson, Lélia Justin. *Manuel de littérature haïtienne et textes expliqués. Littérature des Amériques*. Port-au-Prince: Imp. du Collège Vertières, 1945, 1955.

1551 Pompilus, Pradel. *Manuel illustré d'histoire de la littérature haïtienne*, par Pradel Pompilus et Les Frères de l'Instruction chrétienne. Port-au-Prince: Deschamps, 1961.

4. General Anthology

1552 Gouraige, Ghislain. *Meilleurs Poètes et romanciers haïtiens*. Port-au-Prince: Imp. La Phalange, 1963.

5. Study

1553 Trouillot, Hénock. *Les Origines sociales de la littérature haïtienne*. Port-au-Prince: N. A. Théodore, 1962.

6. Poetry

1554 Garrett, Naomi M. *The Renaissance of Haitian Poetry*. P.: Présence Africaine, 1963.

1555 Lubin, Maurice A. *L'Afrique dans la poésie haïtienne*. Port-au-Prince: Panorama, 1965.

1556 Saint-Louis, Carlos, et Lubin, Maurice A. *Panorama de la poésie haïtienne*. Port-au-Prince: Deschamps, 1950; rpt., Nendeln, Liechtenstein: Kraus Reprint, 1

7. Novel

1557 Souffrant, Claude. "Le fatalisme religieux du paysan haïtien: Sociologie d'un roman." *Europe*, 501 (1971), 27-42.

8. Theatre

1558 Cornevin, Robert. *Le Théâtre haïtien des origines à nos jours*. Montréal: Leméac, 1973.

III. FRENCH-SPEAKING BLACK AFRICA, MADAGASCAR, REUNION, MAURITIUS

a. BIBLIOGRAPHY

See Baratte (no. 47).

242

b. HISTORY AND CIVILIZATION

1559 Deschamps, Hubert-Jules. *L'Afrique noire précoloniale.*
Nouv. éd. P.: PUF, "Que sais-je?" 1969.

1560 _____, sous la dir. de. *Histoire générale de l'Afrique
noire, de Madagascar et des archipels.* 2 vols.
P.: PUF, 1970-71. Ills., cartes.
I: *Des origines à 1800.* 1970.
II: *De 1800 à nos jours.* 1971.

1561 _____. *Les Institutions politiques de l'Afrique noire.*
P.: PUF, "Que sais-je?" 1965.

1562 Diop, Chiekh Anta. *L'Afrique noire précoloniale, étude
comparée des systèmes politiques et sociaux de
l'Europe et de l'Afrique noire, de l'antiquité à la
formation des états modernes.* P.: Présence Africaine, 1960.

1563 _____. *Nations nègres et culture.* 2e éd. P.: Présence Africaine, 1965.

1564 _____. *Antériorité des civilisations nègres: Mythe
ou vérité historique?* P.: Présence Africaine,
1967.
_____. *The African Origin of Civilization: Myth or
Reality.* N.Y.: L. Hill, 1974. (Contains translations of sections of the title above.)

1565 Ki-Zerbo, Joseph. *Histoire de l'Afrique noire, d'hier à
demain.* P.: Hatier, 1972.

1566 Wauthier, Claude. *L'Afrique des Africains. Inventaire
de la négritude.* P.: Eds. du Seuil, 1964; rpt.,
1973.

c. LITERATURE

1. Literary Histories

1567 Mercier, Roger; Pageard, Robert; Fellow, David; et Pichois,
Claude, éds. *Littératures francophones et anglo-
phones de l'Afrique noire (Revue de Littérature
Comparée,* vol. 48, Nos. 3-4). P.: Didier, 1974.

1568 Pageard, Robert. *Littérature négro-africaine. Le mouvement littéraire contemporain dans l'Afrique noire
d'expression française.* P.: Le Livre africain,
1966.

1569 Rial, Jacques. *La Littérature camerounaise de langue
française.* Lausanne: Payot, 1972.

2. General Anthologies
1570 Brench, Anthony C., comp. *Writing in French from Senegal to Cameroon*. London: Oxford U. Pr., 1967.

1571 Hughes, Langston, et Reygnault, Christiane. *Anthologie africaine et malgache*. Textes choisis et présentés par Langston Hughes et Christiane Reygnault. P.: Seghers, 1962.

3. Novel
1572 Brench, Anthony C. *The Novelists' Inheritance in French Africa: Writers from Senegal to Cameroon*. London: Oxford U. Pr., 1967.

1573 Colin, Roland. *Les Contes noirs de l'Ouest africain*. P.: Présence Africaine, 1957.

d. REUNION, MAURITIUS

1. Bibliography
1574 Mauritius. Archives Dept. *Bibliography of Mauritius, 1502-1954, covering the printed record, manuscripts, archivalia and cartographic material*, by Auguste Toussaint, chief archivist. Port Louis: Esclapon, 1956.

2. History
1575 Scherer, André. *Histoire de la Réunion*. P.: PUF, "Que sais-je?" 1966.

1576 Toussaint, Auguste. *Histoire de l'île Maurice*. P.: PUF, "Que sais-je?" 1971.

3. Literature
1577 Ithier, James Joseph Wasley. *La Littérature de langue française à l'île Maurice*. P., 1930.

1578 L'Homme, Léoville. *La Littérature française à l'île Maurice*. P.: R. Duval, 1914.

IV. NORTH AFRICA AND THE NEAR-EAST

a. GENERAL BIBLIOGRAPHY

See in Ch. 3: Arnaud, J. *Bibliographie de la littérature nord-africaine d'expression française, 1945-1962* (no. 46). See the preceding section I.

b. GENERAL WORKS

1579 Monteil, Vincent. *Les Arabes*. 2e éd. P.: PUF, "Que sais-je?" 1959.

1580 Nantet, Jacques. "La Littérature arabe d'expression

française aujourd'hui." *Présence Francophone*,
No. 1 (automne 1970), 42-53.

c. NORTH AFRICA

1. History
1581 Ageron, Charles-Robert. *Histoire de l'Algérie contemporaine (1830-1970)*. 4e éd. P.: PUF, "Que sais-je?
1970.

2. Language
1582 Lanly, André. *Le Français d'Afrique du Nord. Etude
linguistique*. P.: PUF, 1962.

3. Literary Histories
1583 Déjeux, Jean. *La Littérature algérienne contemporaine*.
P.: PUF, "Que sais-je?" 1975.

1584 _____. *Littérature maghrébine de langue française.
Introduction générale et auteurs*. Sherbrooke,
Québec: Eds. Naaman, 1973.

1585 _____. *La Littérature maghrébine d'expression française.
I: Naissance et développement. II: M. Feraoun ou
l'homme-frontière. III: J. Amrouche ou l'éternel
Jugurtha*. 3 vols. Alger: Rencontres culturelles,
Centre culturel français, 1970.

4. General Anthologies
1586 Memmi, Albert, sous la dir. de. *Anthologie des écrivains
français du Maghreb*, sous la dir. de Albert Memmi.
Choix et présentation de Jacqueline Arnaud, Jean
Déjeux, Arlette Roth. P.: Présence Africaine,
1969.

1587 _____. *Anthologie des écrivains maghrébins d'expression
française*. P.: Présence Africaine, 1964.

5. Poetry
1588 Lebel, Roland. *Les Poètes français du Maroc*. Tanger:
Editions internationales, 1956.

1589 Lévi-Valensi, Jacqueline, et Bencheikh, Jamel Eddine.
*Diwan algérien. La Poésie algérienne d'expression
française de 1945 à 1965. Etude critique et choix
de textes (Centre pédagogique maghrébin)*. Alger:
Société nationale d'édition et de diffusion, 1967.

d. NEAR-EAST

1. History
1590 Callot, Jean-Pierre. *Le Proche-Orient arabe*. 3e éd.
P.: PUF, "Que sais-je?" 1970.

2. Language
1591 Abou, Selim. *Le Bilinguisme arabe-français au Liban;
    essai d'anthropologie culturelle.* P.: PUF, 1962.

3. Literature
1592 Khalaf, Saher. "Panorama de la littérature libanaise
    d'expression française d'hier, 1900-1950." *Pré-
    sence francophone*, No. 5 (automne 1972), 5-14.

AUTHOR-TITLE INDEX

In the Index only the first author is listed when a work ha[s]
more than one author. Numbers refer to reference numbers, not
pages.

251

253

258

relatives à la littérature
canadienne-française, 1451
Chalumeau, J.-L., Pensée en
France de Sartre à Foucault,
1252
Chamard, H., Histoire de la Plé-
iade, 878
Champion, P., Histoire poétique
du quinzième siècle, 741
Chandler, F. W., Contemporary
Drama of France, 1223
Chanover, P., "Martinique and
Guadeloupe: A Check List
of Modern Literature," 1536
Chansons de geste du cycle de
Guillaume d'Orange, 693
Chansons de geste et l'épopée
. . ., 690
Chansons de geste françaises,
689
Chansons satiriques et bachiques
. . ., 720
Chapelan, M., Anthologie du
poème en prose, 491
Charbonneau, R. Romanciers
canadiens, 1475
Charbonnier, F., Poésie fran-
çaise et les guerres de re-
ligion. . ., 883
Charléty, S., Histoire du
saint-simonisme. . ., 1124
Charlier, G., Histoire illustrée
des lettres françaises de
Belgique, 1424; Mouvement
romantique en Belgique. . .,
1431
Charlton, D. G., France: A Companion to French Studies,
476; Positivist Thought in
France. . ., 1125; Secular
Religions in France. . .,
1126
Charpentrat, P., Mirage baroque,
982
Charvet, P., Literary History of
France, 636, 803, 939, 1052,
1130, 1131; Nineteenth Century. . ., 1130; Nineteenth
and Twentieth Centuries. . .,
1131
Chassang, A., Des essais dramatiques imités. . ., 751;
Recueil de textes litté-
raires français, 486

Chatelain, H. L., Recherches sur
les vers français au XVe
siècle. . ., 742
Check List of Canadian Im-
prints, 57
Check List of Cumulative In-
dexes to Individual
Periodicals. . ., 186
Checklist of Printed Mate-
rials Relating to French-
Canadian Literature, 1763-
1968, 1452
Chemins critiques. . ., 1305
Chérel, A., De "Télémaque" à
"Candide," 1409
Chevalier, J.-C., Grammaire
Larousse du français
contemporain, 395; Histoire
de la syntaxe . . ., 424
Chevallier, C. A., Théâtre
comique du Moyen Age, 669
Chevrier, J., Littérature
nègre. . ., 1509
Chicago University Press,
Manual of Style for Au-
thors. . ., 100
Chinard, G., Amérique et le
rêve exotique. . ., 555;
Exotisme américain dans la
littérature française au
XVIe siècle. . ., 800
Choix de lettres du dix-
septième siècle. . ., 959
Choix de poésies par Joachim
Du Bellay. . ., 873
Choix d'essais du vingtième
siècle, 1333
Cholakian, P. F., Early French
Novella. . ., 745
Chrestomatie de la littérature
en ancien français. . .,
647
Chrétien de Troyes et le mythe
du Graal . . ., 704
Christoflour, R., Spirituels
et mystiques . . ., 917
Chroniqueurs du seizième
siècle . . ., 1442
Chronologie approximative de
la littérature française
. . ., 631
Cinq Mirages américains. . .,
1346
Cinquante Ans de théâtre (1919-
1969), 1379

259

263

264

274

Kesteloot, L., *Anthologie négro-africaine.* . . . , 1518; *Ecrivains noirs de langue française.* . . . , 1513

Khalaf, S., "Panorama de la littérature libanaise . . . ," 1592

Kirkinen, H., *Origines de la conception moderne de l'homme machine.* . . . , 923

Kirsop, W., "Bibliography of French Literary History . . . ," 16

Ki-Zerbo, J., *Histoire de l'Afrique noire, d'hier à demain,* 1565

Klapp, O., *Bibliographie d'histoire littéraire française,* 17

Klein, K. W., *Partisan Voice* . . . , 721

Knowles, D., *French Drama of the Inter-War Years 1918-1939,* 1375; *Réaction idéaliste au théâtre.* . . . , 540

Kohler, P., *Littérature d'aujourd'hui dans la Suisse romande,* 1444

Krailsheimer, A. J., *Studies in Self-Interest.* . . . , 947; *Three Sixteenth-Century Conteurs,* 841

Kujoth, J. S., *Subject Guide to Periodical Indexes.* . . . , 185

Kukenheim, L., *Esquisse historique de la linguistique française.* . . . , 380; *Grammaire historique de la langue française,* 391; *Guide de la littérature française du Moyen Age,* 638

Kunstler, C., *Vie quotidienne sous la Régence,* 1014; *Vie quotidienne sous Louis XV,* 1015

Labrousse, C.-E., *Aspects de l'évolution économique.* . . . *1815 à 1880,* 1116

Lacassagne, J., *L'Argot du "milieu,"* 295

La Chaussée, F. de, *Initiation à la phonétique historique* . . . , 626

Lachèvre, F., *Bibliographie des recueils collectifs de poésies.* . . . , 889

Lacroix, P., *Recueil de farces, soties et moralités.* . . . , 761

Lagarde, A., *Grands Auteurs français du programme,* 487

Lagarde, G. de, *Naissance de l'esprit laïque.* . . . , 737

Lagrave, H., *Théâtre et le public à Paris de 1715 à 1750,* 1102

Lalou, R., *Roman français depuis 1900,* 1348

Lamennais, ses amis. . . . , 1127

Lancaster, H. C., *History of French Dramatic Literature* . . . , 972

Langage parisien au XIXe siècle. . . . , 1110

Langlois, P., *Guide bibliographique des études littéraires,* 18

Language of French Symbolism, 1211

Languages in Seventeenth and Early Eighteenth Century Imaginary Voyages, 898

Langue et le style du théâtre comique. . . . , 543

Langue et littérature des aborigènes d'Ayti, 1547

Langue et sensibilité au XVIIe siècle. . . . , 900

Langue et techniques poétiques . . . , 724

Langue française au XVIIIe siècle, 1005

Langue française au seizième siècle. . . . , 775

Lanly, A., *Français d'Afrique du Nord. Etude linguistique,* 1582

Lanson, G., *Choix de lettres du dix-septième siècle.* . . . 959; *Manuel bibliographique de la littérature française moderne.* . . . , 19; *Manuel illustré d'histoire de la littérature française,* 478; *Nivelle de La Chaussée.* . . . 1103

290

Raymond, M., *De Baudelaire au surréalisme*, 1329; *Poésie française et le maniérisme.* . . , 979

Raynaud, G., *Bibliographie des chansonniers.* . . , 610

Raynaud de Lage, G., *Introduction à l'ancien français*, 619

Reactionary Revolution: The Catholic Revival. . . , 1295

Réaction idéaliste au théâtre . . , 540

Réalisme et Naturalisme. . . (Bornecque), 1200

Réalisme et Naturalisme. . . (Dumesnil), 1198

Recherche des éléments d'une sociologie des peuples africains. . . , 1530

"Recherches bibliographiques dans le domaine de la littérature française contemporaine," 1238

Recherches sur les vers français au XVe siècle. . . , 742

Recherches sur quelques écrivains du XIVe. . . , 734

Reck, R. D., *Literature and Responsibility.* . . , 1359

Recueil de farces françaises inédites. . . , 759

Recueil de farces, soties et moralités. . . , 761

Recueil de l'origine de la langue et poésie française . . , 718

Recueil de textes littéraires français (Chassang), 486

Recueil général des Isopets, 658

Recueil général des soties, 762

Recueil général et complet des fabliaux. . . , 662

Recueil Trepperel, 760

Réforme, 790

Réforme et la littérature française, 884

Regards sur la philosophie contemporaine, 1253

Rémond, R., *Vie politique en France depuis 1789*, 1119

Renaissance (Morçay), 806

Renaissance (Pichois), 809

Renaissance des lettres. . . , 808

Renaissance France. . . , 803

Renaissance in Historical Thought. . . , 781

Renaissance of Haitian Poetry, 1554

Renaissance orientale, 1140

Répertoire alphabétique des thèses de doctorat. . . , 207

Répertoire bibliographique des traductions et adaptations . . , 42

Répertoire chronologique des littératures modernes, 604

Répertoire collectif des quotidiens. . . , 164

Répertoire de la presse bruxelloise, 143

Répertoire de la presse. . . *françaises*, 155

Répertoire de l'édition au Québec. . . , 68

Répertoire des Bibliothèques . . , 108

Répertoire des livres de langue française disponibles, 72

Répertoire des ouvrages pédagogiques du XVIe siècle, 782

Répertoire des périodiques de langue française. . . , 154

Répertoire des périodiques littéraires français de Belgique. . . , 142

Répertoire des périodiques paraissant en Belgique, 140

Répertoire des périodiques québécois, 145

Répertoire des périodiques suisses, 172

Répertoire des plus anciens textes. . . , 680

Répertoire des Publications Sériées Canadiennes, 146

Répertoire des réimpressions anastatiques. . . , 368

Répertoire des thèses de doctorat. . . , 189

Répertoire des thèses de doc-

304

ERRATA

Page 176 no. 865 should be placed before no. 839.
Page 187 no. 988 should be placed after no. 978.
Page 217 no. 1308 should be placed after no. 1364.